From the Upper Room to Joseph's Tomb

From the Upper Room to Joseph's Tomb

Jesus' Final Journey to Calvary and the Grave

CRUCIFIXION: A MULTIDISCIPLINARY INVESTIGATION OF THE DEATH OF JESUS OF NAZARETH

WOODROW MICHAEL KROLL

Foreword by Charles H. Dyer

RESOURCE *Publications* · Eugene, Oregon

FROM THE UPPER ROOM TO JOSEPH'S TOMB
Jesus' Final Journey to Calvary and the Grave

Crucifixion: A Multidisciplinary Investigation of the Death of Jesus of Nazareth

Copyright © 2025 Woodrow Michael Kroll. All rights reserved. Except for brief quotations in critical publications or reviews, no part of this book may be reproduced in any manner without prior written permission from the publisher. Write: Permissions, Wipf and Stock Publishers, 199 W. 8th Ave., Suite 3, Eugene, OR 97401.

Resource Publications
An Imprint of Wipf and Stock Publishers
199 W. 8th Ave., Suite 3
Eugene, OR 97401

www.wipfandstock.com

PAPERBACK ISBN: 979-8-3852-5172-8
HARDCOVER ISBN: 979-8-3852-5173-5
EBOOK ISBN: 979-8-3852-5174-2

This book is dedicated to all the pilgrims who have followed Jesus from the Upper Room to Joseph's tomb. Some of you have traveled to the Holy City and have traced Jesus' final steps on holy ground. Others have made the journey in your mind while reading the Gospel narratives. To all of you, may you find at the end of your journey an empty tomb and a risen Lord.

The Holy City

And then my dream was changed,
The streets no longer rang,
Hushed were the glad Hosannas
The little children sang.
The sun grew dark with mystery,
The morn was cold and chill,
As the shadow of a cross arose
Upon a lonely hill.

Jerusalem! Jerusalem!
Hark! How the angels sing,
Hosanna in the highest!
Hosanna to your King!
　　　　—Frederick E. Weatherly

Contents

Foreword xi
Preface xiii
Acknowledgements xvii
List of Abbreviations xviii
List of Tables xx
List of Maps xx
Introduction xxi

Chapter 1. The Upper Room: Jesus' Journey Begins 1
    A Description of the Upper Room 2
    The Location of the Upper Room 5
    Literary Evidence for the Site 7
    The Valley Route to Gethsemane 11
    The Significance of the Kidron Valley 13

Chapter 2. Gethsemane: Gateway to Golgotha 16
    Why Not Arrest Jesus in the Upper Room? 17
    Where is Gethsemane? 18
    Was Gethsemane a Garden? 21
    The Grotto of Gethsemane 23
    Historical Examples of Sweating Blood 25
    Jesus' Only Concern 30
    Gethsemane: Gateway to Golgotha 31

Chapter 3. The High Priest's Compound: The House of Miscarried Justice 33
    Why Take Jesus First to Annas? 34
    The Lay of the Land 34
    The Importance of Zion 37

Contents

    The Upper City 38
    The Assumptionist Catholic Palace 41
    The History of the Church of St Peter in Gallicantu 41
    The Armenian Palace of the High Priest 45
    The Palatial Mansion 49
    The Chamber of Hewn Stone 51

Chapter 4. Pilate's Judgment Hall: Innocent, Yet Condemned 55
    The Fortress of Antonia 57
    Herod's Palace 58
    Literary Evidence 59
    Grammatical Evidence 61
    Archaeological Evidence 62
    Domestic Evidence 63

Chapter 5. Herod's Passover Bed & Breakfast: A Contemptuous Confrontation 65
    Herod's Passover Bed & Breakfast: A Brutal Circus 66
    The Character of Herod Antipas 66
    The Location of Herod Antipas's Jerusalem Residence 69
    Jesus is Sent Back to Pontius Pilate 71

Chapter 6. The Via Dolorosa: The Road Where Dead Men Walk 73
    What is the *Via Dolorosa*? 74
    The Stations of the Cross 74
    Jerusalem's *Cardo* and *Decumanus* 82
    People Jesus Encountered on the *Via Dolorosa* 86
    How the Exhausted Jesus Carried His Cross 88
    The *Via Dolorosa* Celebrated in Music 92

Chapter 7. The Killing Field of Jerusalem: Crucifixion's Place of the Skull 94
    Two Ideas About Where Crucifixion Should Take Place 95
    A Place Outside the City 96
    The Wall of Jerusalem in Jesus' Day 99
    A Place Called Golgotha 103
    Crucifixion at Qumran 107
    The Mount of Olives 110
    Gordon's Calvary 117
    The Church of the Holy Sepulchre 121

CONTENTS

Chapter 8. The Tomb of Joseph: Jesus' Temporary Resting Place 132
    Tomb Essentials 133
    Lesser Contenders for the Tomb 137
    The Garden Tomb 141
    Evidence for the Authenticity of the Garden Tomb 144
    The Church of the Holy Sepulchre 165
    Evidence for the Authenticity of the Church of the Holy Sepulchre 170
    Conclusion 191
    Epilogue 194

Endnotes 195
Bibliography 205
Name Index 213
Subject Index 216

Foreword

FROM THE TIME JESUS gathered with his disciples in the Upper Room until his lifeless body was placed in Joseph of Arimathea's tomb took less than a day. However, few realize that all the events that unfolded in that small slice of time also took place in a very limited geographical area. If you have been following along in this compelling series—and I hope you have!—you already know this divine drama's major events and actors. And yet, unless you've been to Israel and physically retraced the steps taken by Jesus during this pivotal twenty-four-hour period, you might not appreciate the close geographical proximity of all the events. It's time to lace up your sandals because we're about to walk behind Jesus on that journey!

Many know by heart all the events of that momentous day, but few have a solid grasp of the physical distances traveled, the geographical details of the different locations, or even the significant change in elevation from one site to the next. And it's a shock to realize all the events took place in an area smaller than a square mile. Jesus, the disciples, the soldiers, and the Jewish and Roman authorities crisscrossed that relatively small area multiple times. By the time Jesus was placed in the tomb, he had passed through two gardens, ascended and descended several steep hills and valleys, entered and exited several of Jerusalem's gates, stood trial in multiple palaces, been beaten inside a Roman army quarters, and then paraded through the city's narrow streets while carrying the wooden beam to which he would be nailed.

We don't fully grasp the physical exhaustion, thirst, and excruciating pain experienced by Jesus during those twenty-four hours. It's hard for us to imagine what it must have been like for him to walk on those rugged Roman paving stones and climb uneven stairs worn down to a dangerous, glassy smoothness by countless sandals. And then to realize he did so while carrying a heavy wooden beam across his shoulders, having already

Foreword

endured significant bodily trauma from a severe Roman lashing. Reading the Bible from the comfort of our home, it's hard to envision what Jesus went through on that fateful day.

Thankfully, this is where Dr. Woodrow Kroll's knowledge and experience come to the fore. In this volume, Dr. Kroll will help you trace Jesus' journey from the Upper Room to the Garden of Gethsemane, back into Jerusalem for the Jewish and Roman trials, and then along a city roadway that led to Golgotha and a nearby tomb in a garden. Combining his deep biblical knowledge with first-hand experience leading more than seventy-five groups to Israel, Dr. Kroll pulls together all the details you might have overlooked to help these events take on greater texture, depth, and spiritual significance.

So grab your Bible and keep it beside you as you walk with Jesus up and down the steep hills of Jerusalem on his journey from the Upper Room to Joseph's tomb!

Dr. Charles H. Dyer
Professor-at-Large of Bible,
Host of *The Land and the Book* radio program
Moody Bible Institute

Preface

THE NUMBER OF PILGRIMS who have traveled to the Holy Land to "walk where Jesus walked" is inestimable, but certainly in the multiple millions. From the days of Helena, Roman Emperor Constantine's mother, men and women have made the journey by boat, by plane, by horse or donkey, and many by foot. With the advent of modern transportation, flights have been packed with Christians and non-believers alike flying to Lod International Airport to deplane on holy ground.

I first visited the Holy Land, spending the summer of 1964 there, while most of the holy sites were in the Hashemite Kingdom of Jordan. What I saw with my own eyes far superseded what I was taught in college, seminary, and graduate school. Not that my formal education was lacking; it wasn't. But for an understanding of the land, the people, and the history of both, there's nothing like seeing it for yourself. I told myself, "If ever I am a teacher, I must bring my students here to let their eyes do what only the eye can do." In 1970 I became that teacher and traveled with students and other Christians to the land of the Bible annually for 50 years.

Often I have told potential travelers, "I have met people who did not want to go to the Holy Land, but I've never met anyone who didn't want to go back"! There is no substitute for seeing for yourself where Jesus fed the 5,000 (Matt 14) or where he healed the man born blind (John 9).

But how do you know when you visit a site that it is the actual place where Jesus performed a miracle or where the Last Supper was held? How do you know those mentioned in the Passion narratives are the correct locations for Jesus' stopovers on his journey to Calvary?

In the following chapters, we will encounter each stopover on the way to the cross mentioned in the Gospel narratives. We will identify the location of the site, learn something about the site, and get a feel for what happened when Jesus stopped there on the day he died.

Preface

As you read this book or any of my works, you will quickly notice that I appeal often to the four Gospels for accurate historical information. I believe these writings are the earliest, most accurate, and best documents we have to inform us of the life and times of Jesus of Nazareth. I accept the Bible at face value, and while I incorporate the valuable insights and research of other scholars into my own, I also come to common sense conclusions that are often not evident in much of modern liberal scholarship. As the final authority, I appeal to those "men [who] spoke from God as they were carried along by the Holy Spirit" (2 Pet 1:21).

Some decades ago many scholars adopted the designations of B.C.E. and C.E. to indicate dates on the calendar. I completely understand why this change was made. The B.C.E. and C.E. designations are more inclusive because they do not specifically relate to Christianity. However, most of the Western world is steeped in the use of BC and AD; even many highly influential scholars have chosen to retain these designations.[1] But I use BC and AD for a strikingly different reason.

Greek scholar Vincent Taylor noted:

> We are bound to consider how we think of time, whether past events are only isolated points in a series, or whether God invades history with abiding consequences. This issue seriously engages the attention of theologians today. It is best considered by reflecting upon (1) events as points in the time series; (2) events with permanent significance; and (3) events as divine invasions in time."[2]

I do not believe the advent of God's Son was part of a mere point-in-time series. I see the birth of the Messiah and Savior as an invasion of time by God himself. Thus, despite scholarly arguments that Christians should adopt the BCE/CE dating system, I will use the designations BC and AD to reflect that incredible moment God changed the world forever by invading time, not simply indicating a timeshare with multiple religious communities.

> "The death of the Incarnate Son of God on a Roman cross marks the central point in the history of mankind." —F. W. Mattox

Now, some technical information. The Scripture references in this book are from the English Standard Version (ESV) of the Bible unless

Preface

otherwise noted. The ESV is based on the Greek text in the 2014 editions of the Greek New Testament (5th corrected edition), published by the United Bible Societies (UBS), and *Novum Testamentum Graece* (28th edition, 2012), edited by Nestle and Aland. The Hebrew words in the text are from the Masoretic text of the Hebrew Bible, as found in *Biblia Hebraica Stuttgartensia* (2nd edition,1983). Words in Greek are taken from the 1993 editions of the Greek New Testament (4th corrected edition) and *Novum Testamentum Graece* (27th ed).

Since multiple words in the Greek language may be used for the same word in English, wherever I have highlighted a Greek word, and there is more than one Scripture associated with it, I have always used the Greek of the first Scripture listed, as found in the 28th revised edition of the Nestle-Aland Novum Testamentum Graece.

All that said, let's walk in the footsteps of Jesus from the Upper Room to Joseph's tomb, and discover the reasons to believe these locations are authentic and accurate. The dusty streets of Roman Jerusalem never met the sandals of a more perfect sacrifice for our sins. Trace with me his steps, feel his passion, and "walk where Jesus walked" on his journey to Calvary.

Woodrow Michael Kroll
Ashland, Nebraska

Acknowledgements

THIS IS BOOK NUMBER five in the series CRUCIFIXION: A Multidisciplinary Investigation of the Death of Jesus of Nazareth. Many of those I have acknowledged before are worthy of acknowledgment again. Among them are my wife, Linda. She has put up with my semi-absence during nine years of research and writing this series. To me, she has made the greatest sacrifice. I thank her for her patience, support, and assistance during this process.

The highest praise, too, must go to Tina Work, who has tirelessly "worked" to bring my writing into compliance with Wipf and Stock Publishers' guidelines. Without her, the books in this series would still be on my computer, in a rather large study, in a small town in the heartland of America. While I can capably adjust many technical issues, some are clearly beyond my ken.

Thanks, too, to my dear friend Dr. Charles Dyer. He has led so many groups to Israel that we usually only see one another in the Holy Land. His knowledge of Israel's topography has been helpful in my own understanding of the land and the Book.

I wish to acknowledge the work of my publisher, Wipf and Stock Publishers of Eugene, Oregon. Special thanks to Matt Wimer, Managing Editor, Emily Callihan, Assistant Managing Editor, and George Callihan, Editorial Administrative Assistant.

Finally, I want to acknowledge decades of work by dedicated historians and archaeologists who have made the journey from the Upper Room to Joseph's tomb historically believable, and to the hundreds of physical guides who have made it highly personal. Thanks to you all.

List of Abbreviations

BIBLE TRANSLATIONS AND ABBREVIATIONS

ASV	American Standard Version
CSB	Christian Standard Bible
CEV	Contemporary English Version
ESV	English Standard Version
GNT	Good News Translation
HCSB	Holman Christian Standard Bible
JBP	J. B. Phillips
KJV	King James Version
TLB	The Living Bible
MSG	The Message
NASB	New American Standard Bible
NCB	New Catholic Bible
NET	New English Translation
NIV	New International Version
NKJV	New King James Version
NLT	New Living Bible
NRSV	New Revised Standard Version
RSV	Revised Standard Version

List of Abbreviations

SCHOLASTIC ABBREVIATIONS

Antiq.	The Antiquities of the Jews, Flavius Josephus
BA	Biblical Archaeologist
BAR	Biblical Archaeology Review
BDB	A Hebrew and English Lexicon of the Old Testament
BibSac	Bibliotheca Sacra
CT	Christianity Today
DSS	The Dead Sea Scrolls
EBib	Études Bibliques
EH	Eusebius, Ecclesiastical History
EQ	Evangelical Quarterly
ExpTim	Expository Times
HSNTA	E. Hennecke and W. Schneemelcher, New Testament Apocrypha
HTR	Harvard Theological Review
HUCA	Hebrew Union College Annual
IEJ/IEQ	Israel Exploration Journal/Quarterly
ISBE	International Standard Bible Encyclopedia
JAAR	Journal of the American Academy of Religion
JBL	Journal of Biblical Literature
JETS	Journal of the Evangelical Theological Society
JJS	Journal of Jewish Studies
JQR	Jewish Quarterly Review
JRS	Journal of Roman Studies
JSNT	Journal for the Study of the New Testament
JTS	Journal of Theological Studies
LXX	The Septuagint
NTS	New Testament Studies
NTG	Novum Testamentum Graece
PEF	Palestine Exploration Fund
PEQ	Palestine Exploration Quarterly
RevArch	Revue Archéologique

List of Abbreviations

RB	Revue Biblique
RevQum	Revue de Qumran
SBLSP	Society of Biblical Literature Seminar Papers
SPCK	Society for Promoting Christian Knowledge
SWJT	Southwestern Journal of Theology
TalBab	The Babylonian Talmud
TalJer	The Jerusalem Talmud
TDNT	Theological Dictionary of the New Testament
TZ	Theologische Zeitschrift
Wars	Wars of the Jews, Flavius Josephus

LIST OF TABLES

Major Old Testament Figures Who Donned Sackcloth in Sorrow
Historical References to Bloody Sweat
From Jesus' Arrest in Gethsemane to Caiaphas' Courtroom
The Armenian Church in Jerusalem
The Praetorium in Modern Translations
Who Was Herod Antipas?
A History of Jerusalem's Walls
The Temple of Jerusalem
Use of the Greek mégas in the New Testament
Maps of Jerusalem

LIST OF MAPS

Madaba Map Site Identification
The Armenian Compound in Jerusalem
The Jerusalem Cardo Maximus and Decumanus Maximus
Jerusalem's Three Walls
The Three Walls of Jerusalem

Introduction

ALMOST EVERYONE LOVES A journey. That's why people go on cruises, hike mountain trails, and walk the cobbled streets of out-of-the-way European villages. We all love a journey.

There is one journey, however, that brings us to tears, not to the joy of our triumphs. That's the journey to the cross. In this series on Roman crucifixion and the death of Jesus, we have now come to those final, fateful steps that lead to the end of the Nazarene's life. Jesus has spent perhaps the last three years of his life healing the sick, raising the dead, feeding the hungry, and teaching them about a kingdom unlike any they have witnessed before. Along the way, he has tramped the dusty trails of Galilee, walked on the water of the sea there, and disappeared at times to be alone to talk with his Heavenly Father.

While much of the Savior's ministry was localized in Galilee, and some of his greatest teachings, such as the Sermon on the Mount, were delivered there, it was in Jerusalem that the paramount experiences of his life took place. In Jerusalem, he cleansed the Temple, twice. In Jerusalem, he confronted the religious leaders of Judaism. In Jerusalem, he observed the annual Passover and other Jewish festivals. In Jerusalem, the "center of the world," Jesus died and rose again.

In this series of books on crucifixion, our investigations into Roman crucifixion and the death of Jesus have always been limited to the last twenty-four hours of Jesus' life. We have not concerned ourselves with his baptism in the River Jordan, his burning-bright face on the Mount of Transfiguration, or even his Triumphal Entry into Jerusalem. We have been laser-focused on the period between the Last Supper and his burial in the tomb of Joseph of Arimathea. Thus, in the present book, we explore each stopover, each location where something happened to Jesus on his way to

INTRODUCTION

the cross, and ultimately the tomb. We are following Jesus from the Upper Room to Joseph's tomb.

Come along and receive the spiritual and instructional benefit of following Jesus' final steps. Prepare to gasp. Prepare to cringe. Prepare to cry. Prepare to walk behind Jesus of Nazareth as he was brutally crucified for you and me.

Endnotes

1. Witherington, "Biblical Views," *BAR* 43.6 (2017): 26.
2. Taylor, *The Cross*.

Chapter 1

The Upper Room

Jesus' Final Journey Begins

He would eat his final meal, not in the magnificent dwelling of a Roman governor or a Jewish ruler, where a retinue of servants would attend to him. He would eat it in a simple room with friends. His feet would not be washed, but he would wash their feet. Jesus came not to be served but to serve.

A Description of the Upper Room
The Location of the Upper Room
Literary Evidence for the Site
The Valley Route to Gethsemane
The Significance of the Kidron Valley

The Upper Room plays a pivotal role in the last hours of Jesus' life and the first hours of the Jerusalem church. It is one of the most meaningful sites of the Christian faith and a "must" on your pilgrimage to the Holy City. Think about the importance of this one room to those first-century Christ-followers.

- It was here, in this room, that Jesus ate his Last Supper with his disciples (Matt 26; Mark 14; Luke 22; John 12).
- Jesus met his disciples in the Upper Room after his resurrection (John 20).

- He met these same disciples again a week later, this time with Thomas present (John 20).
- It was here, in this Upper Room, that the disciples met to seek God's replacement for Judas (Acts 1).
- And it was here that the Holy Spirit descended on the followers of Jesus on Pentecost (Acts 2).

This was a very significant room indeed for Jesus and his first-century followers. It is the most appropriate place to begin following Jesus on his journey to Calvary. But is the traditional site of Jesus' Last Supper actually where the meal was eaten? Can we say anything definitive about the location or description of the Upper Room? Let's see, as we begin to follow Jesus' footsteps.

A DESCRIPTION OF THE UPPER ROOM

Luke provides the following account of the Last Supper site:

> Jesus sent Peter and John, saying, 'Go and prepare the Passover for us, that we may eat it.' They said to him, 'Where will you have us prepare it?' He said to them, 'Behold, when you have entered the city, a man carrying a jar of water will meet you. Follow him into the house that he enters and tell the master of the house, "The Teacher says to you, Where is the guest room, where I may eat the Passover with my disciples?" And he will show you a large upper room furnished; prepare it there.' And they went and found it just as he had told them, and they prepared the Passover" (Luke 22:7–13).

There is not much to be said of this room because the word for the room (Greek: ἀνάγαιον; English: *anagaion*) is used only by Mark in 14:15 and by Luke here in 22:12. It is found nowhere else in Scripture. However, there are three descriptors Luke used that help us understand the character of the room. Notice what they are.

The room was oversized

Peter and John were led to "a large upper room furnished." The room had to be large enough to accommodate Jesus and his disciple band. We are familiar with the word large (Greek: μέγας; English *megas*) because μέγας is the common Greek word describing anything oversized. The word μέγας is especially significant in the crucifixion story. Here are some examples.

"And about the ninth hour Jesus cried out with a loud (μεγάλῃ) voice, saying, '*Eli, Eli, lema sabachthani?*'" (Matt 27:46).

"And Joseph took the body and wrapped it in a clean linen shroud and laid it in his own new tomb, which he had cut in the rock. And he rolled a great (μέγαν) stone to the entrance of the tomb and went away" (Matt 27:59, 60).

"There was a great (μέγας) earthquake, for an angel of the Lord descended from heaven and came and rolled back the stone and sat on it" (Matt 28:2).

The traditional Upper Room in Jerusalem

The Upper Room was as large as Jesus' cry, "*Eli, Eli, lema sabachthani?*" was loud. It was an oversized room, easily capable of handling Jesus and his disciples, with room to spare.

From the Upper Room to Joseph's Tomb

The room was on the second story

Secondly, we know the location of the room relative to the rest of the house. It was an "upper room," referring to a space located on the second floor or higher in the building. This may not have been a traditional room with four walls as we think of it. It could have been a balcony or even the rooftop itself. Today, families in the Middle East frequently use the roof of their homes as a gathering place, a sprawling place where it is cool and comfortable in the evening. I have an Arab friend in Jerusalem who insists on preparing barbequed lamb for me each time I visit him. We always eat on the rooftop about 9:00 pm.

Whether a rooftop or a second-story room, we do not know, but the Upper Room was a higher room than the rest of the house. The word for "room" is a composite made from the term for "above" or "on top" (Greek: ἄνω; English: *ánō*) and the term for the "land" or "ground" (Greek: γῆ; English: *gē*). Hence, the word means "above ground" or the second floor of a building, therefore the upper room.

The room was furnished

Here is a detail that often escapes us. Luke says it was "a large upper room furnished." Doctor Luke chose another rare word (Greek: στρώννυμι; English: *strōnnymi*) to describe this Upper Room. The word means to spread out, as you would an Oriental carpet, or to position couches around the room.

Strōnnymi is not a common word, used only five times in the New Testament, two of which describe the Triumphal Entry and two the Upper Room. Still, we can picture the room from Matthew and Mark's description of Jesus' Triumphal Entry into Jerusalem. Mark says, "And they brought the colt to Jesus and threw their cloaks on it, and he sat on it. And many spread (*strōnnymi*) their cloaks on the road, and others spread (*strōnnymi*) leafy branches that they had cut from the fields" (Mark 11:7, 8).

From understanding how the word is used elsewhere, we can deduce that the Upper Room was not empty. As the palm fronds were spread on Jesus' pathway, the furniture was spread around the Upper Room. Perhaps Peter and John had to move some of it around to prepare for Jesus' Last Supper, but what they needed was already in the furnished room. If the

Greek implies a carpeted room, that would likely signal a relatively wealthy family. However, we cannot say this with certainty.

One final observation. While a well-to-do family may have owned the Upper Room, it was not in the same echelon as Herod's palace or the High Priest's residence. It may have been comfortable, but it was not ornate or elaborate. Even in the final hours before his date with destiny, Jesus did not seek an environment of greatness, grandeur, or luxury. He would eat his final meal, not in the magnificent dwelling of a Roman governor or a Jewish ruler, where a retinue of servants would attend to him. He would eat it in a simple room with friends. His feet would not be washed, but he would wash their feet. Jesus came not to be served but to serve, which is evident at the Last Supper.

THE LOCATION OF THE UPPER ROOM

I spent the summer of 1964 in Europe and the Middle East. It would not be my last journey to either, as I would return to the Holy City at least annually for more than 50 years. One of the obligatory stops for any first-time Christian visitor to the Holy City is the Upper Room. However, first-time visitors entering the room often express a faceful of surprise, if not disappointment. There is nothing there. The well-appointed room of the first century is quite unlike the room it is today. It is virtually empty, and it's not even in the Old City.

The Cenacle

A two-story stone building atop Mount Zion is traditionally called the Cenacle (from the Latin *coenaculum* meaning "upstairs" or "upper room"). It is located just outside the present-day Old City walls. Oddly enough, since the Middle Ages, the first floor of this building has been associated with the tomb of David. There is a cenotaph in a small room that is also used as a synagogue. It is the purported burial place of Israel's most important king.

This building has seen its share of destruction and disaster over the centuries. It has been a church, a mosque, and a synagogue. Nevertheless, the question remains: "Is this the spot? Did the Last Supper actually take place on this site?"

Most helpful in answering these questions is a relatively recent book by David Clausen, former adjunct lecturer in Religious Studies at the

University of North Carolina at Charlotte. He examined the evidence for the various claims involving the Cenacle or Upper Room.[1] Specifically, Clausen focused on when this building was established, how it functioned throughout the centuries, and, most significantly, whether it can be identified as the actual site of Jesus' Last Supper and/or David's Tomb.

The Hagia Sion

While some pilgrims to the Holy Land complain about the ornate, almost gaudy, churches they visit, I am grateful for such churches. Not for the gaudiness because I think that diverts our attention from true worship. However, I am pleased that the church is there, for had these churches not been built over the site of something important to Christians, a McDonald's or KFC might occupy that sacred site, and we would never know what was beneath. It was customary to build a church over a holy place, a site identified in the Bible's text, where the early church gathered because Jesus had performed a miracle there.

So, did subsequent churches occupy the place of today's Cenacle to honor and preserve the Upper Room location? Yes, indeed. A succession of churches was built at the site of the original Upper Room. The Church of Hagia Sion, the grand Byzantine basilica known as the "Mother of all Churches," covered the entire area now occupied by the Dormition Abbey, the Upper Room, and the tomb of David.

During Israel's 1948 War of Independence, a shell exploded on the site of King David's traditional tomb on Mount Zion. This bloody war began on November 29, 1947, and lasted until January 5, 1949. In 1951, Israeli archaeologist Jacob Pinkerfeld was tasked with repairing the damage done to David's tomb. Pinkerfeld first discovered a niche behind the cenotaph of King David. Assuming it to be evidence of a synagogue, he took the opportunity as an archaeologist to remove the marble floor slabs and dig down about 12 centimeters (5 inches), where he discovered a Crusader floor. Approximately 48 centimeters (18 inches) below that, Pinkerfeld uncovered another floor covered with mosaics in geometric patterns. Ten centimeters farther (4 inches) down, he found the building's original plaster floor and what appeared to be a stone pavement. Pinkerfeld believed this was the original floor of the Hagia Sion ("Holy Zion") church built between 379 and 381 AD. The church commemorated the site of the Upper Room.

At this lowest layer, Pinkerfeld identified some plaster with graffiti on it that he believed came from the original synagogue wall. Jacob Pinkerfeld gave this graffiti to Professor Moshe Schwabe for examination. Unfortunately, both Professor Schwabe and archaeologist Pinkerfeld died before this graffiti could be published. That task fell to a team of experts from the *Studium Biblicum Franciscanum* led by Professors Emmanuele Testa and Bellarmino Bagatti.

Testa and Bagatti described the graffiti saying, "One graffito has the initials of the Greek words which may be translated as 'Conquer, Savior, mercy.' Another graffito has letters which can be translated as 'O Jesus, that I may live, O Lord of the autocrat.'"[2] This archaeological evidence tended to authenticate the site as the Upper Room.

LITERARY EVIDENCE FOR THE SITE

In addition to archaeological evidence, there is a substantial amount of literary evidence indicating that this site is indeed the location of the original Upper Room.

Bishop Epiphanius (315–403 AD), the Bishop of Cyprus, was born and raised in central Israel. Epiphanius provided the following information about the church on Mount Zion when the Roman emperor Hadrian visited Jerusalem in 130/131 AD. He said there was standing on Mount Zion, "A small church of God. It marked the site of the *Hypero-on* (Upper Room), to which the disciples returned from the Mount of Olives after the Lord had been taken up [see Acts 1:13]. It had been built on that part of Sion."[3]

Eusebius (265–349 AD), writing in his *Demonstratio Evangelica* (c. 312 AD), even before the Council of Nicea (325 AD), said, "This is the word of the Gospel, which through our Lord Jesus Christ and the Apostles went out from Sion and was spread to every nation. It is a fact that it poured forth from Jerusalem and Mt. Sion adjacent to it, on which our Savior and Lord had stayed many times and where he had taught much doctrine."[4]

Basing his work on Jerome and other earlier sources, Eucherius, Bishop of Lyon (c. 380 – c. 449 AD) and an influential ecclesiastic in the church of Gaul, wrote, "The plain upper part [of Mount Zion] is occupied by monks' cells, which surround a church. Its foundations, it is said, have been laid by the Apostles in reverence for the place of the resurrection of the Lord. It was there that they were filled with the Spirit of the Paraclete [the Holy Spirit] as promised by the Lord."[5]

The church on this site was known as the Church of the Apostles for two reasons. First, the apostles frequented the Upper Room both before and after Jesus' crucifixion and resurrection. Additionally, the building was constructed under the guidance of Simon, son of Cleophas. Kleophas (Cleophas) was thought to be the brother of Joseph of Nazareth.[6] This would make Simon, the builder of the original Church of the Apostles, Jesus' cousin. That means the original building must date before the destruction of Jerusalem in 70 AD.

The first Byzantine church on Mount Zion was authorized by Emperor Theodosius 1 (379–394 AD). Theodosius was also responsible for building the first Byzantine church in Gethsemane. The emperor wanted Christians to venerate the Zion church, so he had the supposed column at which Jesus was scourged retrieved from the ruins of Caiaphas' house and set up in the portico of the Church of the Apostles. In the second iteration of this Byzantine Zion Church, the Column of Flagellation was moved to the center of the church.[7]

The pilgrim Egeria visited Jerusalem around 394 AD. She described a double sanctuary on Mount Zion, i.e., the Church of the Apostles and the Theodosian Church, which stood separate from it, in front.[8]

John II, bishop of Jerusalem from 387 to 417 AD, is revered as a saint by both the Orthodox Church and the Roman Catholic Church. It appears that in the late fourth century AD, John II built the great Hagia Sion Church, which is depicted in the Madaba mosaic map on the floor of the Byzantine Church of Saint George in Madaba, Jordan. Bishop Arculph describes this fabulous mosaic, which dates back to the sixth century AD.[9]

The traditional building housing the Upper Room

At the dedication of the *Hagia Sion,* Bishop John delivered a hard-hitting homily in which he alluded to the coming of the Holy Spirit to the Upper Room (Acts 1:13)[10] Michel van Esbroeck, Belgian scholar at the University of Munich, asserted the homily delivered by John II was preserved in Armenian, though not published until 1973.[11]

In 1984, van Esbroeck published texts discovered in a Georgian monastery in Russia. These texts were from a bishop of Jerusalem named John. They record that the feast of dedication for the Church of Hagia Sion was held on 15 September. The bishop wrote, "And the 15th of the same month was the dedication of the Holy and Glorious Zion, which is the mother of all churches, that had been founded by the Apostles, which emperor Theodosius the Great has built, enlarged, and glorified, and in which the Holy Spirit had come down on the holy day of Pentecost."[12]

Nonetheless, the location of the Hagia Sion as the site of the Upper Room has been called into question by two outstanding mosaics. One is the St. George Church in Madaba, Jordan, a town of 60,000 inhabitants. Unearthed in 1896, the mosaics of the Greek Orthodox Church date to the sixth century AD and are composed of approximately 2,000,000 stone pieces.

Notably, the detailed mosaic map of ancient Jerusalem features the Roman cardo running through the heart of the city. I once had a local Jordanian artisan craft a table for me, replicating this map of Jerusalem with thousands of stone pieces forming the mosaic. It is the most handsome piece in my house.

Handcrafted mosaic map table, a facsimile of the Madaba Map

The Madaba map of Jerusalem does not support the Hagia Sion Church as built over the Upper Room site. Instead, it shows an independent structure south of the Hagia Sion that marks the Upper Room.

This independent, autonomous structure is also depicted in the fifth- to sixth-century mosaics in the Basilica of Santa Maria Maggiore in Rome. The mosaics are visible underneath the windows of the church. While they depict many Old Testament scenes, the triumphal arch has golden mosaics dating back to the fifth century that display scenes from Christ's life. Here also is depicted the location of the Upper Room, distinct from the Hagia Sion Church.

This independent structure within a mosaic, however, is not surprising and has a clear explanation. You cannot place one edifice over another in a mosaic unless you make it 3-D. The ordinary course of action in a case like this is to identify the buildings side by side. This does not necessarily indicate they are at two separate locations. It may simply suggest the artisan was unable to place them on top of each other.

MAP 1

Madaba Map Site Identification

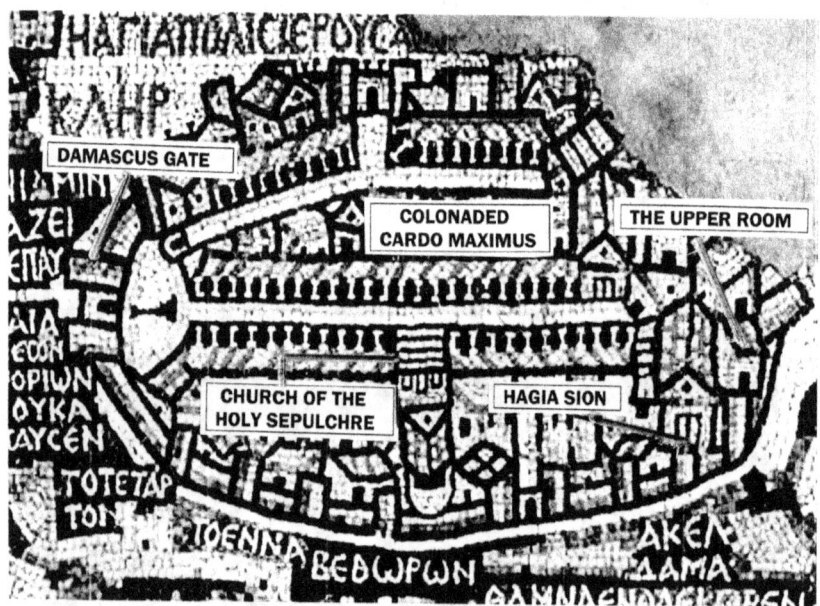

Any thoughtful reader may ask, "Are these really critical questions"? and the answer is no. They do not impact the quality of our faith, nor are they historically or archaeologically problematic. However, they demonstrate that, given the scarce and often conflicting evidence, the Upper Room location and the buildings that commemorate it are subject to some question.

Scholars, such as Amit Reem of the Israel Antiquities Authority (IAA), maintain that the structures detected under the Cenacle are merely the remains of a late fourth-century Byzantine church, the Holy Zion Basilica. However, David Clausen argues that the Cenacle's oldest elements originated before the Byzantine Period (fourth to fifteenth century AD). Final determinations as to the location and configuration of the Upper Room await further evidence.

Our inability to settle the question of the Upper Room's location should not diminish our appreciation for the events that occurred there. As mentioned earlier in this chapter, the Upper Room is the most crucial in the New Testament, maybe in history itself. There is good evidence that the present Cenacle is located over the original site of the Upper Room, even though the present 700- to 800-year-old building may give the impression otherwise.

THE VALLEY ROUTE TO GETHSEMANE

Jesus' footsteps to Calvary began at the Upper Room. From there, he would go to the Garden of Gethsemane to pray and then be arrested. The distance from the Upper Room to the garden is about three-quarters of a mile. Jesus and his now eleven disciples could have wound their way through Jerusalem's streets to the eastern side of the city and passed out the Golden Gate to the garden. However, it was Passover, and Jerusalem's streets were jammed with pilgrims. It would be less crowded for them to descend a set of Roman steps into the valley below. These steps, which are still both visible and usable today, are quite remarkable and likely the authentic ancient steps the Savior used. They were Roman-built, and whatever the Romans built, they built to last.

They are located just to the north of the present Church of Saint Peter in Gallicantu, situated on the eastern slope of Mount Zion, outside the Old City of Jerusalem. Once down in the valley, Jesus and his disciples would have passed the Lower Pool and moved toward the Fountain Gate. On the left was the tiny village of Gihon. Further along, they passed the village of Siloam, now known as Silwan, which clings to the mountain on the opposite side of the Kidron.

*First-century Roman steps from
the Upper City of Jerusalem*

Because it was Passover, they would have passed by hundreds of families camped outside the Holy City, smelling the smoke from tiny fires these pilgrims had built to cook their evening meal. "Some pilgrims may have been able to stay with relatives or friends or in hostels attached to synagogues. Most of them probably camped out in designated areas outside the walls of Jerusalem."[13] Pilgrims coming from Galilee and Perea probably camped on the Mount of Olives, the top of which was not cultivated nor covered with buildings in the New Testament era.[14]

On the last leg of their walk, Jesus and his disciples would curve around the Temple's southeastern corner and up the wadi known as the Kidron Valley. A wadi is a dry creek bed most of the year but can run heavily in the rainy season. The winter rains are gone now, but within the next twenty-four hours, this valley will run red with the blood of the lambs sacrificed for Passover.

Finally, Jesus and his disciples would reach the garden, where they made it their habit to pray, rest, and sometimes sleep. Under normal conditions, this walk would take about fifteen minutes, but it may have taken a few minutes longer on this eventful night.

THE SIGNIFICANCE OF THE KIDRON VALLEY

The Hebrew letter Shin ש, used by Jewish people to represent God—El Shaddai—is geographically formed by the three primary valleys of Jerusalem: the Kidron Valley, the Hinnom Valley, and the Tyropoeon Valley. Jews claim the Creator signed His name on the earth of His city! The Kidron Valley was likely the most important of the three valleys trisecting Jerusalem. According to the biblical texts, when you "crossed the Kidron" from the East, you effectively entered the Holy City (2 Sam 15:23; John 18:1).

The word "Kidron" or "Cedron" comes from a Hebrew word meaning an "ashy dark color." This is the color of sackcloth, the rough material made of animal hair. The name is fitting for those who wore sackcloth, often did so to indicate they were in mourning (1 Kgs 21:27; Job 16:15; Joel 1:13). Wearing sackcloth often symbolized repentance. For example, the people of Nineveh donned sackcloth in response to Jonah's warning, demonstrating their genuine repentance (Jonah 3:5).

Many important events took place in the Kidron Valley, some of which were:

- The poor people of the land were buried at Kidron. It was like a modern-day potter's field. (2 Kgs 23:6; Jer 26:20–23);
- Shimei, an opponent of King David, was not allowed to cross the brook of Kidron under the threat of death at the hands of David's son, Solomon (1 Kgs 2:36–46);
- After Absalom took his throne by force, David was forced to flee over the brook Kidron. Symbolically, this was a picture of the temporary end, or "death", of David's reign. (2 Sam 15:13–23);

TABLE 1

Old Testament Figures Who Donned Sackcloth in Sorrow

Individual/Group	Scripture
Jacob	Genesis 37:34
David	2 Samuel 3:31; 1 Chronicles 21:16; Psalms 30:11; 35:3; 69:11
Rizpah	2 Samuel 21:10
Ahab	1 Kings 21:27
Jehoram	2 Kings 6:30
Hezekiah	2 Kings 19:1; Isa 37;1
Eliakim	2 Kings 19:2; Isa 37:2
Mordecai	Esther 4:1, 4
The People of Israel	Nehemiah 9:1; Esther 4:3; Ezekiel 7:18; Amos 8:10
Job	Job 16:15
Isaiah	Isaiah 20:2
Daughters of Israel	Jeremiah 6:26
Jerusalem's Elders	Lamentations 2:10
The People of Tyre	Ezekiel 27:31
Daniel	Dan 9:3
Israel's Priests	Joel 1:13
The People of Nineveh	Jonah 3:5–8

- Often in Israel's history, it was at Kidron, where the false idols of Israel were destroyed, thus symbolically representing the temporary termination, or "death", of idolatry in Israel. This took place on three different occasions: under the rule of Asa (1 Kgs 15:13), under the rule of

Josiah (2 Kgs 23:4–12), and under the rule of Hezekiah (2 Chr 29:16 and 2 Chr 30:14).
- Most likely, Judas Iscariot traveled the same path to Gethsemane, resulting in the betrayal and arrest of Christ Jesus (John 18:2).

Without question, however, the most important events that occurred in the ashy dark Kidron Valley are related to Jesus' desire to pray to his Heavenly Father and the trek from the garden to the High Priest's complex after he was arrested in Gethsemane.[15]

When Jesus arrived at Gethsemane, he intended to pray, but he knew much more than communing with the Almighty was about to take place. Much more did, as we will see when our journey continues.

Chapter 2

Gethsemane

The Gateway to Golgotha

When Jesus was in the greatest depths of his struggle, not only did he not give up and quit praying to the Father, but he "prayed more earnestly." When it appears we are losing, that is when we must fight the hardest. Failure is found more often in losing heart rather than losing strength.

Why Not Arrest Jesus in the Upper Room?
Where is Gethsemane?
Was Gethsemane a Garden?
The Grotto of Gethsemane
Jesus' Agony in Gethsemane
Historical Examples of Sweating Blood
Jesus' One Concern
Gethsemane: Gateway to Golgotha

If someone asked you to name the five most prominent locations mentioned in Jesus' crucifixion narrative, certainly Gethsemane would be one of your choices. After Golgotha, Gethsemane could be next on your list. However, most people are surprised to learn that Gethsemane is only mentioned twice in the Bible–Matthew 26:36 and Mark 14:32. Luke does not mention Gethsemane; John does not mention it; neither do any of the

New Testament epistles. John does mention a garden that we associate with Gethsemane (John 18:1, 26), but he does not actually name that garden.

In this chapter, we focus on the famous place that was such a critical stopover as we follow Jesus to Calvary. It was Jesus' second stop on his journey to the cross. It was here that Jesus prayed. Here, Judas betrayed the Lord. Here, Peter demonstrated his impetuousness most dramatically. Furthermore, here, Jesus was chained and led away to trial and crucifixion. This is a significant stop on the road to Calvary. However, we must first answer a question that invariably arises in any discussion of the arrest of Jesus.

WHY NOT ARREST JESUS IN THE UPPER ROOM?

Arresting Jesus with his disciples in the Upper Room may indeed have been Plan A. The cenacle would have been the natural place to apprehend and arrest the innocent Nazarene. It was isolated; there were no crowds and no witnesses except those in the room itself. All the High Priest's Temple police had to do was surround the building where the Upper Room was located, push their way into the house, and take Jesus by stealth. This would have worked, too, if God had not planned otherwise.

The Gospels do not explain why Caiaphas failed to arrest Jesus in the Upper Room. Judas knew Jesus was there. He had left that very same room not long before. Surely he would have told Caiaphas and the Temple police. Judas would also have known how much more time Jesus would have spent with the disciples before leaving this upper room. The traitor knew where Jesus would leave, the traitor knew when he would leave, and the traitor knew where Jesus would go when he left. Why wait until the garden where hundreds of Passover pilgrims would have bedded down for the night?

There appears to be no factual explanation for why Jesus was not arrested in the most logical place. The Synoptic Gospels appear to place Jesus' predictions about his disciples scattering and deserting him, as well as the announcement of Peter's triple denial, in the Upper Room context (Matt 26:30–35). John concurs, writing, "When Jesus had spoken these words, he went out with his disciples across the brook Kidron, where there was a garden, which he and his disciples entered" (John 18:1).

Geographically speaking, Sir William Ramsay argued that the predictions of Peter's denials and the disciples' scattering had to occur in the Upper Room because the steps down from the Upper Room to the Kidron were steep, and Jesus and the disciples would have to walk single file to negotiate them. The words of Jesus recorded in John 14–17 appear to have been spoken before he and his disciples left the Upper Room.[16] This may not be a strong argument, but it indicates that much of John 14–16 occurred before they reached Gethsemane. However, neither the Bible nor archaeology answers the question, "Why not arrest Jesus in the Upper Room."

WHERE IS GETHSEMANE?

"The garden has many ancient olive trees today, some of which may have grown from the roots of the trees that were present in Jesus' time. All trees in and around Jerusalem were cut down when the Romans conquered the city in 70 AD. However, olive trees can regenerate from their roots and live for a thousand years or more. I have seen a freshly cut, flat-to-the-ground olive tree stump in March that had shoots rising from it by October.

The name *'Gethsemane,'* comes from the Hebrew *Gat Shmanim*, meaning 'oil press.'"[17] Gethsemane is located on the western slope of the Mount of Olives (Luke 22:39). John Briggs Curtis notes this about the mountain range:

> There are six Old Testament references (2 Sam 15:30; I Kgs 11:7; 2 Kgs 23:13; Ezek 10:23; Neh 8:15[?]; Zech 14:4) to the spur of the mountain range that has three summits or mounts running parallel to Jerusalem for some two and a half miles on the east, separated from the city by the Kidron valley and rising some 300 feet higher than the Temple area.[18]

The highest peak of this mountain range is the northernmost summit, Mount Scopus, which is 826 meters (2,710 feet) above sea level. The Mount of Olives is the center peak and is 818 meters (2,684 feet) high. The southernmost peak is the Mount of Corruption at 747 meters (2,451 feet). The ridge acts as a watershed, with rainfall either flowing toward the Mediterranean Sea or the Judean Desert and the Jordan Valley.

Gethsemane itself faces the city of Jerusalem and rises from the Kidron Valley on the western side of the Mount of Olives. According to the Gospels, this was a place Jesus and his disciples customarily visited when in Jerusalem. It was his sanctuary from the crowds. More importantly, it was Jesus' prayer sanctuary, where he could talk with his Father in solitude.

Near the Church of All Nations, located at the foot of the Mount of Olives, recent archaeological excavations have revealed the remains of a

Second Temple Period ritual bath, known as a mikveh. This discovery is significant because it is one of the first archaeological confirmations of what was present at Gethsemane when Jesus agonized in prayer there.

The earliest reference to Gethsemane's location, apart from the Gospels, comes from Eusebius (290–325 AD), who suggests it is the "place where Christ prayed before the Passion." Eusebius notes that "it is right by the Mount of Olives, in which even now the faithful are zealous in offering prayers." He distinguishes the site from Cheimarrous Kedron (John 18:1), "the Torrent of Kedron," meaning the Brook Kidron.

> "All the historians agree that the arrest of Jesus took place in the Garden of Gethsemane at a late hour on the evening immediately preceding the day of the Crucifixion, and there is strong justification for believing that it could not possibly have been earlier than eleven-thirty."
> —Frank Morrison

The Bordeaux Pilgrim (c. 334 AD) said that "if one left Jerusalem via the gate that is east in order to ascend the Mount of Olives, one passes through a valley called Josaphat." The Pilgrim continued, "On your left, where there are vineyards, is a rock where Judas Iscariot betrayed Christ."

From his description, it appears that the site of Judas' betrayal was associated with a rock formation in the Kidron Valley. This would be on the northern side of the path that led to the summit of the Mount of Olives. It may be the "Rock of Agony," associated with the Church or All Nations, or the rock face of the so-called Grotto of the Betrayal (see below).

Egeria is a fourth-century woman who authored the Peregrinatio, also known as the *Itinerarium Egeriae*. It is a detailed account of her pilgrimage to the Holy Land. Egeria noted that during the Holy Week, pilgrims descend from the Church of the Ascension on the Mount of Olives (now a mosque) "to that place where the Lord prayed." She noted that this was a place where "there is a fine church," apparently a reference to the Church of the Holy Sepulchre in Gethsemane. Jerome Murphy-O'Connor added:

> "The traditional site of Gethsemane has much to recommend its authenticity. When the church historian and bishop Eusebius of Caesarea wrote his *Onomasticon* (an alphabetic list of biblical places with descriptions of their history and geography) at some point between 324 and 336, Gethsemane was already a well-established

place of prayer, based on a tradition transmitted by the Christian community of Jerusalem, which had never abandoned the city."[19]

Nevertheless, four locations claim to be the actual site where Jesus prayed on the night he was betrayed.[20] They are:

1. The Church of All Nations at the foot of the Mount of Olives, containing the so-called "Rock of the Agony";
2. The Grotto of Gethsemane near the Tomb of the Virgin Mary to the north;
3. The Greek Orthodox location to the east; and
4. The Russian Orthodox orchard, next to the Church of Mary Magdalene.

Lieutenant General Sir William Montgomery was a British army commander who served in Sudan, the Middle East, and the Caucasus region of Azerbaijan. Well-traveled, Sir William authored a book entitled *The Land and the Book,* which was first published in 1880. In it, he wrote:

> When I first came to Jerusalem, and for many years afterward, this plot of ground was open to all whenever they chose to come and meditate beneath its very old olive trees. The Latins, however, have within the last few years succeeded in gaining sole possession, and have built a high wall around it. The Greeks have invented another site a little to the north of it. My own impression is that both are wrong. The position is too near the city, and so close to what must have always been the great thoroughfare eastward, that our Lord would scarcely have selected it for retirement on that dangerous and dismal night. I am inclined to place the garden in the secluded vale several hundred yards to the northeast of the present Gethsemane.[21]

When Christian pilgrims visit Jerusalem today, they are almost always taken to the Church of All Nations, officially known as the Basilica of the Agony, at the foot of the Mount of Olives. Here, in this dimly-lit Roman Catholic Church, you see a flat outcrop of rock known as the "Rock of the Agony." Tradition holds that it was here, at this very site, that Jesus fell to his knees in prayer before his Heavenly Father.

The Rock of Agony, Garden of Gethsemane

Gustaf Dalman writes of the location of Gethsemane:

> Josephus (*Wars* 6.1.1) reports that the trees on the east side of the city were cut down in the Roman siege of Jerusalem (some forty years after Jesus' death), and so it is impossible to be sure exactly where the Mount of Olives Gethsemane was. Since the fourth century, a site at the bottom of the mountain (where olive trees grow more abundantly than on the upper slopes) has been venerated, and in particular, a rock formation or cave that might have housed an oil press.[22]

He was speaking of the Church of All Nations.

Nevertheless, much of the discussion about the place where Jesus prayed centers around whether or not Gethsemane was actually a garden. That question may be the elephant in the room for any discussion related to Gethsemane.

WAS GETHSEMANE A GARDEN?

The Gospels indicate that after finishing the Last Supper in the Upper Room, Jesus and his eleven disciples, excluding Judas, departed from there and went out to the Mount of Olives. Matthew 26:30–35 says:

> And when they had sung a hymn, they went out to the Mount of Olives. Then Jesus said to them, "You will all fall away because of

me this night. For it is written, 'I will strike the shepherd, and the sheep of the flock will be scattered.' But after I am raised up, I will go before you to Galilee." Peter answered him, "Though they all fall away because of you, I will never fall away." Jesus said to him, "Truly, I tell you, this very night, before the rooster crows, you will deny me three times." Peter said to him, "Even if I must die with you, I will not deny you." And all the disciples said the same.

Mark 14 records much the same words. Luke documents that after the Last Supper, "he came out and went, as was his custom, to the Mount of Olives, and the disciples followed him" (Luke 22:39).

When Jesus and the eleven disciples came to the Garden of Gethsemane, what exactly did they enter? Was it an olive garden? Was it just a group of trees? What was Gethsemane?

What does the Bible say?

Matthew 26:36 and Mark 14:32 call the place by the name Gethsemane (Greek: Γεθσημανῆ; English: *Gethsēmanē*), a transliteration from the Hebrew and Aramaic phrase (*gat shemane*) signifying an "oil press." Luke and John do not use the name Gethsemane at all. So, what exactly are we talking about when we identify this place as Gethsemane? The Gospels describe it in different ways.

Matthew 26:36 and Mark 14:32 are relatively non-descript about Gethsemane, each calling it a "place" (Greek: χωρίον; English: *chorion*), meaning a field, a plot of ground, or any location that is not populated. Luke 22:39–40 uses an even less descriptive term (Greek: τόπος; English: *tópos*) meaning merely a "spot" or "place." There is no evidence or even a hint in the Synoptics that this place was a garden of any sort. Only John refers to this "place" as a garden, but he does so twice in chapter 18, verses 1 and 26.

John's choice of words each time (Greek: κπος: English: *kēpos*) means a location where you grow things. Gustaf Dalman writes, "John refers to the site as a garden (*kēpos*, applicable to a place with vegetables, flowers, or trees)."[23] Still, no arguments to the contrary change the clear impression that Gethsemane was an olive garden, an orchard of olive trees growing on the western slopes of the Mount of Olives.

So, if Matthew 26:36 and Mark 14:32 call the place by the name Gethsemane, and John 18:1 and 26 call the same place a garden, there should be no reason not to identify the location where Jesus prayed and was arrested as "the garden of Gethsemane."

THE GROTTO OF GETHSEMANE

Some suggest that Gethsemane should be identified with the Grotto or Cave of the Betrayal, about 90 meters (295 feet) north of the Church of All Nations. Excavations indicate that this grotto was once used for the production of olive oil. This would certainly fit with the meaning of Gethsemane.

According to some traditions, Jesus left his disciples in this cave when he went out among the olive trees of Gethsemane to pray. Later, upon his return, tradition claims it was here the Gethsemane group encountered Jesus, where Judas betrayed him, and where he was arrested.

The cave itself is 10 meters by 19 meters square (33 feet deep by 62 feet wide). The speculation is that Jesus and the eleven disciples spent the night in a warm, dry, and roomy cave with a cistern to provide the needed water. Pilgrims from Galilee would have accommodated Jesus and his disciples regardless of the hour they arrived at the cave.

The cave is situated in an area frequently flooded by spring rains. In 1955, a major flood necessitated the renovation and restoration of some of the grotto's damaged areas. Friar Virgilio Canio Corbo undertook the upgrades from 1956 to 1957. (Friar Corbo by himself famously excavated the ruins of Capernaum on the north shore of the Sea of Galilee). What was found in the cave neither confirmed nor denied that this could have been where Jesus was arrested on the night he was betrayed.

Historical references to the grotto

The earliest pilgrim records, however, do not mention a cave in Gethsemane. The oldest reference to the cave dates back to Theodosius (ca. 520 AD). Nonetheless, this reference is suspect because Theodosius confused the site of the Last Supper with the location of Jesus' betrayal, both of which he says occurred "in a cave."

The first document to suggest Christ's agony took place in this grotto was written in 1333 AD by a German Dominican named Wilhelm von Boldensele. He, too, was likely mistaken.

As mentioned above, Adomnán was an abbot at the abbey on the Isle of Iona, Scotland. He wrote a treatise called *De Locis Sanctis* ("On Holy

Places"), which was an account of the great Christian holy places and sites of pilgrimage. Adomnán got most of his information from the Frankish bishop Arculf, who had personally traveled to Rome, Constantinople, Egypt, and the Holy Land. The name Gethsemane is not mentioned in Admonán's treatise, but it is clear that this is the cave the pilgrim referred to.

> Not far above the tomb of Saint Mary on the Mount of Olives, there is a cave which faces the Valley of Jehoshaphat. In it are two very deep wells: one goes down to an untold depth below the mountain, and the other is in the floor of the cave. It has a huge shaft sunk deep, which goes down straight. Over these wells there is a permanent covering . . . According to what the holy Arculf says, this cave has a small entrance which is closed by a wooden door, and he paid it many visits.[24]

Jack Finegan comments:

> [About 333 AD], "the Bordeaux Pilgrim went out from the city to the gate which is to the eastward (*contra oriente*) in order to ascend the Mount of Olives . . . He says: 'On the left, where there are vineyards, is a rock where Judas Iscariot betrayed Christ; on the right is a palm tree from which the children broke off branches and strewed them when Christ came . . . The Bordeaux Pilgrim was therefore quite plainly in the vicinity of what we know as the Grotto of the Betrayal and the Garden of Gethsemane.[25]

"They went to a place which was called Gethsemane; and he said to his disciples, 'Sit here, while I pray'" (Mark 14:32). Gerhard Kroll (no relation), *In the Footsteps of Jesus. His Life. His Work. His Time* commented further:

> At the time of Jesus, in this terrain on the slopes of the Mount of Olives, there was a farmstead with an oil press for crushing the olives . . . The farmstead was named Gethsemane on account of the oil press . . . Nearby was a large natural cave, which could have offered Jesus and his disciples a safe, if not a particularly comfortable place to spend the night.[26]

We know from the pilgrim Egeria that a "magnificent church" existed here by the end of the fourth century AD. "Completed in 1924, the present-day Church of Jesus' Agony not only encompasses the site of the '*ecclesia elegans*' [Egeria's church], it once more surrounds the rock on which tradition tells us that Jesus prayed."[27]

While this mix of ancient travelers and modern scholars reports similar but not always identical information about the garden and its cave, there is enough correspondence to suggest that the grotto and the garden were and are real places and that Jesus and his disciples met together there for the last time before his crucifixion.

John 18:1–4 gives us insight into what happened the night Judas kissed his Master and set in motion the most significant weekend in history. John says:

> When Jesus had spoken these words, he went out with his disciples across the brook Kidron, where there was a garden, which he and his disciples entered. Now Judas, who betrayed him, also knew the place, for Jesus often met there with his disciples. So Judas, having procured a band of soldiers and some officers from the chief priests and the Pharisees, went there with lanterns and torches and weapons. Then Jesus, knowing all that would happen to him, came forward and said to them, "Whom do you seek"?

However, some scholars are not on board with the idea that Jesus and his disciples were accosted in the cave of Gethsemane. Max Kuchler remains skeptical, suggesting that the verb (Greek: ἐξέρχομαι; English: *exérchomai*), translated as "came forward" in John 18:4, refers to the garden (John 18:1, 3), not to a cave, which none of the Gospel writers mention.[28] Kuchler asserts that the words "came forward" meant that Jesus stepped forward from the disciples to speak directly to the Temple guards and the rest of the Gethsemane group.

Many scholars believe that Jesus' agony occurred in the Garden of Gethsemane, while his betrayal may have taken place in this grotto.[29] Should this cave be the actual place where Jesus frequented, it means Jesus left eight disciples in the cave to rest, took the primary three from the cave into the treed area to pray, and went even further into the olive grove to talk with his Heavenly Father.[30]

In the garden, as he wrestled with the will of God, Jesus is said to have sweated drops of blood. How is this possible? We must examine that next.

HISTORICAL EXAMPLES OF SWEATING BLOOD

Jesus was not the only person to experience the phenomenon of losing blood through sweating. "Of medical significance is that Luke mentions him [Jesus] as having sweat like blood. The medical term for this is '*hemohidrosis*' or '*hematidrosis*.' It has been seen in patients who have experienced extreme stress or shock to their systems."[31]

There is no reason to believe that Luke meant his words figuratively or symbolically because there is no inherent meaning to the expression. For example, phrases like "he spilled the beans" or "he let the cat out of the bag" are figurative expressions that have inherent meanings we can all relate to. Luke's words do not.

There is a rare medical condition called hematidrosis, also known as Sudorcruentus, Sudor Sanguineus, Suerdesany, or *hemorrhagia percutem*. This condition has a long documented history. Here are some examples of the phenomenon known as bloody sweat.

The fourth century BC

The great Greek philosopher Aristotle (384–322 BC) has been called the "Father of Western Philosophy." A Greek native of the island of Lesbos, Theophrastus was the successor to Aristotle in the Peripatetic school. He lived from 371 to 287 BC and was a prolific writer, addressing topics such as physics, metaphysics, moral character, and the properties of stones, among others. He mentions the phenomenon of hematidrosis.

The first century AD

More commonly known as Lucan, Marcus Annaeus Lucanus was the nephew of the philosopher Seneca the Younger. Born in 39 AD in Cordoba, Spain, he died in Rome in 65 AD. This Roman poet and republican patriot wrote the epic work *Bellum Civile*, better known as the *Pharsalia*. Lucan also mentions people sweating blood.

The sixteenth century

In his Commentaries on the Four Gospels, sixteenth-century author Joannes Maldonato mentions, "A robust and healthy man at Paris who, on hearing the sentence of death passed on him, was covered with a bloody sweat."

One of the more influential authorities on medicine during the late Renaissance was Joannes Schenck. His *Observationum medicarum rariorum* about rare medical observations, published in 1584, contained a description of "a nun who fell into the hands of soldiers; and, on seeing herself encompassed with swords and daggers threatening instant death, was so terrified and agitated, that she discharged blood from every part of her body, and died of hemorrhage in the sight of her assailants."[32]

Sixteenth-century French statesman and historiographer Jacques-Auguste de Thou wrote a multi-volume Latin work called *Historia sui temporis* (*History of His Own Time*). In this series of books on historical subjects, de Thou had much to say about crucifixion and the sweating drops of blood. He mentions the following case.

> An Italian officer who commanded at Monte-Maro, a fortress of [the] Piedmont, during the warfare in 1552, having been treacherously seized by order of the hostile general, and threatened with public execution unless he surrendered the place, was so agitated at the prospect of an ignominious death, that he sweated blood from every part of his body.

De Thou also tells of a young Florentine in Rome who was unjustly put to death by order of Pope Sixtus V. He notes, "When the youth was led forth to execution, he excited the commiseration of many, and through excess of grief, was observed to shed bloody tears, and to discharge blood instead of sweat from his whole body."[33]

The seventeenth century

Paulus Zacchias, a seventeenth-century Italian physician, medical science and forensic medicine teacher, and personal physician to two popes, wrote the book *Quaestiones medico-legales* (*Medical and Legal Questions*) in which he examined hematidrosis. He also mentioned a young man who sweated blood when he was condemned to die in flames.[34]

The eighteenth century

Samuel A. A. D. Tissot, an eighteenth-century Swiss Calvinist, neurologist, and physician, wrote *Traité des nerfs et de leurs maladies* (*Treatise on the Nerves and Nervous Disorders*). In this work, he described "a sailor who was so alarmed by a storm, that through fear he fell down, and his face sweated blood, which during the whole continuance of the storm returned like ordinary sweat, as fast as it was wiped away."[35]

German author Gottlieb Heinrich Kannegiesser explains the cause of bloody sweat.

> Violent mental excitement, whether occasioned by uncontrollable anger, or vehement joy, and in like manner sudden terror, or intense fear, forces out a sweat, accompanied with signs either of anxiety or of hilarity . . . If the mind is seized with a sudden fear of death, the sweat, owing to the excessive degree of constriction, often becomes bloody.[36]

Kanneigiesser then cites several examples of those who have sweated blood when under extreme duress. "A young boy, who, having taken part in a crime for which two of his elder brothers were hanged, was exposed to public view under the gallows on which they were executed, and was thereupon observed to sweat blood from his whole body."

The nineteenth century

"While hematidrosis has been reported to occur from other rare medical entities, the presence of profound fear accounted for a significant number of reported cases, including six cases in men condemned to execution, a case occurring during the London blitz, a case involving a fear of being raped, [and] a fear of a storm while sailing, etc."[37]

The twentieth century

Both Dr. Ryland Whitaker, in his article "The Physical Cause of the Death of our Lord" (1935), and Dr. A. LeBec, in *"Death of the Cross: A Physiological Study of the Passion of Our Lord Jesus Christ"* (1925), documented several instances of hematidrosis on record. A search of the vast medical literature revealed that a significant number of cases of hematidrosis were associated with a severe anxiety reaction triggered by fear.

This association with fear was the most strikingly seen in a review of reported cases by J. H. Pooley in 1884. "The capillaries around the sweat pores become fragile and leak blood into the sweat. A case history is recorded in which a young girl who had a fear of air raids in WWI developed the condition after a gas explosion occurred in the house next door."

In 1918, Dr. C. T. Scott described an instance of an intelligent young girl of eleven whom her parents sheltered because she was very nervous about air raids. The child experienced frequent bouts of hematidrosis.[38]

During the waning years of the twentieth century, seventy-six cases of hematidrosis were studied and classified according to causative factors: "Acute fear and intense mental contemplation were found to be the most frequent inciting causes."[39]

TABLE 1

Historical References to Bloody Sweat

Author	Work	Account
Aristotle	The History of Animals, l.3.19	Bloody sweat arising from malnutrition
Aristotle	The Parts of Animals, l.3.5	Bloody sweat arising from illness
Thuanus	Historia sui Temporis, 1.1.8, 804–805	Captured governor facing ignominious death
Thuanus	Historia sui Temporis, 4.1.82, 69	Florentine man sweat blood at execution
Maldonato	Classic Jesuit author	Paris man sweats blood when convicted
Diodorus	Bibliotheca Historica	Snakebite brings sweat-like blood
Julius Solin	Polyhistor, c. 40	Snakebite causes bloody sweat
Isidor	Hispalens. Etymolog. l.12.c.4	Snakebite causes bloody sweat

Indeed, the stress Jesus endured facing the torture of the cross would be enough to cause real blood to sweat through his pores.

Hematidrosis is not a person oozing blood instead of sweat. It is the capillaries surrounding the sweat pores that become fragile and, under severe stress, leak blood into the sweat that appears on the body's surface. In Jesus' case, his stress level was so elevated that his sweat was generously mixed with blood so that its color and consistency were as if it had been wholly blood.

Was it really blood? Yes. Was it really sweat? Yes. It was a phenomenon that mixed blood and sweat. The result is bloody sweat, and Jesus experienced it while his humanity, which naturally loathed the idea of being crucified, wrestled with his divinity, which knew the eternal plan required him to be crucified.

JESUS' ONLY CONCERN

Determination is a profound factor in success. Giving up when your life situation is cruel, unfair, or painful always results in defeat. In the Garden of Gethsemane, Jesus of Nazareth exhibited the ultimate display of determination. He set his mind to see his Father in heaven glorified through what would transpire in the next seventeen hours. With the glory of God as his only concern, his instincts were subdued by his determination to accomplish the divine plan of redemption.

> "Jesus accepted the cross out of a motive of love for God even more than, and before, he accepted it because of his love for man."
> —Geerhardus Vos

Some see the psychological and emotional agony Jesus experienced in the garden was a battle of two wills. No one wants to die, especially in shame and pain. Nevertheless, Jesus knew full well why he came to Earth. Everything he said and everything he did was leading up to this very moment. He could not allow his human inclinations to impact his divine instructions. When Jesus was in the greatest depths of his struggle, not only did he not give up and quit praying to the Father, but he "prayed more earnestly." When it appears we are losing, that is when we must fight the hardest. Failure is found more often in losing heart rather than losing strength. Premier twentieth-century German Catholic Theologian Joseph Ratzinger, who later became Pope Benedict XVI, made this comment about the two wills of the Savior.

> The two parts of Jesus' prayer are presented as the confrontation between two wills: there is the 'natural will' of the man Jesus, which resists the appalling destructiveness of what is happening and wants to plead that the chalice pass from him; and there is the 'filial will' that abandons itself totally to the Father's will.[40]

I understand the agony in Gethsemane not so much a battle of Jesus' will as it was the subduing of what is natural to achieve what is not natural. Jesus' determination to carry out the Father's purpose in our salvation would not allow this last-minute agony to invalidate the eternal redemptive plan of God.

During the most challenging hour of his life, what pushed Jesus toward the cross? What was the motivation to take on the pain, the shame, and the suffering of crucifixion? Was it a sense of duty? No, it was his stated commitment to glorify the Father. Jesus came to glorify the Father. He lived to glorify the Father. He would die to glorify the Father. His only concern was the Father's glory.

GETHSEMANE: GATEWAY TO GOLGOTHA

St. Louis, Missouri, has its arch, the Gateway to the West. In the decades following World War II, San Francisco was called the Gateway to the Pacific. Mumbai has the Gateway of India. But history's most significant gateway was the one that led to Golgotha and the sacrifice of the Son of God for our sins. The gateway to Golgotha was a garden called Gethsemane.

Had he wanted, when the mob approached Gethsemane to arrest Jesus, the Savior could have escaped (see Luke 4:30). He was already deep into the garden. Along with a myriad of others, the soldiers and police approached from the Kidron Valley. If his desire to do the will of the Father had not been so strong, Jesus could have climbed higher up the slopes of the Mount of Olives, crossed east over the crest of the mountain, and from there, it was downhill to Jericho and the Jordan Valley. Across the river, he could escape into obscurity. However, this was not God's plan, and as a result, it was not his Son's choice.

F. J. Huegel authored the book, *The Cross of Christ—The Throne of God*. In it, he observed:

> Would you have the key to the Saviour's deepest thought? Here it is. You need to look no further. You need to ask no theologian. You need to ask no preacher. Jesus speaks. His language is clear: "For this cause I came." "This," says the Master, in effect "is my hour. Here my genius will find its real expression. This is the real reason for my descent from Heaven. I came to pour out my lifeblood for sinners."[41]

Jesus was determined that nothing would deter him from the cross because, in the eternal plan of the Holy Trinity, the cross would ultimately bring glory to the Father.

This is not easy to understand, but it demonstrates once again the truth of the LORD's words in Isaiah 55:8, 9: "For my thoughts are not your thoughts, neither are your ways my ways, saith the Lord. For as the heavens are higher than the earth, so are my ways higher than your ways, and my thoughts than your thoughts."

> "'Not my will but yours be done' does not ensure there will be no Friday afternoon, but it does guarantee there will be a Sunday morning."
> —Woodrow Michael Kroll

What of God's Word we can see and investigate, we believe. What we cannot see or investigate, we either accept by faith or reject by choice. What is true is not determined by whether or not we understand it, accept it, or believe it. Truth is truth because it is authentic, factual, accurate, and genuine. That describes God's truth every time.

The journey to Golgotha had to start somewhere. It began in a peaceful garden. Gethsemane was the gateway to Golgotha.

> All those who journey, soon or late,
> Must pass within the garden's gate;
> Must kneel alone in darkness there.
> And battle with some fierce despair.
> God pity those who cannot say,
> 'Not mine but thine'; but only pray,
> 'Let this cup pass'; and cannot see,
> The purpose in Gethsemane.
> —Anonymous

Chapter 3

The High Priest's Compound

The House of Miscarried Justice

Certainly, Zion played a pivotal role in the hopes and expectations of the people of God. But the importance of Zion was not just a covenantal importance; it was also geographical.

Why Take Jesus First to Annas?
The Lay of the Land
The Importance of Zion
The Upper City
The Assumptionist Catholic Palace
The Armenian Palace of the High Priest
The Palatial Mansion
The Chamber of Hewn Stone

What was Jerusalem like when Jesus taught in its Temple? How luxurious were the accommodations for the Jewish High Priest at the time? Where was the palace of the High Priest located? Did Annas and his son-in-law Caiaphas live in a palace compound, or did they have separate palaces in different parts of the city? Furthermore, why did the Temple police take Jesus first to Annas after his arrest when Caiaphas was the High Priest?

These are the kinds of questions this chapter will attempt to answer. Let's begin with that last question first.

WHY TAKE JESUS FIRST TO ANNAS?

Jesus' trial before Annas and Caiaphas was anything but typical. Almost everything about it was atypical. It began with a preliminary interrogation by Annas around 11:00 pm, just before the day of Preparation for Passover was about to start, according to Roman time. While the High Priest Caiaphas was the head of the Sanhedrin, Jesus was first taken to Annas for questioning. The trial itself lacked many of the features typically found in standard Jewish judicial procedures. The separation between the interrogation of Annas and the late-night tribunal of Caiaphas is evident in the Gospels.

Table 1 presents the various events in the life of Jesus that occurred late on Thursday evening and into Friday morning. Take note of the distinction between the events that happened at the house of Annas and those at the house of Caiaphas.

It was the Apostle John who informed us, "So the band of soldiers and their captain and the officers of the Jews arrested Jesus and bound him. First, they led him to Annas, for he was the father-in-law of Caiaphas, who was High Priest that year" (John 18:12, 13). This was a journey of approximately 1,500 meters (4,921 feet; just a football field short of a mile).

To appreciate this stop on Jesus' journey to Calvary, we must first gain a clear understanding of Jerusalem's geography.

THE LAY OF THE LAND

Jerusalem, as Jesus knew it, bore little resemblance to the city David had conquered in the tenth century BC. In David's day, Jerusalem was a small, isolated hill fortress valued more for its location than for its splendor. From the day David and his men conquered this small outcrop of land, it became known as the City of David. It was David's son, Solomon, who enlarged and beautified the city.

THE HIGH PRIEST'S COMPOUND

TABLE 1
From Jesus' Arrest in Gethsemane to Caiaphas' Courtroom

The Interrogation by Annas	
The officers arrested and bound Jesus	John 18:12
They first led Jesus to Annas	John 18:13
Annas questioned Jesus about his teaching	John 18:19
Jesus remarked that he spoke in public, and nothing was hidden. Ask the people what he taught.	John 18:20
One of the officers struck Jesus for being insolent	John 18:22
Annas sent Jesus to Caiaphas, the High Priest.	John 18:24
The Trial by Caiaphas	
The Temple police seized Jesus, led him to Caiaphas	Mark 14:53; John 18:12
The "chief priests and the whole council" were present	Matt. 26:59
They all sought false testimony to put Jesus to death	Matt. 26:59; Mark 14:55
No credible witnesses could be found	Matt. 26:60; Mark 14:56
Two witnesses said Jesus vowed in 3 days to rebuild the Temple. Even their testimonies didn't agree.	Matt. 26:61; Mark 14:58
Caiaphas demanded that Jesus respond to the charges	Matt. 26:62; Mark 14:60
Jesus remained silent	Matt. 26:63; Mark. 14:61
Caiaphas asked, "Are you the Christ?"	Mark. 14:61
Jesus said he'd be "seated at the right hand of Power" and "coming with the clouds of heaven."	Mark 14:62; Luke 22:68
Religious leaders pled Jesus say if he was the Christ	Luke 22:67
Jesus said if he told them, they would not believe him	Luke 22:68
They then asked, "Are you the Son of God?"	Luke 22:70
Jesus answered, "You say that I am."	Luke 22:70
Caiaphas tore his robes, claimed Jesus blasphemied	Matt. 26:65; Mark 14:63
Caiaphas asked the council for a judgment	Matt. 26:66; Luke 22:71
In lock-step, they responded, "He deserves death"	Matt. 26:66; Mark 14:64
The Sanhedrin members spat in Jesus' face	Matt. 26:67; Mark 14:65
They covered his head and struck Jesus	Mark 14:63; Luke 22:63
Some of the Sanhedrin slapped Jesus.	Matt. 26:67
They mocked him: "Prophesy… Who struck you?"	Mark 14:65; Luke 22:64
The guards tortured Jesus by beating him	Mark 14:65
At daylight, the council again gathered together	Luke 22:66

In the sixth century BC, the army of Nebuchadnezzar leveled Jerusalem and carried off most of its citizens into exile. During the years of captivity in Babylon, the Jews in exile both prayed and longed for that distant Holy City (see Ps 79:1–4; 137:1–6). Nevertheless, when they finally returned and rebuilt Jerusalem, the Temple was far inferior to its former splendor. Ironically, it was the despised autocrat Herod the Great who restored Jerusalem and its Temple to their former grandeur.

In the 33 years of his reign (37–4 B.C.), Herod the Great transformed the city as no other ruler had since Solomon. Building palaces and citadels, a theatre and an amphitheater, viaducts, and public monuments was just the beginning of Herod's building efforts. These ambitious building projects, some of which were completed after his death, were part of the king's single-minded campaign to increase his capital's importance in the eyes of the Roman Empire.

> "Whoever has not seen Jerusalem in its splendor has never seen a fine city." — Babylonian Talmud (*Succah*, 51b)

Even today, no visitor seeing Jerusalem for the first time can fail to be mesmerized by its magnificent splendor. For pilgrims, the steep and difficult ascent from Jericho in the Jordan Valley to the Holy City was worth it when the pilgrim rounded the top of the Mount of Olives. There, suddenly, you caught a magnificent panorama like few others in the world. Your view across the Kidron Valley focused on "the perfection of beauty" (Ps 50:2), "the joy of all the world" (Lam 2:15), the Holy City (Neh 11:1, 18; Isa 48:2; 52:1; Matt 4:5; 27:53; Rev 21:2, 10, 19)—Jerusalem.

In Jesus' day, the view from the Mount of Olives was dominated by the gleaming, magnificent Temple. The importance of this location cannot be overstated. It was the LORD's earthly dwelling place. It was here, in the holy of holies within the Temple, that YHWH met once a year with the High Priest and spoke to the people. Here, the Jewish people performed rituals and ceremonies that foreshadowed the coming of the Messiah, the Kinsman Redeemer, the Lamb of God who takes away the sin of the world.

The Temple stood as the primary marker for everything else in the city, much like the Colosseum does in Rome or the Eiffel Tower in Paris. The city was geographically divided into four distinct areas: the Mount of Olives, the Temple Mount (also known as Mount Moriah), the Lower City, and the Upper City.

The High Priest's Compound

To the southwest of the Temple was the Lower City. Here, you would find dusty streets lined with limestone houses, somewhat yellowed from the burning Palestinian sun, sloping downward toward the Tyropean Valley. This valley, also known as the "Valley of the Cheesemakers," ran essentially north to south through the center of Jerusalem, separating the Temple Mount from the Upper City and Mount Zion.

Mountains surrounded the city itself. "As the mountains surround Jerusalem, so the LORD surrounds his people, from this time forth and forevermore" (Ps 125:2). A high, thick stone wall also enclosed it. The wall was often damaged, repaired, and enlarged over the centuries. When Jesus entered the gates of the city, the wall was about four miles in circumference. Within that wall, approximately 25,000 people resided in an area of about one square mile. Just inside each gate was a customs station. Here, publicans collected taxes on all goods entering or leaving the city of Jerusalem.

That is Jerusalem. It is one of the most mesmerizing cities in the world. Sometimes visitors are so enthralled by the Golden City that they become afflicted with what has been called the "Jerusalem Syndrome." When so captivated by the City of David that you feel you belong there, that God has called you there, that you leave your companions or fellow pilgrims, abandon your home country, and suddenly call Jerusalem your home, you may be afflicted with "Jerusalem Syndrome." Fortunately for most, after a couple of weeks, they seem to overcome the syndrome and return home.

THE IMPORTANCE OF ZION

To say that Mount Zion and Jerusalem were important to the Jewish people and their God is a colossal understatement. The Scriptures intensely and frequently suggest that YHWH loves Zion, that he lives there on Earth, and that Mount Zion is the apple of his eye. "Many peoples shall come, and say: 'Come, let us go up to the mountain of the Lord, to the house of the God of Jacob, that he may teach us his ways and that we may walk in his paths.' For out of Zion shall go forth the law, and the word of the Lord from Jerusalem" (Isa 2:3).

Zion is associated with the power of the LORD in battle. "The Lord of hosts will come down to fight on Mount Zion and its hill (Isa 31:4). Zion was not just "a sight for sore eyes," but a source of joy for those exiles who returned to the hill of God. "And the ransomed of the Lord shall return and come to Zion with singing; everlasting joy shall be upon their heads"

(Isa 35:10; 51:11). Zion is the home of the Almighty. "So you shall know that I am the LORD your God, who dwells in Zion, my holy mountain. Furthermore, Jerusalem shall be holy" (Joel 3:17, see also Pss 74:2; 135:21; Isa 8:18; 18:7; Jer 31:6; Joel 3:21; 3:17; Mic 4:12). To the Jew (and many others around the world), Jerusalem is the most significant city on Earth, and with good reason.

Zion is often directly identified with the city of Jerusalem. "O Zion; put on your beautiful garments, O Jerusalem, the holy city" (Isa 51:2, see also Isa10:32; 30:19; 40:9; 64:10; Jer 26:18; Joel 3:17; Amos 1;2; Mic 3;12; 4:12; Zeph 3:16; Zech 1:14, 17; and 9:9). Referring to Jerusalem, the prophet says, "They shall call you the City of the LORD, the Zion of the Holy One of Israel" (Isa 60:14). Even when not designated "Mount Zion," it is identified with a hill or a mountain. "Go on up to a high mountain, O Zion, herald of good news; lift up your voice with strength, O Jerusalem, herald of good news" (Isa 40:9, see also Isa 46:13; Jer 31:12; Joel 2:1; 3:17; Mic 4:12).

One of the great prophecies of the Old Testament links Zion with Jerusalem. "Rejoice greatly, O daughter of Zion! Shout aloud, O daughter of Jerusalem! Behold, your king is coming to you; righteous and having salvation is he, humble and mounted on a donkey, on a colt, the foal of a donkey" (Zech 9:9). That phrase "daughter of Zion" is a popular one, meaning the people of Jerusalem. "Daughters of Jerusalem" is found in the Bible fourteen times, but "Daughters of Zion" thirty-two times.

Certainly, Zion played a pivotal role in the hopes and expectations of the people of God. However, the importance of Zion was not just covenantal; it was also geographical.

THE UPPER CITY

Perhaps only the Mount of Olives is better known to Holy Land pilgrims than Mount Zion. The first leg of Jesus' journey to Calvary was between these two mountains. Rising to the west of the Temple was the Upper City, located on Mount Zion. Here stood the white marble villas and palatial residences of the rich and famous. Two large arched passageways spanned the valley, crossing from the Upper City to the Temple Mount. The Upper City was the equivalent of Chaoyang Park in Beijing, Leblon in Rio de Janeiro, or the Upper West Side in New York. It is here that the rich and the famous of Jerusalem lived.

The High Priest's Compound

The historic residences of the High Priests

Mount Zion did not always refer to the exact geographical location it now occupies. It was a mountain on the move. The Old Testament tersely describes David's conquest of the Jebusite city. "David took the stronghold of Zion, that is, the city of David" (2 Sam 5:7). Zion was identified as the City of David. While the traditional tomb of David is located on Mount Zion, the biblical texts place David's tomb in the City of David overlooking the Kidron Valley (1 Kgs 2:10; Neh 3:14–16). The third-century *Tosefta Baba Bathra* 1.11–12 also places the tomb near the Kidron Valley. However, in the twelfth century, the Sephardic Jewish philosopher Maimonides (1135–1204 AD) believed David's tomb was associated with the Lower City overlooking the Tyropean Valley (*Mishnah Torah* 8: *Avodah*). We are not so much concerned here with the location of the tomb of David as we are with the "upper crust" choosing to live in the Upper City near his tomb.

The hill southeast of Herod's Palace encompassed the Upper City on Mount Zion. It was inhabited during biblical times but deserted after the Babylonian conquest of Jerusalem in 586 BC. During Herod the Great's reign in the first century BC, the Upper City once more was inhabited. It was during that time this area became Jerusalem's residential quarter for the aristocracy and priestly families. It was also during this time that the area designated "Mount Zion" became associated with the upper hill west of the Temple rather than the hill overlooking the Kidron.

Before the days of Jesus and as far back as the time of Nehemiah, the High Priest resided on the western side of the Temple court area. During the time of the Maccabees, the High Priest lived in the Hasmonaean Palace in the Upper City overlooking the valley below. Josephus mentions that, during Jesus' time, the house of Ananias, located in the prefecture of Gessius Florus, stood near the Palace of the Hasmonaeans on the eastern ridge of the Upper City.

From the Upper Room to Joseph's Tomb

*Model of the Hasmonean Palace
in the Second Temple Period*

The palace of the Hasmoneans was located on the eastern side of the Upper City. It contained a roof called the Xystus, where the people in the large square below could be addressed. It had large courts, living quarters, baths, and a service court. Josephus' description of the Hasmonean palace is quite precise. He placed it "over the gallery, at the passage to the Upper City, where the bridge joined the Temple to the gallery."

With these landmarks, it is possible to approximate the position of the palace in front of the Temple, slightly north of the modern Jewish Quarter. This location would make good sense both topographically, as it is situated at a lofty elevation and administratively, since it is adjacent to the wealthy and priestly quarters in the Upper City. Because it overlooked the Temple, both the Roman prefect and the Jewish High Priest could constantly observe the goings-on in the Temple.

We must remember, however, that Jerusalem was destroyed in 70 AD. Its citizens were scattered; both Jews and Christians were persecuted throughout the empire. The exact location of the sacred Christian places was not easy to find upon their return. Many houses were looted and burnt, and according to Josephus, the city of Jerusalem was unrecognizable. Even if anyone returning to the city after its destruction knew the exact location of the palace of Caiaphas, it would have been nearly impossible to find it.

After Constantine's conversion in the early fourth century, when the influx of Christian pilgrims to Jerusalem began to grow, the location of many previously forgotten sacred places was, for lack of a more euphemistic term, "invented" because there was simply no other way to determine their exact locations.

As of now, the precise location of Caiaphas' palace remains unknown. However, if the High Priests lived somewhere in the Upper City, is it possible to identify a potential location? Maybe, yet as always, there are multiple contenders for the honor. Let's examine each. Likely, at one of them, Jesus received an unfair trial.

THE ASSUMPTIONIST CATHOLIC PALACE

The traditional site of the High Priest's house, and the site most frequently visited by pilgrims to Jerusalem, is located on the eastern slope of Mount Zion. Here is the beautiful church of St. Peter in Gallicantu. The site was chosen because of the remains of a sixth-century AD church found beneath it.

Saint Peter in Gallicantu commemorates the appearance of Jesus before Caiaphas, his death sentence compelled by the Sanhedrin, Peter's denial, and his regret when the rooster crowed. Within this neo-Byzantine church with its impressive mosaics, you will find a model of the Byzantine Jerusalem, a crypt, a deep pit believed by some to be the dungeon where Jesus was held overnight before his crucifixion, several archaeological sites, and a belvedere offering a panoramic view of Jerusalem.

THE HISTORY OF THE CHURCH OF ST PETER IN GALLICANTU

One of the reasons for believing this is that the actual site of the High Priest's compound is marked by churches that have been built, destroyed, rebuilt, destroyed again, and rebuilt. That would not be the case if, throughout history, people held this location to be authentic.

In the year 457 AD, a church was built here, but it was severely damaged in 529 AD during the Samaritan Revolt. The church was destroyed by the Persians in 614 AD. However, because many believed this to be the site of Peter's denials in Caiaphas' courtyard, the church was rebuilt around 628 AD. Unfortunately, it was destroyed again in 1009 AD by the mad Caliph Hakim. Continuing to bounce back, the Church of St. Peter in Gallicantu was rebuilt around 1100 AD by the Crusaders but destroyed again in 1219 AD by the Turks. A chapel was built in this location and destroyed around 1300 AD. The present church, a fusion of art and history, was completed in 1932. So far, so good.

Today, St. Peter in Gallicantu stands majestically on the sharp eastern slope of Mount Zion. It is one of the finest churches in the Holy City.

A description of the church

The Church of St. Peter in Gallicantu is constructed on four distinct levels: the upper church, the middle church, the guardroom, and the dungeon. The upper and middle churches are beautifully decorated with both ancient and contemporary art. The guardroom and dungeon have bare walls and dirt floors that have been pounded hard by the feet of pilgrims for decades.

The Roof

On the roof of the church rises a golden rooster atop a black cross—recalling Christ's prophesy that Peter would deny him three times "before the rooster crows" (Matt 26:34). Peter's denials of his Lord are recorded in all four Gospels, most succinctly in Matthew 26:69–75. Three of the Gospels also record his bitter tears of remorse (see Matt 26:74; Mark 14:72; Luke 22:62).

The scene of Peter's denials was the courtyard of the High Priest's palace. The Assumptionist Catholics, who built St Peter in Gallicantu over the ruins of a Byzantine basilica, maintain it stands on the site of the High Priest's house.

The Upper Church

Entrance to the church is gained through two amazing wrought iron doors with skillfully carved bas-reliefs of Jesus with the eleven disciples. After you pass through the doors, to the right are two Byzantine-era mosaics. These were discovered during excavations beneath the church and are most likely a portion of the floor of the fifth-century Byzantine Church.

The High Priest's Compound

The back wall and two side walls are covered with three large mosaics; the one facing the entrance depicts a bound Jesus being questioned in the house of Caiaphas. The fourteen stations of the cross line the walls and are marked with simple crosses.

Perhaps the most striking feature of the upper church is the ceiling. It features a beautiful, multi-colored, stain-glass window in the shape of a cross. The amount of light entering through this window is minimal, but the artistic effect is maximal.

The Middle Church

Downstairs, the middle church incorporates the stone from ancient grottos for part of its walls. There is an altar that depicts Peter's tragic denials of Jesus, accompanied by icons above it. The scenes above the altar represent Peter's denials, his repentance for those denials, and the Master on the shore of the Sea of Galilee after his resurrection, depicting Peter's gracious restoration.

In this chapel's sanctuary is a hole. If you look down through it, you can see caves that some interpret as part of a Byzantine shrine. The walls are engraved with crosses left by fifth-century followers of Jesus.

Since most of the inscriptions in the church are in French, some may have difficulty understanding them. The Assumptionists are a French religious order established in 1887 and named for Mary's alleged assumption into heaven.

The Guardroom

On the next level down, there are several caves from the Second Temple Period. Here is the guardroom where the private police force of the High Priest would hold prisoners in cells awaiting trial by Caiaphas. Clearly visible in the guardroom are wall fixtures that are understood to have been used to attach prisoners' chains. Holes in the stone pillars could have been used to fasten a prisoner's hands and feet to prevent escape when he was flogged.[42]

Depressions carved into the bedrock floor before the "cells" may have been bowls for salt and vinegar to disinfect the prisoner's wounds.

The Dungeon

Further down into the bedrock, a dungeon was cut, which may have operated as a prison cell. The only access to the bottle-necked cell was through a shaft from above. This means the prisoner would be lowered and raised in and out of the dungeon using a rope harness. A mosaic depicting Jesus in such a harness is outside on the south wall of the church.

A small window from the guardroom may have served as an overlook for a guard on the level above. There is even a stone that some believe is there for the guard to stand on to get a better look down into the dungeon.

Since tradition places the house of Caiaphas on this site, many Christians believe that Jesus may have been imprisoned in one of these underground cells after his arrest. While this is entirely possible, it is not altogether necessary. Caves like these often were found in Roman-era homes. They served as cellars, baths, and even water cisterns.

The Courtyard

The church takes its name from the Latin word "Gallicantu," meaning "cock's crow." Mark 14:29, 30 tells us, "Peter said to him, 'Even though they all fall away, I will not.' And Jesus said to him, 'Truly, I tell you, this very night, before the rooster crows twice, you will deny me three times'" (see also Matt. 26:69–75; Luke 22: 57; 27: 34–61).

Today, in the courtyard of the church stands a finely crafted statue representing the infamous denial of Peter. The characters featured in the statue are a young maiden who identifies Peter, a rooster atop a tall pillar, a Roman soldier standing guard, and, of course, Peter.

Evidence for St. Peter in Gallicantu Church

Some scholars believe this church is too far removed from the Upper City, too far "down the hill" on the slopes of Mount Zion to be the actual site of Caiaphas' palace. Jerome Murphy-O'Connor considers it "much more likely that the house of the High Priest was at the top of the hill." However, biblical scholar and archaeologist Bargil Pixner, a former prior of the Dormition Abbey, disagrees, saying, "This late and astonishing theory [suggesting Caiaphas' palace was on top Mount Zion] originated at the time of the Crusaders and is quite improbable."

The High Priest's Compound

While there is no smoking gun to confirm that St. Peter in Gallicantu was the site of Jesus' appearance before Caiaphas, as well as Peter's denials, there is some evidence to support this claim.

- Excavations at St Peter in Gallicantu have revealed a water cistern, corn mill, storage chambers, and servants' quarters. All of these would be needed for the priests' allotment of grain for food and the bevy of servants attached to the High Priest's family.
- Excavation in 1889 uncovered three Byzantine crosses engraved in the opening at the top of the sacred pit. Seven red and four black oxide crosses have also been discovered on the walls of the dungeon, and the silhouette of a praying figure is on the lower south wall. These indicate early veneration of the site.
- Artifacts discovered at the site include a complete set of weights and measures for liquids and solids as used by the priests in the Temple and a door lintel with the word "Korban" [sacrificial offering] inscribed in Hebrew.
- While the churches on this site have often met with disastrous ends, the fact that the faithful over the centuries kept building here to commemorate Jesus' appearance before Caiaphas and Peter's denials provides some justification for believing this was the historical site of these historical events.
- According to the Bordeaux Pilgrim in his *Itinerarium Burdigalense*, ". . . going up to the Pool of Siloe to Mount Zion one would come across the House of the High Priest Caiaphas." The pilgrim's description would fit the location of the Church of St. Peter in Gallicantu nicely.

This site, likely due to its location and proximity to the nearby beautiful church, is one of the most popular destinations for pilgrims visiting Jerusalem.

THE ARMENIAN PALACE OF THE HIGH PRIEST

Equally credible as the site of Caiaphas' house is on the grounds of the Armenian Monastery of Jerusalem. Dating back to the fifteenth century, this monastery is also situated on the site of a much older church.

The Armenian Quarter is the smallest among Jerusalem's Quarters. Fundamentally, it is just the ancient monastery and the abode of the Armenian Patriarchate. The Armenians originally were from the Lake Van region of northeastern Turkey. This is the area of the Ararat Mountains where the Bible records that Noah's ark came to rest (Gen. 8:4). Armenia was the first nation to officially adopt Christianity in 301 AD, under King Tiridates III.

MAP 1

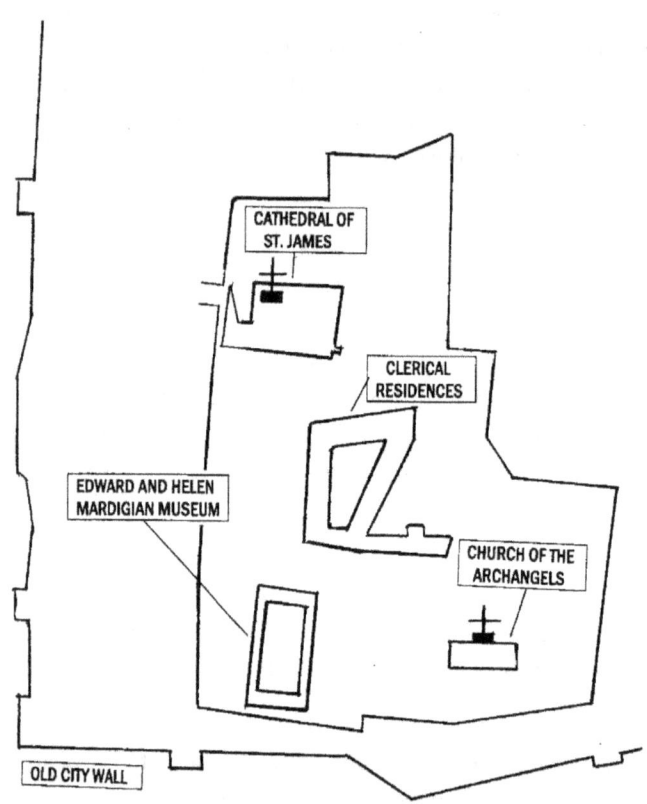

The Armenian Compound in Jerusalem

During the Roman era, the Armenians fought against Rome's Tenth Legion. When Christianity was introduced to the Holy Land, Armenian pilgrims began arriving at Jerusalem in large numbers. According to tradition, the Armenians received a special permit from Mohammad to practice their traditions in the Holy Land. They also received written approval from the Umayyad Caliph Omar ibn al-Khattab in Damascus.

The High Priest's Compound

Following the genocide of the Armenians in Turkey during World War I, many Armenian refugees migrated to Jerusalem, taking refuge in the monastery. Since then, the monastery has been used as living quarters. Most of the Armenians living in Jerusalem today are descendants of the genocide survivors. The compound enabled Armenians to live safely here for hundreds of years.

The Armenians of Jerusalem are considered one of the oldest communities in the area. The members of the clergy comprise only a small portion of the monastery's residents, who are primarily secular Armenian citizens renting apartments and rooms within the monastery but are obligated to abide by its rules. The prevailing language in the monastery is Armenian, and in every corner, there are signs and flags in this language.

The Armenian Quarter's major church is St. James Cathedral, which was originally built as a monastery and serves as the seat of the Armenian Patriarchate of Jerusalem. The church was constructed during the Crusader Period of the twelfth century, as evident by its massive construction style and pointed, intersecting arches.

To the left of the entrance is a chapel believed to mark the spot where James, the son of Zebedee, was beheaded in 44 AD on the orders of Herod Agrippa I (Acts 12:1–3). According to tradition, only his head is buried here, as his body was transported to the Crusader city of Santiago de Compostela in northwestern Spain. Below the high altar is the tomb of another St. James, the one to whom this cathedral is dedicated. This is James, the brother of Jesus and the first bishop of Jerusalem, who was stoned to death in 62 AD.

Also within the compound, on a much less grandiose scale than the Cathedral of St. James, is the Church of the Holy Archangels. Here, according to traditional Armenian belief, is the location of the House of Annas. It is located on the opposite side of the Armenian compound from the cathedral, on the northern edge.

Within the compound is a walled-up olive tree that has been sacred to Armenians since early Christian times. The tree never seems to grow or die. On the evening of Good Friday, faithful Armenians come to this tree, and a ceremony is held there. According to one of Armenian Catholicism's greatest heroes and historians, Archbishop Maghakia Ormanyan, "The fruits of the tree are gathered while spiritual songs and hymns are sung and with the stone of the fruit [olive pits] rosaries are prepared which are spread by the pilgrims everywhere" (*Armenian Jerusalem*, 1931[not available in English]).

During the recent restoration of the church, workers discovered some ancient Armenian inscriptions buried behind layers of plaster. Some of these date back to the thirteenth century AD.

However, the most significant archaeological discoveries were made within areas of the small Armenian Quarter excavated by Israeli archaeologists in the 1970s. Those digs revealed many luxurious homes from the Herodian era. These homes were large, two- or three-story houses with running water, cisterns, baths, and pools, all decorated with mosaic floors. One particularly remarkable house had frescoes depicting birds.

Model of the High Priest's compound

These were the houses of the wealthiest citizens. The estimated area of the place also aligns better with a description provided by Theodosius the Great, the Roman emperor from 379 AD to 395 AD.

Many scholars prefer this location to the St. Peter in Gallicantu Church site. However, some scholars argue that not all of these houses belonged to Jewish households. Others claim that the High Priest's compound could not have been located this close to the site of the Last Supper, the Church of Holy Zion, which is less than fifty meters away. As is so often the case, the jury is still out on the location of Caiaphas's palace compound.

Among these luxurious homes discovered in the Jewish Quarter of Jerusalem's Old City were some mansions belonging to wealthy priests dating to the first century. Following the 1967 reunification of Jerusalem, extensive archeological excavations were carried out in the Jewish Quarter. These excavations were conducted between 1969 and 1982 under the auspices of the Institute of Archaeology of the Hebrew University of Jerusalem, the Israel Exploration Society, and the Israel Antiquities Authority. The chief archaeologist in charge was Nahman Avigad.[43]

In 1970, one of the key findings of the Avigad excavations was the Burnt House, located six meters (19.68 feet) below the current street level of the Jewish Quarter.[44] The house is only part of a much larger complex, which could not be fully excavated and still lies under the Jewish Quarter. Coins were found in the house that were issued by the Roman governors of Judea, as well as those issued by the Jewish rebels between 67 and 69 AD. However, no coins from a later date were found, indicating that the house was burned down in 70 AD.

Also found in the house was a round stone weight, ten centimeters (3.937 inches) in diameter. On it, in square Aramaic script, was the Hebrew inscription "Bar Kathros," meaning the "son of Kathros." This inscription would indicate that the house belonged to the priestly Kathros family, which had abused its sacred position in the Temple. The Talmud lists the abusive priestly families in *Pesahim* 57A, saying, "Abba Saul ben Batnit in the name of Abba Joseph ben Hanin said: 'Woe is me through the 'house of Kathros' and through their pens.'" The reference to misusing their pens may imply that the Kathros family disseminated misinformation.

THE PALATIAL MANSION

Concerning the third possible location for the High Priest's compound, a palatial mansion was excavated in 1973–1974. Archaeological architect Leen Ritmeyer was a member of the Avigad team that excavated this large palace near the Burnt House, as well as the Temple Mount in Jerusalem. It became known as the "Palatial Mansion" or "Herodian Mansion."

Ritmeyer has identified the mansion as that of Annas, who ruled as High Priest from 6 to 15 AD and was the *de facto* ruler for many years afterward. Ritmeyer pointed out that there remains little question that the Palatial Mansion housed priests, for no less than four mikva'ot [ritual baths] were found at this palace, the most discovered in any ancient dwelling in Israel.

The Palatial Mansion was restored from 1985 to 1987 and is now part of the Wohl Museum located at 1 Hakara'im Street, off the central Hurva Square in the Jewish Quarter. This impressive structure contains 603.87 square meters (6,500 square feet) of floor space. However, since it was a two-story building, the usable living space was about twice as ample. In all of Israel, no other private residence of this size has been excavated.

Archaeological digs have revealed that the remains of this mansion display the kind of wealth Annas would have accumulated, much of it dishonestly. It contains both mosaic floors and fresco-adorned walls. The mansion itself was arranged around a large, paved, central courtyard. There was a reception hall west of the courtyard. Suppose this mansion can be identified with the High Priest's compound. In that case, it is possible that Annas interrogated Jesus in his residence while Peter warmed himself by the fire in the courtyard of the compound.

In *Wars* 2.17.6, Josephus records that the Palace of Annas was burnt in 70 AD.

> The others then set fire to the house of Ananias the High Priest, and to the palaces of Agrippa and Bernice . . . And when they had thus burnt down the nerves of the city, they fell upon their enemies; at which time some of the men of power, and of the High Priests, went into the vaults underground, and concealed themselves, while others fled with the king's soldiers to the upper palace, and shut the gates immediately; among whom were Ananias the High Priest, and the ambassadors that had been sent to Agrippa.

Upon excavation, there was plenty of evidence that the Palatial Mansion had been destroyed by fire.[45] Charred walls can be seen today. While the Palatial Mansion fits the general description of what may have been the palace of Annas the High Priest, and while it is located in the general area you would expect the High Priest's compound to be, to date, there is no definitive evidence that certifies this as Annas' residence.

Just as we do not know precisely where in Gethsemane Jesus was arrested, we do not know exactly where the palaces of Annas and Caiaphas were located. I have proposed throughout this and other works of mine on crucifixion that there existed a High Priest's compound, with a courtyard between Annas' wing of the compound and Caiaphas' wing. Family compounds were not uncommon, especially for wealthy families.[46] No evidence definitively indicates that the wealthy High Priests in the Roman era did not live in a compound, in the courtyard of which Peter warmed himself and denied his Lord. Without archaeological confirmation, the location of the High Priest's palace is yet open for discussion.

TABLE 2
The Armenian Church in Jerusalem

The National Church of Armenia is an Oriental Orthodox Christian community.
Tradition claims Apostles Bartholomew and Thaddeus evangelized Armenia.
About 300 AD, Armenia was the first country to adopt Christianity as a national religion.
At the Council of Dvin in 506 AD, the Armenian Church rejected the ruling of the Council of Chalcedon (451 AD) that confirmed Jesus Christ is one person consisting of two natures.
Roman Catholic and Eastern Orthodox theologians refer to the Armenian Church as a *monophysite* religion (Jesus, the incarnate word, has only one nature—divine).
However, Armenians deny this, claiming instead that Christ incarnate was one being where both divine and human natures were united (*miaphysitise*).
The Armenian Church severed ties with Rome and Constantinople in 610 AD.
The Creed of the Armenian Church is the formal declaration of Armenian beliefs.
An Armenian presence in Jerusalem dates back to the fourth century AD.
The Armenian Quarter covers 0.126 km (0.078 mi) or 14 percent of the Old City.
The quarter can be accessed through the Zion Gate or the Jaffa Gate.
St. James Monastery dominates the quarter housing the Jerusalem Patriarchate.
The Armenian Patriarchate is the *de facto* administrator of the quarter's tiny welfare state consisting of approximately 2,500 Armenian residents.

There is yet another building that is important to and associated with the High Priest, especially Caiaphas and the crucifixion narrative. It is the seat of the Sanhedrin.

THE CHAMBER OF HEWN STONE

Regardless of the location of the High Priest's compound, Jesus' trial before Caiaphas was a two-stage event. The "real" trial was the one held in the late-night hours when Jesus was both interrogated by Annas and then shuffled across the High Priest's compound to the house of Caiaphas. The "legal" trial was held the next morning at the Temple in the Chamber of Hewn Stone.

Concerning the trial conducted at night by Caiaphas and the quorum of Sanhedrin, David W. Chapman and Eckhard J. Schnabel maintain, "Recent investigations of the legal situation in Roman provinces, in particular in Judea, have suggested that an interrogation of Jesus by the Sanhedrin, convened *ad hoc* by the High Priest, is historically plausible."[47] Josef Blinzler, Raymond Brown, Erika Heusler, and other scholars also contend that the late-night event was an *ad hoc* trial conducted by Caiaphas and a quorum of the Sanhedrin.

Edwin M. Yamauchi points out, "It was only legal to pronounce the actual death sentence in the Chamber of Hewn Stone, in the innermost court of the Temple."[48] For these reasons, a nighttime trial without a daytime hearing seems impossible.

One prominent Catholic theologian wrote:

> The fundamental decision to take action against Jesus, reached during that meeting of the Sanhedrin, was put into effect on the night leading from Thursday to Friday with his arrest on the Mount of Olives . . . It now seems reasonable to assume that what took place when Jesus was brought before the Sanhedrin was not a proper trial, but more of a cross-examination that led to the decision to hand him over to the Roman Governor for sentencing.[49]

A prominent Evangelical theologian, years ago, one of my treasured seminary professors, wrote:

> The purpose of the night meeting was to find a valid reason to sentence Jesus to death. Matthew states specifically that the council was seeking false witness against Jesus (Matt 26:59). Many came forward, but no two of them agreed with each other in every detail, as was required by law. Bear in mind that in Jewish legal practice witnesses were not allowed to hear each other's evidence, and that in capital cases, the unanimous testimony of two was required for conviction (Num 35:30; Deut 17:6; 19:15; *Ant.* 4.8.115).[50]

So, where did the Sanhedrin meet early in the morning? Luke 22:66–67 says, "When day came, the assembly of the elders of the people gathered together, both chief priests and scribes. And they led him away to their council, and they said, 'If you are the Christ, tell us.'"

The High Priest's Compound

At Caiaphas' house, the Jewish authorities condemned Jesus to death. Then they ratified their judgment a few hours later when "they led him away" to the whole Sanhedrin gathered at the Chamber of Hewn Stone. From there, they sent Jesus to Pontius Pilate for execution, just as the Gospels say.

The Mishnah corroborates the Gospel narratives, indicating the Great Sanhedrin met in the Chamber of the Hewn Stone (*Lishkat hagazit*). This was their usual meeting place during the Second Temple Period (sixth century BC to first century AD).

The term for "hewn stone" in the Septuagint is translated as ξυστός or Xystos (see 1 Chr 22:2; Amos 5:11). Xystos was a term in Greek architecture for the covered portion of the gymnasium where exercises took place during winter months or rainy weather.

According to the entry for "Xystus" in the *Encyclopeadia Britannica*, page 889, the Romans applied the term to a covered garden walk or portico. In front of the portico, which was divided into flower beds with borders of small evergreen shrubs, a promenade would be located between rows of large trees.

Some have translated the word as "the Hall beside the Xystos," meaning a large hall adjacent to a portico—a bridge connecting the Temple Mount and the Xystos. Wilson's Arch was part of that bridge over the Tyropoean Valley.

That this chamber was designed as a special place is indicated by its name—"Chamber of the Hewn Stone," as opposed to being constructed with untooled stone. The stones of this chamber had been "dressed" or chiseled with smooth surfaces and intricate designs crafted by Israel's finest masons and artisans. The Holy of Holies and Holy Place may have had more precious trappings and furniture, but the Chamber of Hewn Stone was the premier appendage to the Temple enclosure.

The Chamber of Hewn Stone was built into the north wall of Jerusalem's Temple with the northern half built outside of the Temple courtyard and thus left unconsecrated, while the corresponding southern half was on the inside of the courtyard (*Sanhedrin* 11:2). Doors would permit the Sanhedrin to enter from the outside and pass into the Temple without returning outside. The chamber was approximately eleven meters (36 feet) by twelve meters (40 feet), certainly large enough to hold all seventy-one members of the Sanhedrin.

As the home of the Sanhedrin, the Chamber of Hewn Stone served as the seat of Israel's supreme court, where life-or-death decisions were often made. Mishnah *Sanhedrin* 11 speaks of "the great court of the Chamber of Hewn Stone from whence instruction issued to all Israel" [seventy plus the High Priest].

John Wilkinson writes:

> This was the formal session of the Sanhedrin (Luke 22:66), sitting under the presidency of Caiaphas (John 18:24 . . . the result of this purely formal meeting is to ratify the charge formulated by the night committee (court) and make their proposal into an official act of the Sanhedrin so that Jesus can be taken as a condemned man to Pilate.[51]

Jesus' third layover on his foreordained journey to Calvary was associated with the High Priestly family in Jesus' day. This meant an inquiry at the house of Annas and an *ad hoc* trial at the house of Caiaphas. I have labeled this location "the house of injustice" for obvious reasons. It was here that Jesus was slapped, spat upon, and beaten on the head while being questioned by the religious authorities of Jerusalem. No justice was witnessed at any of these locations where justice was supposed to be found. None.

If being betrayed by his friend Judas was the low point in Jesus' journey to the cross, being unjustly accused and convicted must have been close to it.

Chapter 4

Pilate's Judgment Hall

Innocent, Yet Condemned

Since, as Theodor Mommsen noted, emperors and governors held court where they lived, it is unlikely Procula, Pilate's wife, who accompanied him to Jerusalem on his official visits, would have been subjected to living in a military barracks when a glorious palace was available to her. Pilate may have been shifty, but he wasn't stupid.

The Fortress of Antonia
Herod's Palace
Literary Evidence
Grammatical Evidence
Archaeological Evidence
Domestic Evidence

After the miscarriage of justice at the residences of Annas and Caiaphas and the ratification of that injustice at the Chamber of Hewn Stone, Jesus was taken to the residence of the Roman prefect, Pontius Pilate, in Jerusalem. John 18:28 informs us, "They led Jesus from the house of Caiaphas to the governor's headquarters." However, Mark 15:16 in the NIV says, "The soldiers led Jesus away into the palace (that is, the Praetorium)." There is no contradiction here.

TABLE 1

The Praetorium in Modern Translations

Scripture	ESV	KJV	NIV	CSB
Matt 27:27	governor's headquarters	common hall	Praetorium	Governor's Residence
Mark 15:16	governor's headquarters	the hall, praetorium	palace, the praetorium	Governor's Residence
John 18:28	governor's headquarters	judgment hall	the palace	Governor's Headquarters
John 18:33	headquarters	judgment hall	the palace	Headquarters
John 19:9	headquarters	judgment hall	the palace	Headquarters
Acts 23:35	Herod's praetorium	Herod's judgment hall	Herod's palace	Herod's Palace
Phil 1:13	imperial guard	palace guard	palace guard	Imperial Guard

The governor's palace, the governor's headquarters, and the governor's Praetorium are different names for the same location.[52] Like the emperor in Rome, provincial governors held court in the palaces where they resided.[53] The word "praetorium" (Greek: πραιτώριον; English: *praitórion*) is a loanword from the Latin *praetor*, which meant the official seat of a provincial governor.[54] Although the judgment hall or praetorium often was the governor's residence,[55] essentially wherever the prefect was, there was the praetorium as well.

> "Where MacGregor sits, there is the head of the table."
> —Robert MacGregor from Sir Walter Scott's *Rob Roy*

The key issue regarding Jesus' layover at the Roman governor's headquarters is its location. This question has been the subject of tenacious and sometimes abrasive debate. There are but two options for the location of the Jerusalem praetorium. One gained favor early but has been losing favor for some time. The other became popular more recently but seems to have all the evidence on its side. We will examine both.

Some say that when Pilate visited Jerusalem, he established both his headquarters and living quarters in the Fortress of Antonia. Others understand Herod the Great's palace to be more suitable for the governor. Here are the arguments for both locations.

THE FORTRESS OF ANTONIA

In 1879, giant stone slabs were unearthed in Jerusalem's East Hill just north of the Temple precincts. This led some to believe that it confirmed the twelfth-century tradition that Pilate's judgment hall was located in this vicinity.

Père L. H. Vincent excavated the site in the 1930s.[56] It is located under the convent of *Les Dames de Sion* (Sisters of Sion) on the Via Dolorosa and has been understood for hundreds of years as the first two stops on the Via Dolorosa.[57]

Emil Schürer held that "in Jerusalem, there was stationed only one cohort."[58] He explained, "This is the *tagma* spoken of by Josephus in his *Jewish Wars* 5.5.8 as always stationed in the Antonia." The Gospel authors record that when Jesus was crowned with thorns, Pilate's soldiers gathered together the whole cohort (Greek: σπεῖρα; English: *speira*: Matt. 27:27; Mark 15:16). Schürer argued that this gathering would have been impossible unless Pilate was living where the troops were already stationed. This led to the conclusion that all the events of Jesus' trial before Pilate took place in the army barracks of Jerusalem.

A Model of the Fortress of Antonia

Schürer reasoned that Herod the Great's royal palace in Jerusalem could hardly be garrisoned effectively anywhere else if the cohort was in the Antonia Fortress, which it was. However, even Schürer admitted that Herod's palace "was not only a princely dwelling but at the same time a strong castle, in which at times [during the rebellion in 4 BC and again 66 AD] large detachments of troops could maintain their position against the assaults of the whole mass of the people."[59]

> "Herod's palace was not a building—it was a compound. The compound was ideal for Roman governors." —Shimon Gibson

As mentioned, the tradition that goes back to the medieval era is that the Roman prefect's Praetorium was housed in the Antonia Fortress. However, archaeologist Shimon Gibson measured the base of the Antonia Fortress and argues that it is not large enough to have functioned as anything but a Roman outpost and observation tower overlooking the Temple area. If this is so, is there an alternative location for Pilate's Praetorium? There is, and many today believe, that Herod's royal palace was located in Jerusalem's Upper City. That is where his Praetorium was stationed.

Gibson notes, "Today, a consensus of opinion exists among scholars that Herod's Palace on the west side of the city was the same as the Praetorium and that in its immediate vicinity Jesus was tried and condemned to death."[60]

HEROD'S PALACE

Since mounting evidence now favors Herod's Palace as the prefect's Jerusalem residence, we must carefully explore this location. The palace stood in the western part of the Upper City, today just inside the Jaffa Gate. It served as a luxurious residence and a military fortress.

Antonia was a military fortress in which one of the five cohorts commanded by the prefect of Judea was garrisoned. Its comforts and conveniences would have been quite spartan. On the other hand, the royal palace in Jerusalem, constructed by Herod the Great, rivaled the famed southern Italian city of Sybaris in luxury. Two of the palace wings—the Caesareum and Agrippium—were large enough to accommodate the prefect and his entourage, as well as a military escort traveling with him.

David's Tower

LITERARY EVIDENCE

The historian Josephus described the size and grandeur of Herod's royal palace in Jerusalem. "Herod rebuilt the Temple and encompassed a piece of land about it with a wall, which land was twice as large as that before enclosed. The expenses he laid out upon it were vastly large also, and the riches about it were unspeakable" (*Wars* 1.21.1). The impression Josephus gives is that this was a massive complex with inexhaustible splendor.

The premier Jewish historian also says that within the palace, there were...

> Rooms of great magnificence, and over them upper rooms, and cisterns to receive rainwater. They were many in number, and the steps by which you ascended up to them were every one broad: of these towers then the third wall had ninety, and the spaces between them were each 200 cubits [300 feet]; but in the middle wall were forty towers, and the old wall was parted into sixty, while the whole compass of the city was thirty-three furlongs [21,780 feet] (*Wars* 5.4.3).

Josephus also described the amenities of Herod's palace.

He built himself a palace in the Upper City, raising the rooms to a very great height, and adorning them with the most costly furniture of gold, and marble seats, and beds; and these were so large that they could contain very many companies of men. These apartments were also of distinct magnitudes (*Ant.*15.9.3).

Without question, the Jerusalem palace of Herod the Great was massive and well-fortified. Josephus also recorded that, after a Roman soldier "mooned" the crowd of Jews, the prefect Cumanus (48–52 AD) sent reinforcements from this palace to the Antonia Fortress (*Ant.* 20.5.3; *Wars* 2.12.1), to watch over the disgruntled Jews in the Temple area. This demonstrated that soldiers could easily and adequately be housed in Herod's palace.

There is an account in the writings of Flavius Josephus that helps us identify the location of Pilate's residence while he was in Jerusalem. It is found in the *Wars of the Jews* 2.14.8, 9 and records the tyranny and slaughter of the innocents by Gessius Florus, the most wicked of all the Roman governors of Judea. Florus had been ridiculed and rebuffed by certain Jews and responded with his usual bloodthirsty actions.

> Now at this time Florus took up his quarters at the palace; and on the next day he had his tribunal set before it, and sat upon it, when the High Priests, and the men of power, and those of the greatest eminence in the city, came all before that tribunal; upon which Florus commanded them to deliver up to him those that had reproached him [which they did not] . . . Florus was more provoked at this and called out aloud to the soldiers to plunder that which was called the Upper Marketplace, and to slay such as they met with.

Here are the facts we learn from this Josephus passage.

- Florus's (and all prefects) residence while in Jerusalem was in the palace of Herod the Great.
- The High Priests, the men of power, and those of the greatest eminence in the city all belonged to the same class of people and thus were considered a group by the Romans.
- To cause the most tremendous pain for the High Priests, Florus ordered the Roman soldiers to plunder and slaughter all those who frequented the Upper Marketplace.

Josephus continues in *Wars* 2.14.9:

So the soldiers, taking this exhortation of their commander in a sense agreeable to their desire of gain, did not only plunder the place they were sent to, but forcing themselves into every house, they slew its inhabitants ... they also caught many of the quiet people and brought them before Florus, whom he first chastised with stripes, and then crucified. Accordingly, the whole number of those that were destroyed that day, with their wives and children, (for they did not spare even the infants themselves,) was about three thousand and six hundred. And what made this calamity the heavier was this new method of Roman barbarity; for Florus ventured then to do what no one had done before, that is, to have men of the equestrian order whipped and nailed to the cross before his tribunal; who, although they were by birth Jews, yet were they of Roman dignity notwithstanding.

Again, from Josephus, we learn the following:

- Many innocent (quiet) people were brouht before Florus, who first scourged them and then had them crucified.
- Florus also whipped and nailed to the cross men of the equestrian order, which was not acceptable in the Roman social class order.
- By the time Gessius Florus was the Roman prefect of Judea (64–66 AD), death by crucifixion was an established Roman practice. The Jews who died by Florus' hand were nailed to a cross, not impaled on a stake.

The literary evidence for Herod's Jerusalem palace as the home of the Roman prefect is quite strong, but there is more.

GRAMMATICAL EVIDENCE

There is also grammatical evidence that favors the palace of Herod the Great for the site of Jesus' trial. Secular literature uses the word *aulē* (Greek: αὐλή; English: *aulē*) when it speaks of Herod's Jerusalem palace [Josephus uses this term often], but never is *aulē* used for the Antonia Fortress.[61]

The Gospel reference that speaks most strongly to this identification is Mark 15:16, which says, "And the soldiers led him away inside the palace (that is, the governor's headquarters), and they called together the whole battalion." For "palace," Mark used the word αὐλή. For the "governor's headquarters," he chose the word πραιτώριον (praetorium). Moreover, for "battalion," Mark went with σπεῖρα (military cohort).⁶² Each of these choices by Mark indicates that a formidable force of Roman soldiers could be housed at the residence of Jerusalem's prefect, along with his praetorium.

ARCHAEOLOGICAL EVIDENCE

In Jerusalem, the Kishle is the name of an abandoned Ottoman Period prison. It is within the Tower of David complex. Excavations in 1999–2000 beneath the Kishle provided archaeological evidence that Pontius Pilate's praetorium was located in Herod the Great's Jerusalem palace. Israel Antiquities Authority archaeologist Amit Re'em uncovered the foundation walls of the palace and the sewage system that serviced it.

The archaeological dig at Herod's Palace in Jerusalem
Photo Credit: The Tower of David Museum

University of North Carolina at Chapel Hill archaeologist Jodi Magness⁶³ reminds us that this was not the first time archaeology pointed to this location as the site of Herod's palace. Senior Associate Fellow at the Albright Institute, Shimon Gibson, conveys the majority academic opinion that Pilate's praetorium was located in Herod's palace complex.

> [T]here can be no doubt that on the occasions when [Pilate] stayed in Jerusalem, particularly during the Jewish festivities, he took up residence at Herod's old palace situated on the west side of the city, also known as the praetorium. The word praetorium might

refer to a palace or a judicial, military seat, but it is likely that in Jerusalem, it referred to the entire palace compound, which on the north included palatial buildings used for residential purposes and on the south, military barracks.[64]

It is evident, therefore, that the literary, grammatical, and archaeological evidence for Herod's Jerusalem Palace as Pilate's residence is exceptionally strong. Nevertheless, there is still more.

DOMESTIC EVIDENCE

This is not empirical evidence. I refer to it as "domestic" evidence because it reflects a common-sense approach to Pilate's home life. Since, as Theodor Mommsen noted, emperors and governors held court where they lived, it is unlikely Procula, Pilate's wife, who accompanied him to Jerusalem on his official visits, would have been subjected to living in a military barracks when a glorious palace was available to her.[65] Pilate may have been shifty, but he wasn't stupid.

The New Testament states only that Jesus' trial before Pilate took place at Pilate's praetorium, which was any location where a Roman magistrate chose to hold court.[66] "That the actual chamber or hall in the palace or praetorium where trials were held was called *secretarium* confirms the secrecy of the proceedings."[67] The living quarters in Herod's royal palace in Jerusalem were second to none, with the possible exception of Herod's palace in Caesarea Maritima, where the Roman prefects spent most of their time.

From literary, grammatical, and archaeological evidence, as well as common sense, we must conclude that the judgment hall in which Jesus stood before Pilate was not located along the northeastern corridor of Old Jerusalem but rather on the southwestern hill, the Upper City residential area for the wealthiest Jews of Jesus' day.

Archaeologist Shimon Gibson attested, "There is little doubt that the trial occurred somewhere within Herod's palace compound. In the Gospel of John, the trial is described as taking place near a gate and on a bumpy stone pavement—details that fit with previous archaeological findings near the prison."[68]

The spiritual sentimentality of walking the Via Dolorosa and the pavement beneath the Sisters of Sion Convent will keep pilgrims on that route for years to come. However, the archaeological and historical evidence has shifted to a different route, and different layover stops on Jesus' journey to

Calvary. In the future, the new Via Dolorosa will replace the path where pilgrims walk today. They will sing. They will bear crosses. And they will walk along with Jesus on his way to crucifixion.

Chapter 5

Herod Antipas' Passover Bed and Breakfast

A Contemptuous Confrontation

Jesus found that he had nothing he wished to say to Herod.
Herod Antipas had a great desire to see Jesus; Jesus had no desire to see him.

Herod's Passover Bed & Breakfast: A Brutal Circus
The Character of Herod Antipas
The Location of Herod Antipas's Jerusalem Residence
Jesus is Sent Back to Pontius Pilate

Juvenal was a Roman poet active in the late first and early second centuries AD. He wrote sixteen known poems divided among five books, all in the genre of satire. The sixth and tenth satires are the most renowned works in the collection. In Satire ten, Juvenal created a phrase that has almost become synonymous with ancient Rome. Juvenal wrote, "The People who once upon a time handed out military command, high civil office, legions—everything, now restrains itself and anxiously hopes for just two things: bread and circuses." [69]

HEROD'S PASSOVER BED & BREAKFAST: A BRUTAL CIRCUS

In the political context in which Juvenal wrote, he was decrying the prevailing means of generating public approval in first-century Roman society. This noble cause was not based on Rome's excellence in public policy or public service but instead on diversion or distraction by satisfying the baser needs of the population rather than appealing to higher moral values. The people did not want education, culture, or even religion; all they wanted was their government to feed and entertain them. Juvenal was referring to the Roman practice of providing free wheat [bread] to Roman citizens, as well as extravagant and costly circus games and other forms of entertainment as a means of gaining or keeping political power.

However, the cry "Give us bread and the circus," meaning gladiatorial contests and other grandiose spectacles, began long before the end of the first century AD. According to the late prominent linguist and New Testament scholar Bruce Metzger, it was a familiar cry in the days of Nero and before.[70] The people simply wanted the empire to feed them and entertain them, a bellwether for every society in moral and cultural crisis.

The lack of willingness to work to contribute to society as a whole was a systemic problem in Rome. It was evident at every level of society, from top to bottom. This attitude was vividly displayed by Antipas when Pilate sent Jesus to him for trial.

THE CHARACTER OF HEROD ANTIPAS

While they had never met, Herod was well aware of Jesus' miracles and his growing popularity. However, Jesus was equally well aware of Antipas's character and his multiplying vulgarity. This is evidenced by Jesus referring to Herod Antipas as "that fox" (Luke 13:32). The word Jesus used (Greek: ἀλώπηξ; English: *alōpēx*) refers to a cunning person. He was painting the son of Herod the Great as a beguiling, conniving rascal.

Herod Antipas possessed an unprincipled intelligence. "Unprincipled intelligence is an intelligence that, unguided by the laws of men or God, seeks only its own interests. In Herod's case, he would never do anything that wasn't in his own interest."

Herod Antipas' Passover Bed and Breakfast

Antipas divorced his first wife, Phasaelis, the daughter of King Aretas IV of Nabatea, to marry Herodias, the wife of his half-brother Herod II. This reprehensible act, as well as his treatment of the Savior during Jesus' layover on his way to Calvary, certainly corroborates Antipas' innate selfishness.

Herod was in Jerusalem that day the world turned dark because he was part Jewish by birth, and it was Passover weekend. He had traveled south from Galilee and Perea, where he was the tetrarch, down the Jordan Valley and up the mountains to Jerusalem. He had no foreknowledge of what would transpire that Good Friday, not to mention Resurrection morning. Luke 23:4–12 records Jesus' appearance before Herod. Here are some excerpts.

> Pilate said to the chief priests and the crowds, "I find no guilt in this man." But they were urgent, saying, "He stirs up the people, teaching throughout all Judea, from Galilee even to this place." When Pilate heard this, he asked whether the man was a Galilean. And when he learned that he belonged to Herod's jurisdiction, he sent him over to Herod, who was himself in Jerusalem at that time. When Herod saw Jesus, he was very glad, for he had long desired to see him, because he had heard about him, and he was hoping to see some sign done by him. So he questioned him at some length, but he [Jesus] made no answer. The chief priests and the scribes stood by, vehemently accusing him. And Herod with his soldiers treated him with contempt and mocked him. Then, arraying him in splendid clothing, he [Antipas] sent him [Jesus] back to Pilate. And Herod and Pilate became friends with each other that very day, for before this they had been at enmity with each other.

When Herod Antipas journeyed from Galilee to Judea and entered Jerusalem, he did not even know Jesus was in the city. In fact, he was surprisingly pleased when he learned that Pilate was sending the Nazarene to him for judgment. Antipas wanted Jesus to perform some magic for him, to do some tricks. This is another hint at his character.

"He stood before Jesus, without shame, without any stirring of moral delicacy, and put to Jesus some idle and curious questions. Nevertheless, Jesus answered him nothing. Jesus found that he had nothing he wished to say to Herod."[71] Herod Antipas had a great desire to see Jesus; Jesus had no desire to see him.

From the Upper Room to Joseph's Tomb

TABLE 1

Who Was Herod Antipas?

Herod Antipas (21 BC-39AD) was one of fourteen sons of Herod the Great by ten wives.
Upon Herod's death, Antipas became the tetrarch of Galilee in northern Israel, as well as the land of Perea, east of the Jordan River and the Dead Sea.
Antipas was not Herod's first choice as heir. It was only after Aristobulus and Alexander were executed and another brother, Antipater, was convicted of trying to poison his father that the elderly Herod fell back on his youngest son, Antipas.
Not the builder his father was, Antipas built Tiberias and rebuilt Sepphoris.
Although they never met, Jesus grew up in Nazareth while Antipas ruled Galilee.
Antipas married Phasaël, daughter of King Aretas IV of Nabatea.
While in Rome, he fell in love with half-brother, Herod Philip II's wife, Herodias.
Antipas divorced his Nabatean wife, Phasaël, and married Herodias. Enraged, King Aretas IV went to war against Antipas, a war that Antipas lost.
Aretas was upset due to pride, but John the Baptist was upset for moral reasons.
John reproached Herod Antipas for his dodgy marriage, Herodias wanted revenge.
Herodias goaded Antipas into imprisoning the Baptist and then persuaded her daughter, Salome, to ask for John's head in return for dancing at her stepfather's birthday feast.
Antipas gave the order for John's execution, but when Jesus' miracles were reported to him, he thought John had been resurrected and was Jesus.
When Pilate sent Jesus to Antipas because he was a Galilean, Antipas only wanted to see some miracles, which he thought would be entertaining.
In 39 AD, Antipas was accused of conspiracy against the Roman emperor Caligula. He was promptly sent to Gaul in exile, according to Josephus. Antipas was never heard of again.

I refer to the time Jesus spent in the Jerusalem palace as Herod Antipas' Passover "bed and breakfast," not because he slept or ate there, but because of the short length of time Jesus spent there. While Luke 23:9 says, "So he [Herod Antipas] questioned him [Jesus] at some length, but he [Jesus] made no answer," it appears that Jesus' face time with Antipas was an hour or less. The expression "at some length" (Greek: ἱκανός; English: *hikanós*) refers to the barrage of questions Antipas asked, not the length of time it took to ask them. Jesus found that he had nothing he wished to say to Herod. Herod Antipas had a great desire to see Jesus; Jesus had no desire to see him.

The New International Version translates this verse, "He plied him with many questions, but Jesus gave him no answer." When the Messiah refused to recognize the authority of the man who had been plotting to kill him (Luke 13:31), resulting in his absolute silence, the questioning process was short-lived.

But, in this book, we're interested in following Jesus' footsteps from the Upper Room to Joseph of Arimathea's tomb. So, it is legitimate to ask, "Where did this antagonistic encounter take place?"

THE LOCATION OF HEROD ANTIPAS'S JERUSALEM RESIDENCE

When Jesus was marched from Pilate's Jerusalem residence to Herod's Jerusalem residence, where did he go? How far did he go? What route would he have taken? Those are the questions that interest us here.

Bear in mind that, for different reasons, both Pontius Pilate and Herod the Tetrarch were only in Jerusalem because of the Passover weekend. Herod lived in Tiberias, Galilee, where, along with Perea, he served as the Roman administrator. Pilate lived in the luxurious palace built by Herod the Great in Caesarea Maritima on the Mediterranean coast. It was Passover that brought these two enemies to town, but it was Jesus who brought them together. "And Herod and Pilate became friends with each other that very day, for before this they had been at enmity with each other" (Luke 23:12).

Although Antipas was the son of Herod the Great, Jerusalem was located in Judea, where Pontius Pilate served as the Roman prefect. Consequently, on Pilate's visits to Jerusalem, his entourage and he stayed in Herod's royal palace located just inside the western wall, near the Jaffa Gate today. Herod Antipas' palace was approximately halfway between Herod's royal palace and the Temple Mount.

Harold Hoehner noted, "After Pilate's hearing that Jesus was from Galilee, Luke switches the scene to Jesus being tried by Herod [Antipas]. He was no doubt escorted by some guards as well as by some of the Sanhedrin from Pilate's residence to the Hasmonaean palace, which was Antipas's Jerusalem residence located west of the Temple."[72]

Although not an expert builder like Herod, during the Hasmonean rule over Jerusalem (140 BC—37 BC), the city saw two major landmarks constructed. One of these was the Hasmonean Baris, which was a fortress thought to have stood at the northwestern corner of the Temple Mount.[73] Josephus commented, "Now on the north side [of the Temple] was built a citadel, whose walls were square, and strong, and of extraordinary firmness. This citadel was built by the kings of the Asamonean race, who were also High Priests before Herod, and they called it the Tower, in which were reposited the vestments of the High Priest, which the High Priest only put on at the time when he was to offer sacrifice" (*Ant.* 15.11.4).

Little is known of the Baris' form except that it had several high towers, one of which was known as "Straton's Tower." Josephus reports that Hyrcanus I, the Hasmonean leader and Jewish High Priest (134 BC until he died in 104 BC), spent more time in the Baris than in the Hasmonean palace in Jerusalem's Upper City. The Baris housed the sacred vestments worn by the High Priest.[74] Herod the Great renovated and refurbished the Baris and renamed it Antonia in honor of his patron Mark Antony (*Wars* 4.21.1; *Ant.* 13.11.2; 15.11.4; 18.4.3). Some remains north of the Temple Mount have been tentatively identified with the Hasmonean Baris.[75]

The second Hasmonean building project in Jerusalem was the Hasmonean palace itself. Josephus provides a helpful description of the palace's location.

> He therefore called the multitude together into a large gallery and placed his sister Bernice in the house of the Asamoneans, that she might be seen by them, (which house was over the gallery, at the passage to the Upper City, where the bridge joined the Temple to the gallery) (*Wars* 2.16.3).

"Over the gallery." "At the passage to the Upper City." "Where the bridge joined the Temple to the gallery." From these descriptive phrases, it's quite possible to establish the approximate location of this palace. It would have been facing the Temple, slightly north of the modern Jewish Quarter.

This location makes a great deal of sense. It makes topographical sense because this places the Hasmonean palace on a lofty spot, which would set it above the surrounding buildings. It contained a roof called the Xystus, from where people in the large square below could be addressed. It also made social sense because the palace would be adjacent to the wealthy and priestly quarters in the Upper City. It had large courts, living quarters, baths, and a service court.

In addition, it made strategic sense because overlooking the Temple would give the king and the High Priest a vantage point from which to observe any trouble brewing in the Temple courtyard. If discontent was fermenting, they knew it immediately.

Luke informs us concerning Herod Antipas and his soldiers. "They treated him [Jesus] with contempt and mocked him." Herod and his soldiers despised Jesus. What began as a frivolous desire to be entertained devolved into disdainful taunting, insulting, heckling, and scornful mocking. This contemptuous behavior likely lasted through the journey back to Pilate at King Herod's royal palace. "Arraying him in splendid clothing, he [Antipas] sent him [Jesus] back to Pilate." Their verbal barbs at Jesus were accompanied by dressing Jesus in fine clothing to further mock him as a king.

JESUS IS SENT BACK TO PONTIUS PILATE

After this fruitless layover on Jesus' journey to the cross, he was returned to Pilate. Jesus' layover at the residence of Herod Antipas produced more heat than light. Luke tells us, " Herod asked him many questions, but Jesus did not answer. Then, the chief priests and the teachers of the Law of Moses stood up and accused him of all kinds of bad things. Herod and his soldiers made fun of Jesus and insulted him. They put a fine robe on him and sent him back to Pilate" (Luke 23:9–11 CEV).

While only Luke records Jesus' stopover at the residence of Herod Antipas, and even he provides little information about that stop, nevertheless, we learn something from the verbs the good doctor used.

- Herod Antipas "questioned" (Greek: ἐπερωτάω; English: *eperōtáō*) Jesus. The verb connotes a simple interrogation, but it can also insinuate a demand or an accusatory question. In fact, in the Gospel of Mark, the writer uses this verb twenty-six times, ten of which appear to be an unfriendly demand. Antipas demanded Jesus respond to his barrage of curiosities, but Jesus, fully aware that Antipas only wanted entertainment, not information, refused to answer. This sent Antipas into a rage.

- The chief priests and scribes "stood by," but Luke does not say they "stood idly by" or they "stood peaceably by." No, derived from this verb, Luke adds that these religious leaders were "vehemently accusing him." Jesus may have been silent, but the chief priests and Jewish scribes certainly were not. They not only accused Jesus of things he did not say or do, but they did so "vehemently" (Greek: ευτόνως; English: *eutónōs*) meaning vociferously, forcefully, and loudly. There must have been chaos at Herod Antipas' palace during Jesus' brief visit there.

From Gethsemane to the residence of Annas. From Annas to the house of Caiaphas. From the residence of Caiaphas to the Chamber of Hewn Stone. From the chamber to Herod's royal palace, where Pontius Pilate was in residence. From there to the Hasmonean Palace, where Herod Antipas was in residence. Then, back to Pilate. The journey to Calvary can now only mean one street is left—the Via Dolorosa.

Chapter 6

The Via Dolorosa

The Road Where Dead Men Walk

Carrying one's cross was not just part of the punishment; it was part of the spectacle. It must have been quite a sight, especially for the Father in heaven who ordered his Son's crucifixion.

What is the Via Dolorosa?
The Stations of the Cross
Jerusalem's *Cardo* and *Decumanus*
People Jesus Encountered on the Via Dolorosa
How the Exhausted Jesus Carried His Cross
The Via Dolorosa Celebrated in Music

For the Christian faithful, certain words or phrases trigger an emotional response. Say the word "Calvary," and the heart fills with gratitude. Say the words "Via Dolorosa," and the heart fills with a sense of foreboding. And yet, these emotions could be completely reversed and still be appropriate. For followers of Jesus Christ, the Passion story is the greatest story ever told, and the Via Dolorosa is a considerable part of it.

Jesus had been apprehended in the Garden of Gethsemane. He had undergone the interrogation by Annas and two trial events with Caiaphas. He had been shuffled from the palace of the High Priest to the palace of the Roman prefect. His "non-trial" with Pilate ended with a sentence of death on a cross. All that is left is for Jesus to struggle to the "Place of the Skull," be nailed to a wooden cross, and die, making atonement for our sins.

In this chapter, we focus on the journey from Pilate's Jerusalem headquarters to "the place of the skull." This part of the story focuses on perhaps the most famous street in the world. Paris can keep its Champs-Élysées. Washington, DC can have its Pennsylvania Avenue, Shanghai its Nanjing Road, and Rome its Via Appia. The most famous, most important, most venerated street in the world is Jerusalem's Via Dolorosa.

WHAT IS THE VIA DOLOROSA?

Via Dolorosa is Latin for "Way of Sorrows," "Way of Suffering," or simply the "Painful Way." Around 1350 AD, Franciscan friars began walking and praying on the supposed route of Jesus' Passion. They started at the Church of the Holy Sepulcher and proceeded to what they understood to be Pilate's headquarters in the Antonia Fortress, traveling in the opposite direction from our Lord's trek.[76] The route was not reversed until 1517 AD when the Franciscans began following the chronological footsteps of Jesus rather than the geographical ones. Thus, they started at the Antonia and ended at Golgotha.[77]

In the second half of the sixteenth century, the name Via Dolorosa was first given to this street by the Franciscan Boniface of Ragusa. He conducted devotional walks through the streets of Jerusalem, retracing the route on which it was believed Jesus lugged his cross to Golgotha. For this reason, the Via Dolorosa is sometimes referred to as *Via Crucis* or the "Way of the Cross."

The winding route from the Antonia Fortress to the Church of the Holy Sepulcher is about 600 meters (2,000 feet). The current route was established in the eighteenth century, replacing several earlier versions of the route.[78] However, we must ask, "Did the historic Via Dolorosa indeed follow the route that Jesus took"? We need to answer this question.

THE STATIONS OF THE CROSS

Christian visitors of the Holy City of Jerusalem invariably walk the pilgrim way on the Via Dolorosa. It begins north of the Temple Mount at the Convent of the Sisters of Zion, where Lion's Gate Street becomes the Via

Dolorosa. From here, the "Way of Sorrows" winds its way westward to the Church of the Holy Sepulcher.

The journey from Pilate's praetorium to Golgotha has drawn millions of Christian pilgrims over the centuries. When the Spanish Franciscan Antonio of Aranda described it in 1530 AD, however, there were only three intermediate stops between the house of Pilate and the Holy Sepulcher: (1) Jesus' encounter with Mary, who collapses; (2) Simon of Cyrene takes the cross from Jesus, and (3) Veronica wipes the face of Jesus.[79] Ironically, only two of these three have the Scriptural seal of approval. Today, those three stops have grown to fourteen.

TABLE 1

Stations of the Cross Historically Verified

Station	Event	Biblical Reference	Historically Verifiable
#1	Jesus' Trial before Pontius Pilate	John 19:1–5	Yes
#2	Jesus Takes Up His Cross	John 19:16–18	Yes
#3	Jesus Falls for the First Time	None	No
#4	Jesus Meets His Mother, Mary	None	No
#5	Simon Carries Jesus' Cross	Mark 15:21–22	Yes
#6	Veronica Wipes Jesus' Brow	None	No
#7	Jesus Falls for the Second Time	None	No
#8	Jesus Warns Daughters of Jerusalem	Luke 23:27–31	Yes
#9	Jesus Falls a Third Time	None	No
#10	Jesus is Stripped of His Clothes	John 19:23–24	Yes
#11	Jesus is Nailed to the Cross	Luke 23:33–34	Yes
#12	Jesus Dies on the Cross	Luke 23:44–46	Yes
#13	Jesus' Body Removed from the Cross	Mark 15:46	Yes
#14	Jesus' Body is Placed in the Tomb	Matt 27:57–60	Yes

Out of the fourteen traditional Stations of the Cross, only nine have a foundation in the Gospel narratives. Stations 3, 4, 6, 7, and 9 are not certified by Scripture. In fact, there is no evidence for Station 6 before medieval times, and Station 13 appears to embellish the Gospels' account in ways that are not historically warranted. Nevertheless, these fourteen stations have been venerated for centuries, especially in the Roman Catholic tradition.[80]

Station #1. Jesus' Trial before Pontius Pilate

"Then Pilate took Jesus and had him flogged. The soldiers also twisted together a crown of thorns, put it on his head, and threw a purple robe around him. And they repeatedly came up to him and said, 'Hail, King of the Jews!' and were slapping his face. Pilate went outside again and said to them, 'Look, I am bringing him outside to you to let you know I find no grounds for charging Him.' Then Jesus came out wearing the crown of thorns and the purple robe. Pilate said to them, 'Here is the man!'" (John 19:1–5).

Two crucial events in the Passion Week are celebrated at Station 1. First, the Church of the Flagellation commemorates the flogging Jesus endured, even though he was pronounced innocent. Second, the Ecce Homo Church remembers Pilate's famous "Behold the man" [Ecce Homo] statement. Both of these chapels are located within the Franciscan compound on the Via Dolorosa. This compound was built over a large area of Roman pavement that was traditionally thought to be the Lithostratos described by the Gospels as the location of Jesus' trial before Pontius Pilate.

Station #2. Jesus Takes Up His Cross

"Therefore they took Jesus away. Carrying his own cross, He went out to what is called Skull Place, which in Hebrew is called Golgotha. There they crucified him and two others with him, one on either side, with Jesus in the middle" (John 19:16–18). This station, often referred to as the "Imposition of the Cross," is commemorated in a beautiful little chapel within the Church of the Condemnation and Imposition of the Cross, located inside the Franciscan compound.

Station #3. Jesus Falls for the First Time

As with the first two stations, I would include the Gospel account here if there were any. The fact is that a widespread tradition has shaped the belief that Jesus stumbled three times during his journey to Golgotha; however, in none of the Gospel accounts is it ever recorded that Jesus stumbled or fell (Matt. 27:32; Mark 15:21; Luke 23:26; John 19:16, 17). Be that as it may, the supposed first fall is represented by the third station adjacent to the nineteenth-century Polish Catholic Chapel, next to the Austro-Hungarian hospice. Over the entrance to the chapel is a lunette, a half-moon-shaped space with a bas-relief of Jesus falling under the weight of his cross.

Station #4. Jesus Meets His Mother Mary

Again, the New Testament makes no mention of a meeting between Jesus and his mother on the Via Dolorosa. Nonetheless, this tradition became popular within the Catholic Church. This fourth station, located within a nineteenth-century Armenian Catholic oratory named Our Lady of the Spasm, was built in 1881. Above the entrance to the chapel is another lunette with a bas-relief carved of Mary meeting Jesus, who is carrying his cross. She is grabbing his wrist as he makes his way to Golgotha.

Station #5. Simon of Cyrene Carries Jesus' Cross

"And they compelled a passerby, Simon of Cyrene, who was coming in from the country, the father of Alexander and Rufus, to carry his cross. And they brought him to the place called Golgotha (which means Place of a Skull)" (Mark 15:21, 22). The traditional site for this station is located adjacent to the Chapel of Simon of Cyrene. This chapel was built by the Franciscans in 1895. Before the fifteenth century, however, this location was regarded as the "House of the Poor Man" named Lazarus (Luke 16:19–31). The house dates to the Middle Ages.

Station #6. Veronica Wipes Jesus' Brow

This incident appears to be a Medieval Roman Catholic legend. Even the name Veronica is a composite of two Latin words (*vera* and *icon*), meaning "true image." It is alleged that the veil of Veronica absorbed the image of Jesus' face when Veronica wiped the sweat from his face with a cloth. The location of the sixth station was identified only in the nineteenth century. The Greek Catholics purchased the twelfth-century ruins at that location in 1883 and built the Church of the Holy Face and Saint Veronica. The Greek

Catholic Church claimed that the residence of Veronica had formerly been located in this area. On a meter-tall, old stone pillar located between two doors is an inscription identifying the name of the station. Remember, there is no evidence a woman named Veronica even existed, let alone that she wiped the face of Jesus and miraculously, the image of his face adhered to her veil. This belief became a tradition, and by tradition, for some people, it became a fact.

Station #7. Jesus Falls for the Second Time

Unfortunately, just as Stations #3, #4, and #6 lack historical background and biblical evidence to support them, Station #7 lacks historical background and biblical evidence to support it. A key influencer in shaping the modern stations was Adam Krafft. In the German city of Nuremberg around 1490, Krafft carved seven woodcuts depicting Jesus falling or at least showing weakness during his Via Dolorosa journey. In Krafft's mind, those seven occasions were: Jesus' first fall (3rd Station); Jesus meets his mother (4th Station); Simon of Cyrene carries Jesus' cross (5th Station); Veronica wipes Jesus' face (6th Station); Jesus' second fall (7th Station); Jesus warns the Daughters of Jerusalem (8th Station); Jesus' third fall (9th Station). Again, except for the 8th Station, none of these incidents is historically verifiable.

Station #8. Jesus Warns the Daughters of Jerusalem

"And there followed him a great multitude of the people and of women who were mourning and lamenting for him. But turning to them, Jesus said, 'Daughters of Jerusalem, do not weep for me, but weep for yourselves and for your children. For behold, the days are coming when they will say, "Blessed are the barren and the wombs that never bore and the breasts that never nursed!" Then they will begin to say to the mountains, "Fall on us," and to the hills, "Cover us." For if they do these things when the wood is green, what will happen when it is dry?'" (Luke 23:27–31). Today, the eighth station of the Via Dolorosa is located adjacent to the Greek Orthodox Monastery of St. Charalampos.

Station #9. Jesus Falls a Third Time

This station suffers from the same fate as Stations 3 and 7. It is never recorded in the Bible that Jesus stumbled and fell as he made his way to Golgotha. This surprises most people. However, be mindful that these three Stations of the Cross lack any historical foundation. They are products of religious tradition. That does not mean Jesus did not fall on the Via Dolorosa. He may well have fallen, but we have no biblical or historical record of it.

Station #10. Jesus Is Stripped of His Clothes

"When the soldiers had crucified Jesus, they took his garments and divided them into four parts, one part for each soldier; also his tunic. But the tunic was seamless, woven in one piece from top to bottom, so they said to one another, 'Let us not tear it, but cast lots for it to see whose it shall be.' This was to fulfill the Scripture which says, 'They divided my garments among them, and for my clothing they cast lots'" (John 19:23, 24).

The location for this station and the four that follow are found at or inside the Church of the Holy Sepulcher in Jerusalem. Station #10, known as the Chapel of the Franks, is located outside and to the right of the church entrance. This exterior location provided access directly to Calvary, enabling medieval pilgrims to acquire indulgences even when the church was closed or when they lacked the money to pay the entrance fee.

Station #11. Jesus Is Nailed to the Cross

"Two others, who were criminals, were led away to be put to death with him. And when they came to the place that is called The Skull, there they crucified him, and the criminals, one on his right and one on his left. And Jesus said, 'Father, forgive them, for they know not what they do'" (Luke 23:33, 34).

Just inside the massive doors of the Church of the Holy Sepulcher, and to the right, is a set of well-worn stone steps that lead to the traditional site of Calvary. Presumably, the soldiers would have nailed Jesus' hands to the *patibulum* of the cross on the lower level, then ascended the hill and raised this crosspiece with Jesus nailed to it and fitted it to the top of the *stipes*. They then would have nailed his feet to the upright *stipes*. There is, however, scant evidence that Calvary was on a hill.

Station #12. *Jesus Dies on the Cross*

"It was now about the sixth hour, and there was darkness over the whole land until the ninth hour, while the sun's light failed. And the curtain of the Temple was torn in two. Then Jesus, calling out with a loud voice, said, 'Father, into your hands I commit my spirit!' And having said this, he breathed his last" (Luke 23:44–46). Near the location of Station #11 is Station #12, within the Church of the Holy Sepulcher. Here, Jesus took his last human breath and died as an atonement for our sin.

Station #13. *Jesus' Body Is Removed From the Cross*

"And Joseph bought a linen shroud, and taking him down, wrapped him in the linen shroud and laid him in a tomb that had been cut out of the rock. And he rolled a stone against the entrance of the tomb" (Mark 15:46). Directly inside the enormous doors of the Church of the Holy Sepulchre is the "Stone of Anointing." According to tradition, the body of Jesus was laid on this stone after being removed from the cross. Often referred to as the "Disposition of Jesus," removing the Savior's body from the cross has been the subject of many an artist, but none more impressive than Peter Paul Rubens' *The Descent from the Cross*. It is the central panel of a triptych painting still in its original location within the Cathedral of Our Lady, Antwerp, Belgium. No trip to Belgium is complete without seeing the Rubens.

Station #14. *Jesus' Body Is Placed in the Tomb*

"When it was evening, there came a rich man from Arimathea, named Joseph, who also was a disciple of Jesus. He went to Pilate and asked for the body of Jesus. Then Pilate ordered it to be given to him. And Joseph took the body and wrapped it in a clean linen shroud and laid it in his own new tomb, which he had cut in the rock. And he rolled a great stone to the entrance of the tomb and went away" (Matt 27:57–60). From the "Stone of Anointing," where devotees kneel and kiss the stone, the view shifts to the left, revealing the Rotunda and, within it, the Edicule, the Tomb of Jesus.

From the very beginning, pilgrims have walked the Via Dolorosa as a devotional practice. People from all over the world, but mainly from Europe and the Americas, have come to follow the path they believed led to the praetorium of Pilate, to the place called Calvary. Invariably, two consequences arose from this innate need to identify with Jesus' death.

First, devotional literature developed that expanded on the Gospel accounts of Jesus' trek along this street. From this expansion came tradition, and tradition led to the establishment of more stations than were supported by the Gospels.

Second, with the traditional street of the Via Dolorosa identified and specific stops along the route declared as sacred sites for prayer and meditation, and more pilgrims wished to come to Jerusalem to experience "walking where Jesus walked." Commercial ventures arose. Books of prescribed prayers and recitations became a necessary accouterment to the pilgrimage. The fourteen stations became immortalized in games, stickers, cartoons, and other paraphernalia designed to add to the experience. Travel agencies created pilgrim tours to facilitate getting enthusiastic wayfarers from here to there, "there" being the Via Dolorosa in Jerusalem.

Devotion was still the motive, but the crowds along the route had become huge. Often someone would carry a huge cross at the head of each pilgrim group. The noise was unflinching and unabated. The walk on the Via Dolorosa took on an almost circus-like atmosphere.

And then, it happened. Magazines and TV stations were interviewing credible archaeologists, who said the evidence was quite conclusive that the traditional Via Dolorosa was the wrong street and that all the sacred sites were not sacred at all.

> "The Via Dolorosa in the Old City of Jerusalem, [that] pilgrims have walked for centuries believing it to be the path that Jesus walked to Golgotha, is based on the incorrect assumption that the praetorium was in the Antonia Fortress at the northwest corner of the Temple Mount."
> —Eckhart J. Schnabel

New evidence produces new theories. When new evidence lined up with old facts, a strong argument was presented; it is all related to the streets of Jerusalem.

From the Upper Room to Joseph's Tomb

JERUSALEM'S CARDO AND DECUMANUS

Roman cities were always built or rebuilt with a plan. The Romans were antiquity's most expert builders of almost everything, including theaters, roads, buildings, cities, and more. This is why so many Roman building projects continue to stand today, whether it is the Pont du Gard in southern France, the Amphitheater in Pula in Croatia, or the Library of Celsus in Ephesus. Every city that received the attention of Roman engineers bore a resemblance to its city plan.

Alcantara Bridge, crossing the Tagus River. Alcantara, Spain.

The Romans were master road builders. They constructed their roads in three layers; the bottom layer was called *statumen*, which was made from crushed stone mixed with cement. The middle layer was the *rudera*, composed of fine gravel, rough stone, and sometimes pottery chips. The top layer of a Roman road or street was made of cobblestones, cut mostly square on all sides. They fit tightly together with a thin column of sand filtered between each cobblestone to hold it in place. The Roman engineers even knew how to construct all their roads with a convex surface so that the rain would freely drain off into a curbed ditch on either side.

In the Roman plan, cities typically featured an east-west-oriented street known as a *decumanus*. The main east-west street was called the *Decumanus Maximus*.[81] The *Decumanus Maximus* was crossed with the perpendicular north-south-oriented street called the *Cardo*. The main Cardo was known as the *Cardo Maximus*. In Roman cities, the Forum was

The Via Dolorosa

typically situated near the intersection of the two broad, paved streets—the *Decumanus Maximus* and the *Cardo Maximus*.

In later Roman times, the *Cardo* was about 12 meters (40 feet) wide and lined on both sides with columns. The total width of the street, plus the shopping areas built on either side, was 22 meters (72 feet). That is the equivalent of a 4-lane highway today.

As the map below illustrates, the *Decumanus Maximus* of Jerusalem ran from the Temple Mount west to the current Jaffa Gate. The *Cardo Maximus* carried people and traffic from the Damascus Gate on the north side of Jerusalem deep into the heart of the city. The *Cardo* intersected the *Decumanus*, about halfway between the Temple and the western gate of the city.

In twenty-first-century Jerusalem, the Cardo Maximus would have been approximately where Shuk ha-Basamim Street is located today, running north to south. The *Decumanus Maximus* ran east to west, about where David Street is located in the Old City. Appropriately, the palace of Herod the Great was situated at the western end of the *Decumanus Maximus*, with Golgotha on the west side of the *Cardo Maximus*, north of the *Decumanus Maximus*. These main thoroughfares made Jesus' walk to Golgotha quite direct.

MAP 1

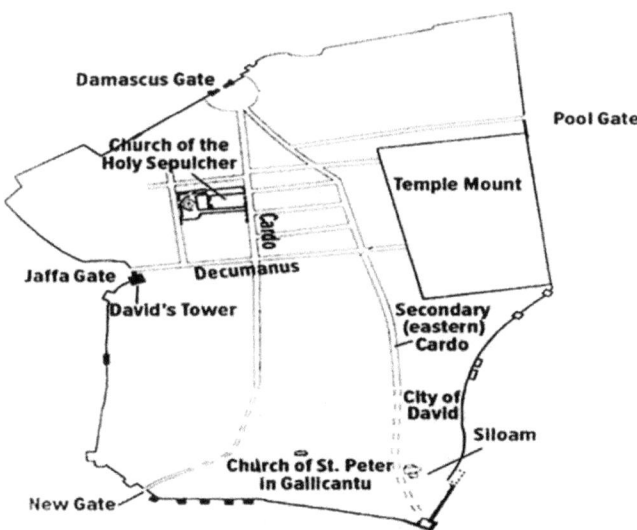

The Jerusalem Cardo Maximus and Decumanus Maximus

There was, however, one huge problem. The *Decumanus* and *Cardo* were not built until after the days of Jesus.[82] Just because these two Roman arteries were not there in Jesus' Jerusalem does not mean that major streets at that location did not exist before the Romans built the *Decumanus* and *Cardo*. Roman engineers would have followed the path of least resistance in cutting a broad street through the center of the city, and likely that meant using existing streets.[83] Nevertheless, the question remains. "Was the location of the future *Cardo* or the *Decumanus* where the Via Dolorosa existed in Jesus' day"?

It appears the Romans also built another east-west street north of the Antonia Fortress, approximately where Lions Gate Street and Via Dolorosa are today. This was because the Temple Mount stood in the way of completing the *Decumanus Maximus* entirely across the city. This street would have been the traditional Via Dolorosa.

> "From a historical point of view, this [the Via Dolorosa] is almost certainly not the route that Jesus took in his final days, in his final hours."
> —Hector Patmore

Over the last several decades, mounting archaeological evidence has suggested that Pilate's praetorium was not located in the Antonia Fortress but rather at Herod's palace on the other side of the Old City of Jerusalem. The physical evidence corroborates the existing literary evidence. Archaeologist Pierre Benoit wrote that "like Philo, the late-first-century writer, Josephus testifies that the Roman governors of Roman Judaea, who governed from Caesarea Maritima on the coast, stayed in Herod's palace while they were in Jerusalem, carried out their judgments on the pavement immediately outside it, and had those found guilty flogged there."[84]

More than two decades ago, plans were made to expand the Tower of David Museum in Jerusalem. However, as archaeologists began peeling away layers under the floor of an old, abandoned building adjacent to the museum, something genuinely amazing appeared. Scholars knew that this site had been used as a prison during the Ottoman Turks' rule and later by the British, but archaeologists did not expect to find what their digging revealed.

Their careful excavation exposed what they suspected to be the remains of a palace—but not just any palace—Herod's palace. This is the palace where it is believed the Roman governor established his headquarters during his visits to Jerusalem. And, this is where Jesus' trial before Pilate would have taken place.[85]

Now, after years of excavation, the suspicions of the early archaeologists have been confirmed. Amit Re'em, the Jerusalem district archaeologist who headed the excavation team in the early days of digging, indicated that this building had yielded a treasure trove of amazing discoveries covering many, many years. Some of those discoveries included symbols that were carved into the walls of old jail cells by prisoners from the Jewish resistance fighters at the founding of the State of Israel. Articles from the Crusader times were also located. Nevertheless, the most exciting find was an underground sewage system that appears to have serviced the expansive palace of Herod the Great himself.

In 2009, Israeli archaeologist Shimon Gibson was digging just south of the Jaffa Gate, the western terminus of the ancient Roman *Decumanus Maximus*. Here, there were two fortification walls with an outer gate and an inner gate leading to a barracks. What Gibson discovered was the remains of a large, paved courtyard that contained a raised platform measuring approximately two square meters (22 square feet). Gibson wrote of the inner courtyard, paved with flagstones, that it "corresponds perfectly with the situation of the place of the Roman tribunal as suggested by Josephus and John."[86]

Josephus indicated that Herod's palace was on the western hill.[87] The work of multiple archaeologists has proven it to be located under a corner, just east of the Jaffa Gate. Furthermore, archaeology has now confirmed that before Hadrian's second-century alterations for the construction of Aelia Capitolina, the area adjacent to the Antonia Fortress was a large open-air pool of water.[88] For Shimon Gibson, there is little doubt that Jesus' trial before Pilate occurred somewhere within Herod's palace compound. "In the Gospel of John, the trial is described as taking place near a gate and on a bumpy stone pavement—details that fit with previous archaeological findings near the prison."[89]

As growing archaeological evidence suggests, if Pilate took up residence in Herod's Palace when he came to Jerusalem, Jesus likely bore his cross on streets that roughly correspond to the locations of the Cardo Maximus and the Decumanus Maximus. If Pilate operated out of the Antonia Fortress, Jesus might have carried his cross for a short distance on the *Cardo,* but not at all on the *Decumanus.*

> "The Via Dolorosa is defined by faith, not history."
> —Jerome Murphy-O'Connor

Does this mean that pilgrims to the Holy City will abandon the traditional Via Dolorosa for a new, more likely route? Perhaps, eventually. We must remember that the journey along the Via Dolorosa is not a journey of facts; it is a journey of faith. However, visitors to Jerusalem should include the Old Citadel and the Tower of David in their itinerary if they want to see where Pilate condemned Jesus to be crucified.

PEOPLE JESUS ENCOUNTERED ON THE VIA DOLOROSA

What would those in the crowd experience when the Roman soldiers shuffled Jesus along the Via Dolorosa to Golgotha? What would they see? Let your mind wander for a few moments.

First, they would see and hear others in the crowd. This was not their first crucifixion; they had witnessed far too many already. Nevertheless, it was a very special crucifixion. It was the execution of a man whom many believed to be the Messiah. Most of them were craning their necks, waiting to get a glimpse of this Nazarene.

Next, they would see a single Roman soldier in front of the others carrying a placard. According to custom, a Roman captain led the procession, usually carrying a small board, often on a pole or stick. On that board was written the name of the convicted and the crime for which he was condemned to death. The Jewish Gemara reports:

> Abaye says: "And the crier must also publicly proclaim that the transgression was committed on such and such a day, at such and such an hour, and at such and such a place, as perhaps there are those who know that the witnesses could not have been in that place at that time, and they will come forward and render the witnesses conspiring witnesses."[90]

In the case of Jesus, this would have been the *titulus* to which the Jewish religious authorities so strongly objected.

Pilate also wrote an inscription and put it on the cross. It read, "Jesus of Nazareth, the King of the Jews." Many of the Jews read this inscription, for the place where Jesus was crucified was near the city, and it was written in Aramaic, in Latin, and in Greek. So the chief priests of the Jews said to Pilate, "Do not write, 'The King of the Jews,' but rather, 'This man said, I am King of the Jews.'" Pilate answered, "What I have written I have written" (John 19:19–22).

After the lead man with the placard, the first soldiers approached, clearing the way and pushing back the crowd when needed. These Roman soldiers were "clad in sandals, legs bare, wearing the skirt-like *pteruges* to cover their loins, sweating profusely beneath the plates of armor on their chests and tinned bronze attic helmets that cover the tops of their heads and the sides of their faces."[91] The Romans were experienced at crowd control. They knew there would be taunts from the crowd. There may be objects thrown, such as rotten fruit, garbage, or worse. The soldiers wanted no trouble until they finished escorting Jesus and the killing squad to the place of death, the place known as Golgotha.

The killing squad likely followed these regular soldiers. These were the men of the crucifixion death squads, soldiers of impressive physiques prone to brutality. Each crucifixion killing squad consisted of four men, known as a *quaternion*. A fifth man, a centurion, known as the *exactor mortis*, oversaw their actions and walked in front of them.

Then, those along the Via Dolorosa would see Jesus battered, bloodied, and barely recognizable as a human being. They would see him bent over as he carried that heavy *patibulum* from Pilate's judgment hall to Golgotha. It was the Roman custom that the prisoner should be stripped naked, hit, and insulted during this passage through the city. According to the Gospels, however, Jesus put on his clothes again before leaving Pilate's house.

Pierre Benoit observed, "He would have left Herod's palace, the present-day 'Tower of David,' taken the present 'David Street' as far as the three parallel 'souks,' followed these northward and ended up at the gate which now stands in the Alexander Hospice. Going out by this gate, he would have been close to Calvary."[92]

Additional Roman soldiers would follow behind Jesus, bringing up the rear. They would prod or whip the Savior to keep him trudging forward. They would also control the crowd closest to Jesus as he passed by. These soldiers were also escorts to the place of death.

Finally, the crowd would close in behind the procession. They would yell delight or displeasure, depending on their attitude toward the one being crucified. This crowd would follow Jesus and the soldiers to Calvary so they could have a front-row seat to the spectacle of death.

HOW THE EXHAUSTED JESUS CARRIED HIS CROSS

It was the Roman custom to compel a condemned man to carry his cross to the crucifixion site. That would be like having the person to be executed load the bullets into the rifles of the firing squad.

There is ample historical and literary evidence to support the notion that the prisoner bears his cross. Andreas J. Köstenberger notes that "traditional reconstruction has Jesus bear the cross, that is, the horizontal crossbar called a *patibulum* until he collapses on the way, at which time Simon of Cyrene is pressed into service (Matt. 27:32)."[93] The third-century BC Roman comic dramatist Plautus wrote, "Carry the cross through the city, then attach to the cross." (*The Charcoal Woman Carbonaria* 2). In *The Braggart Warrior, a.k.a. Miles Gloriosus* 2.4.6, 7, Plautus penned, "Go straight out of the gate, when you have a cross in your hands." Plutarch (*Moralia* 554AB) said, "Every wrongdoer who goes to execution carries out his own cross."[94]

The condemned man was forced to walk through the city as an example to those looking on. In two passages in the *Mostellaria*, a Roman comedy written by Plautus two centuries before Jesus' crucifixion, Plautus said (Frag. *Carbonaria*, 2), '*Patibulum ferat per urbem*,' "Let him carry his cross [*patibulum*] through the city" (see also Josephus, *Ant.* 20.6.3, where Claudius ordered the tribune Celer to be dragged through the city of Jerusalem in front of everybody before being executed). Plautus continued that the condemned "be attached to the upright stake [*crux*]." "If this was regular practice in the Jerusalem of Jesus' day, we ought, therefore to picture him as carrying the 'stretcher' or 'crossbar' to the place where the upright stake was already fixed."[95]

The first-century playwright Chariton, in his novel *Chaereas* or *Callirhoe*, wrote, "Without seeing them or hearing their defense, the master (Mithridates) immediately ordered the crucifixion of the sixteen cellmates. They were brought out, chained together at the foot and the neck, each carrying his cross."[96]

The Via Dolorosa

In his book *"In the Shadow of the Cross,"* Randal Earl Denny recounts a story about a businessman attending the famous once-a-decade passion play in Oberammergau, Germany. Denny says:

> Apparently, the man had more enthusiasm than he did sense because, after the final act of the Passion Play, he rushed on stage to take some pictures. He even got a picture of Anton Lang, who played the part of Jesus that year, still in costume. Mr. Lang gave him a look of displeasure. Then he spied the big cross that Anton Lang carried up the hill of Calvary. The businessman said to his wife, "Quick, take my camera and when I lift the cross onto my shoulder, you take my picture." But when he tried to lift the cross, he found it too heavy. He could not get it off the floor. Anton Lang came over to stop the man's disrespectful actions when the businessman asked, "How did you lift that to your shoulder? It is very heavy. Why don't you use a lighter cross?" To this Anton Lang replied, "Sir, if I did not feel the weight of his cross, I could not play his part."[97]

Ordinarily, the condemned carried his cross to the execution site by the longest street or road possible. This was so that the most incredible crowd of onlookers would see the pathetic man and be deterred from any civil disobedience.

> "I think it's fairly unlikely that crucified victims, including Jesus, would have carried the entire cross, both beams, through the streets. It would have been several hundred pounds and probably almost impossible to walk to the site of the crucifixion." — Jonathan Reed

However, that does not appear to be the case with Jesus. The execution detail took Jesus, and perhaps the other two men, to be crucified from the courtyard of Pilate's praetorium to the Gennath Gate, a distance of about 700 meters (2,300 feet). Assuming the traditional site of the Church of the Holy Sepulcher is the location of Golgotha, this was a relatively short walk. It would take an unencumbered person about twelve minutes to walk that far. We can assume that with the crowd pressing from each side and with the brutalized condition of Jesus' body, it took him more time than that.

Authors Edwards, Gabel, and Hosmer claim:

> It is reasonable to assume that Jesus was in good health before the ordeal that he faced in the hours before his death. Having been a

carpenter and traveling throughout the land during his ministry would have required that he would be in good physical condition. Before the crucifixion, however, he was forced to walk 2.5 miles over a sleepless night, during which he suffered great anguish through his six trials, was mocked, ridiculed, and severely beaten.[98]

The 2.5 miles they speak of would be a calculation of the distance Jesus walked to the Upper Room, from there to Gethsemane, from the garden to the palace of the High Priest, then to Pilate's praetorium, a quick trip to Herod Agrippa's Jerusalem residence and back, then from the governor's judgment hall to the place of execution.

It is reasonable to ask how a man who was so sleep-deprived, someone who had not eaten since the Last Supper, could carry a heavy wooden cross. How could a man subjected to the lictors' abusive scourging, one who had been pummeled by the Roman soldiers, a man whose blood loss must have been as excessive as his thirst, how a man like that could carry a wooden cross? Superimposed upon his physical condition, Jesus had suffered extreme mental and spiritual distress in Gethsemane and had withstood interrogation by Annas, Caiaphas, the Sanhedrin, Pontius Pilate, and Herod Agrippa. How could any man in this condition carry the *patibulum* on his shoulders to the location where he knew he would die?

No human being could. Nevertheless, Jesus was not some human Superman. He was much more. He was the unique, one-of-a-kind God-man. He was a human being, and it was his humanity, not his deity, that bore the cross to Calvary. He died as a sinless man, not as God. His deity was not abused here; his humanity was. What the Roman soldiers demanded, Jesus could not physically do. He was much too weak to bear such a load.

> "As a forensic pathologist, I find it extraordinary that Jesus was able to make the trek to Calvary at all in the condition that he was in."
> —Frederick T. Zugibe

As Jesus and the soldiers left Pilate's praetorium, he carried the *patibulum* on his shoulders. John 19:16, 17 indicates, "So they took Jesus, and he went out, bearing his own cross, to the place called The Place of a Skull, which in Aramaic is called Golgotha." However, the soldiers soon spotted that Jesus was too weak to carry his cross along the Via Dolorosa to Golgotha. That's why Luke 23:26 adds, "They seized one Simon of Cyrene . . . and laid on him the cross, to carry it behind Jesus."

As previously mentioned, the widespread belief that Jesus stumbled and fell beneath the load of his cross is not supported in the Gospel accounts (Matt 27:32–33; Mark 15:20–22; Luke 23:25–26; John 19:16–18). The closest anyone can come to a reference to Jesus' falling beneath the weight of his cross is Psalm 35:15: "But at my stumbling they rejoiced and gathered; they gathered together against me." However, this psalm of David is not generally considered a messianic psalm and therefore cannot be definitively applied to Jesus.

It is an assumption that Jesus fell to the ground. It's based solely on the tradition of the church.[99] It is not an assumption that Simon of Cyrene was conscripted to carry the *patibulum* of Jesus' cross.

If Jesus did fall forward on the Via Dolorosa, a physician would describe what the likely result would be.

> His arms could not brace his fall since they were tied with ropes to the beam. This likely resulted in a full-force fall upon his face and chest, probably knocking the wind out of him. A significant blunt force trauma to the breastbone can result in bruising of the heart muscle (*myocardial contusion*). This could result in a fluid collection around Jesus' heart (*pericardial effusion*), which could lead to shock and low blood pressure, if not to death, making it impossible to finish this otherwise relatively short walk.[100]

The involvement of Simon in bearing Jesus' cross stemmed from both the plan of the Sovereign God and the need of the Roman soldiers to expedite the process. Whether Jesus fell or not, he was too weak to continue carrying the heavy load of his cross. Luke's account makes perfect sense. "And as they led him away, they seized one Simon of Cyrene, who was coming in from the country, and laid on him the cross, to carry it behind Jesus."

The final procession along the Via Dolorosa consisted of the first soldier carrying the titulus, a group of soldiers, the killing squad, Jesus himself, Simon of Cyrene, additional soldiers, and the closing crowd. Carrying one's cross was not just part of the punishment; it was part of the spectacle. It must have been quite a sight, especially for the Father in heaven who ordered his Son's crucifixion.

From the Upper Room to Joseph's Tomb

THE VIA DOLOROSA CELEBRATED IN MUSIC

While the Via Dolorosa translates to "Way of Sorrows," it is clear that this most famous street has stirred the emotions of composers who have grappled with the subject in their musical compositions.

In 1879, the renowned Hungarian composer Franz Liszt composed a *Via Crucis* for mixed choir, soloists, and organ. The work combines unison songs (Stations 1 and 14) with Lutheran chorales (Stations 4 and 12), as well as chorales inspired by another famous composer, Johann Sebastian Bach, and his own chorales (Station 6). The other stations (2, 3, 5, 6, 7, 8, 9, 10, 11, and 13) feature the solo organ (or piano). Liszt himself wanted to perform the *Via Crucis* in the Colosseum of Rome.

A child prodigy, French Organist Marcel Dupré continued to add to his stature as an adult. In 1931, Dupré improvised and transcribed musical meditations based on fourteen poems by Paul Claudel, a six-time nominee for the Nobel Prize in Literature. Each poem corresponds to a Station of the Cross.

David Bowie claimed his 1976 song "Station to Station" was "very much concerned with the stations of the cross."[101] Although he is primarily known as a Broadway composer, Michael Valenti, with librettist Diane Seymour, wrote an oratorio entitled "The Way." The musical piece, which premiered in 1991, depicted the fourteen Stations of the Cross.

Polish composer Paweł Lukaszewski wrote *Via Crucis*, which the Wrocław Opera premiered on Good Friday, March 30, 2018. Italian musician, composer, and poet Stefano Vagnini's 2002 modular oratorio, *Via Crucis*, is a composition for organ, computer, choir, string orchestra, and brass quartet.[102] As the name suggests, Vagnini's *Via Crucis* depicts the fourteen Stations of the Cross.

One of the more popular Christian compositions telling the story of Jesus on the Via Dolorosa is Billy Sprague and Niles Borop's 1984 work entitled *Via Dolorosa*. This piece focuses more on the Savior who walked the Via Dolorosa than on the Stations of the Cross. For that reason, it has won the praise of many gospel singers.

This chapter began by naming some of the most famous streets in the world. Nevertheless, Wall Street, Broadway, 5th Avenue, or any other street in New York City cannot hold a candle to the Via Dolorosa in Jerusalem.[103] It is not just that this is a famous street; it's a meaningful street. It connects an unfair trial with an inhumane crucifixion.

The Via Dolorosa

Even that is not enough, however, to make the Via Dolorosa as special as it is. Take Jesus off that path to Calvary, and you take the meaning out of the Via Dolorosa forever. Just as he gives meaning to life, so too Jesus Christ gives meaning to an otherwise meaningless street in Old Jerusalem and forever will—the Via Dolorosa.

Chapter 7

The Killing Field of Jerusalem

Crucifixion's Place of the Skull

Jesus was not unfamiliar with "the place of the skull." He had passed it dozens of times, arrayed each time with criminals being crucified. He looked at Golgotha with eyes of passion, awaiting his day, his turn, his date with destiny.

Two Ideas About Where Crucifixion Should Take Place
A Place Outside the City
The Wall of Jerusalem in Jesus' Day
A Place Called Golgotha
Crucifixion at Qumran
The Mount of Olives
Gordon's Calvary
The Church of the Holy Sepulchre

The first-century Roman educator and rhetorician Quintilian wrote, "Whenever we crucify the guilty, the most crowded roads are chosen, where the most people can see and be moved by this fear. For penalties relate not so much to retribution as to their exemplary effect" (Quintilian, *Declamations* 274).

Roman law decreed that crucifixions must occur in the most public places so the highest number of passersby could view their indecency. This would have the most significant impact possible on the citizens of occupied territories, such as Judea. In the case of Jesus, this was Passover week when the highest number of Jews would be in the Holy City and able to witness the Calvary event.

Nevertheless, how was it determined where the killing fields would be? Who decided where those to be crucified were crucified?

TWO IDEAS ABOUT WHERE CRUCIFIXION SHOULD TAKE PLACE

Since in the provinces, Roman justice was entirely at the discretion of the governor or those appointed by him, there was little chance for standardization in Roman judicial procedure. The Roman prefect would consider the facts and make his judgment. There was, of course, Roman law that he had to be aware of and had to follow, but laws passed by the Senate in Rome could not possibly address all the nuances of criminal activity in distant provinces. The result was the locals made their own laws. As a consequence, the prefect had a great deal of discretion in how and where justice was applied.

The twentieth-century Dutch Neo-Calvinist theologian and professor Klaas Schilder wrote a trilogy about Jesus' death (*Christ in His Suffering, Christ on Trial,* and *Christ Crucified*). In *Christ on Trial*, writing about the appropriateness of Pilate sending Jesus to Herod Agrippa for trial because Jesus was from Galilee, Schilder reports:

> As it happened, there was a regulation at the time which had it that an accused person might be tried in any of three places: 1) at the place of his birth; 2) at the place where he established his residence, or 3) at the place in which he had committed his crime. According to this regulation, more than one basis could be named to justify calling the tetrarch of Galilee into the trial of Jesus.[104]

This regulation generated a real problem for Pilate and the Romans. The site of Jesus' birth was Bethlehem in Judea (Matt 2:1; Luke 2:4, 15; John 7:42; Mic 5:2). However, very little of Jesus' life is associated with Bethlehem after his birth. Although he was raised in Nazareth, Jesus made Capernaum his home (Matt 4:13; 9:1; 17:24; Mark 1:21; 2:1; 9:33; Luke 4:23; 4:31; 7:1; John 2:12; 4:46; 6:17, 24, 59).

It was the standard Roman practice to execute a lawbreaker where he committed a crime (*Forum Deliciti*). Nevertheless, how does one determine where Jesus committed a crime if his alleged crimes were healing the sick, raising the dead, and teaching the people about God and his love? Jesus was an itinerant teacher. Where would Pilate begin?

Would you hold his execution in Galilee (Mark 1:14); by the Sea of Galilee (Matt 14:14); in Cana (John 2:1); Gennesaret (Matt.14:34); Sychar of Samaria (John 4:5); Caesarea Philippi (Matt 16:13); Capernaum (Matt 17:24); Jericho (Matt 20:29); the land of the Gerasenes (Mark 5:1); Bethsaida (Mark 8:22); beyond the Jordan (Mark 10:1); Tyre and Sidon (Matt 15:21), just to name a few sites where Jesus worked the works of his Heavenly Father?

Holding a trial and executing punishment at the location of the crime seems to be the Jewish preference. The Jewish Talmudist Rabbi Samuel bar Naḥmani (c. 270–330 AD) lived in Babylonia and is known throughout the Talmud only as Rabbah. Rabbah said, "In the place where the brigands rob, there they crucify him." The rabbi demonstrated the common practice of holding court wherever a crime was committed.

> "Jesus was not crucified in a Cathedral between two candles, but on a cross between two thieves; on the town garbage heap . . . at the kind of place where cynics talk smut, and thieves curse, and soldiers gamble."
> —George F. Macleod

It was determined that since most of his "crime" was committed in Jerusalem, it was appropriate to crucify Jesus there. This was likely more for the sake of expedience rather than adherence to any regulation.

A PLACE OUTSIDE THE CITY

Hebrews 13:11, 12, "For the bodies of those animals whose blood is brought into the holy places by the High Priest as a sacrifice for sin are burned outside the camp. So Jesus also suffered outside the gate in order to sanctify the people through his own blood."

In the Pentateuch, the expression "outside the camp" occurs twenty-two times. More than a quarter of those times, it refers to making the sin offering "outside the camp" (Exod 29:14; Lev 4:12, 21; 8:17; 9:11; 16:27). The writer of Hebrews is crystal clear that Jesus would become our sin offering "outside the camp" as well. Thus, the greatest certainty related to the location of Jesus' crucifixion is that it had to occur outside Jerusalem's city walls.

Literary affirmation

There is evidence in the sources that certain cities in the Roman Empire had places of execution permanently established outside the city walls. In *Miles Gloriosus* 2.4.6–7, the Roman playwright Plautus specifies that the person who carried the crossbeam of his cross would be crucified outside the gate.[105]

The Roman historian Tacitus records that there was such a place in Rome on the Campus Esquilinus. It was called Sessorium, the place where enslaved people were crucified, their execution being accomplished by the *carnifex servorum* or executioner.[106] Later, this disgraceful location became known as the "forest of crosses," where the bodies of many executed victims became the prey of vultures and other predatory birds.[107]

Justus Lipsius says their bodies were eaten while the enslaved people hanging on their crosses were still alive.[108] Charles Duane Johnson confirms, "The crucified body was sometimes left to rot on the cross and serve as a disgrace, a convincing warning and deterrent to passersby."[109]

In Jerusalem, those deemed worthy of execution by the Roman prefect were crucified at Golgotha, the place of the skull, outside the city. All four Gospel writers mention this established killing field as the site where Jesus of Nazareth was crucified. (Matt 27:33; Mark 15:22; Luke 23:33; John 19:17).

Golgotha was Jerusalem's equivalent of Rome's Sessorium. Jesus was not unfamiliar with "the place of the skull." He had passed it dozens, perhaps hundreds, of times, arrayed each time with criminals being crucified. He looked at Golgotha with eyes of passion, awaiting his day, his turn, his date with destiny.

Biblical affirmation

Leviticus 24:13, 14 specifies that the blasphemer was to be taken outside the camp and stoned by the entire community of Israel. Similarly, Numbers 15:35, 36 indicates the Sabbath-breaker was to be stoned outside the camp. Raymond Brown remarks:

[In Greek,] both passages use *exagein*, the verb employed here only by Mark 15:20b. When Israel settled in the Promised Land, that directive was understood in terms of outside the city, that is where Naboth was led to be stoned for cursing God and king (I Kgs 21:13), and where Stephen was dragged to be stoned for blasphemy against Moses and God (Acts 7:58; see also 6:1).[110]

Another reason executions took place outside the city was because of the strict Jewish laws regarding the proximity of dead bodies to the living. Coming into contact with a dead body meant a period of ritual cleansing for uncleanness (Num 19:11–22). The Pharisees, in particular, took this very seriously. As a result, those few tombs that happened to be within the city were often whitewashed, so no Jew could accidentally come into direct contact with death.

Besides this restriction, there was a curse upon anyone who was hanged on a tree (Deut 21:22, 23; see also Gal 3:13). Therefore, to avoid a curse from God within the Holy City, all crucifixions had to occur outside the gates.

Grammatical affirmation

The grammar used by the four Gospel writers is not only quite similar, but it is also quite telling. In each of the Gospel accounts of Jesus being led to Golgotha, the verbs confirm that Jesus was led outside of Jerusalem to be crucified. Matthew 27:32, 33 says, "As they went out, they found a man of Cyrene, Simon by name. They compelled this man to carry his cross. And they came to a place called Golgotha (which means Place of a Skull)." The words "they went out" (Greek: ἐξέρχομαι; English: *exérchomai*) are a combination of ἐκ "out of" and ἔρχομαι "to bring, come, or pass") and therefore mean "to pass out of."

Mark 15:20, 22 also indicates, "And they led him out to crucify him." The phrase "led him out" (Greek: ἐξάγω; English: *exágō*), is a combination of ἐκ "out of" and ἄγω "to bring" or "to lead" and means "to lead out." Luke and John agree (see Luke 23:32, 33 and John 19:16, 17, which are the same as Matthew 27:32, 33).

Levitical law and Roman law were both observed when the Roman soldiers led Jesus through the Jerusalem gate to the designated place of execution, Golgotha.

Historical confirmation

The noted church historian Eusebius journeyed to Jerusalem with Queen Helena, mother of Constantine the Great (272–337 AD). The purpose of the journey was to discover, confirm, and preserve the site of the Lord's crucifixion. The local Christians of Jerusalem immediately led Eusebius and the Queen Mother to a site outside the city gates. On this site, liturgical celebrations had been held until 66 AD.[111]

The site's landscape underwent significant changes when Emperor Hadrian (117–138 AD) rebuilt Jerusalem in 135 AD as a Roman city, which he named Aelia Capitolina. Hadrian built temples to Roman deities, including Aphrodite and Jupiter. Still, the local Christians knew the exact spot that followers of Jesus centuries earlier identified as the site of Golgotha and Jesus' crucifixion.

Erich Kiehl summarizes what we know about Jerusalem's execution site. "The place of execution was near Jerusalem (John 19:20), outside the walls of the city (Heb 13:12), and close to a busy street (Mark 15:29). Matthew 26:65, 66 and Mark 14:63, 64 both note that Jesus was condemned for blasphemy. Leviticus 24:14 and Numbers 15:35, 36 stipulate that blasphemers were to be executed outside the camp."[112]

The evidence is incontrovertible. Jesus was executed just outside the gate of the Old City of Jerusalem. He died at a place called Calvary by the Romans and Golgotha by the Jews.

THE WALL OF JERUSALEM IN JESUS' DAY

Look at a map of the Old City of Jerusalem today, and the leading contender for the location of Golgotha has a problem. The Church of the Holy Sepulchre is situated within the existing Old City walls. Does this disqualify it as a candidate for the authentic site of Jesus' death and subsequent burial? Some have felt so in the past, but the traditional site is not disqualified if you understand the history of the walls of Jerusalem.

From the Upper Room to Joseph's Tomb

The Church of the Holy Sepulchre

Visitors to the Holy City today are likely to be impressed by the wall that encircles the Old City. It is indeed massive. The average height of this wall is almost 12 meters (40 feet); the average thickness is just over 2.5 meters (8 feet); the length of the wall is about 4,018 meters (2½ miles). Walking the Ramparts Wall is something everyone under 70 should attempt on a visit to Jerusalem.[113] It's fun; it provides incredible panoramic views, and it gives you a sense of the safety the Jews felt when the gates were closed at night.

However, the current walls were built when Jerusalem was part of the Ottoman Empire. The great Sultan Suleiman the Magnificent ordered the previously ruined city walls to be rebuilt. The work was completed between 1537 and 1541 AD, spanning four years. Today, the Jerusalem wall features thirty-four watchtowers and seven main gates that are open to traffic, with two additional gates recently discovered by archaeologists. In 1981, the Old City of Jerusalem, along with its walls, was added to the UNESCO World Heritage Site list.

Walls have surrounded Jerusalem throughout its history. David prayed to God, asking, "Do good to Zion in your good pleasure; build up the walls of Jerusalem" (Ps 51:18). Elsewhere, David begged, "Pray for the peace of Jerusalem! May they be secure who love you! Peace be within your walls and security within your towers!" (Ps 122:6–7).

Our primary source of information about the walls surrounding Jerusalem in Jesus' day is the historian Josephus. Here is how he described the fortifications of Jerusalem in the late Second Temple Period.

The Killing Field of Jerusalem

The city of Jerusalem was fortified with three walls, on such parts as were not encompassed with unpassable valleys; for in such places it had but one wall. The city was built upon two hills, which are opposite to one another, and have a valley to divide them asunder; at which valley the corresponding rows of houses on both hills end. Of these hills, that which contains the Upper City is much higher, and in length more direct. Accordingly, it was called the "Citadel" by King David . . . the other hill, which was called "Acra" and sustains the lower city . . . Now the Valley of the Cheesemongers, as it was called, and was that which we told you before distinguished the hill of the Upper City from that of the lower, extended as far as Siloam; for that is the name of a fountain which hath sweet water in it, and this in great plenty also (*Wars* 5.4.1).

Table 1 represents the multi-layered history of Jerusalem's walls from the days of the Jebusites to the twenty-first century.

TABLE 1
A History of Jerusalem's Walls

The Wall of the Jebusites (?? BC–1004 BC)
The Wall of David around the City of David (1004–971 BC)
The Wall of Solomon encompassing the Temple Mount (971–931 BC)
The Wall of Hezekiah, "Broad Wall" for western expansion (931–586 BC)
The Wall of Nehemiah and the Returning Exiles (444–442 BC)
The Wall of the Maccabees (134–76 BC)
The Wall in Jesus' Day (76 BC–33 AD)
The Wall of Northern Expansion (37–70 AD)
The Wall of Aelia Capitolina (70–299 AD)
The Wall of Third Century Jerusalem (299–313 AD)
The Wall expanding Jerusalem for Christian Pilgrimages (313–637 AD)
The Walls of the Muslims, Crusaders, and Mamluks (637–1517 AD)
The Wall of Suleiman the Magnificent (1517 AD–present)

Josephus mentions three fortified walls around Jerusalem in his day, the first century AD. A brief description of each follows.

From the Upper Room to Joseph's Tomb

The First Wall (ca. 130 BC)

Josephus called this wall the "old one," beginning on the north at the tower Hippicus and extending as far as the cloister of the Temple. From that same northern starting point, the wall was built westward to the Gate of the Essenes, then above the Pool of Siloam, stretching around to the eastern cloister of the Temple.

MAP 1
Jerusalem's Three Walls

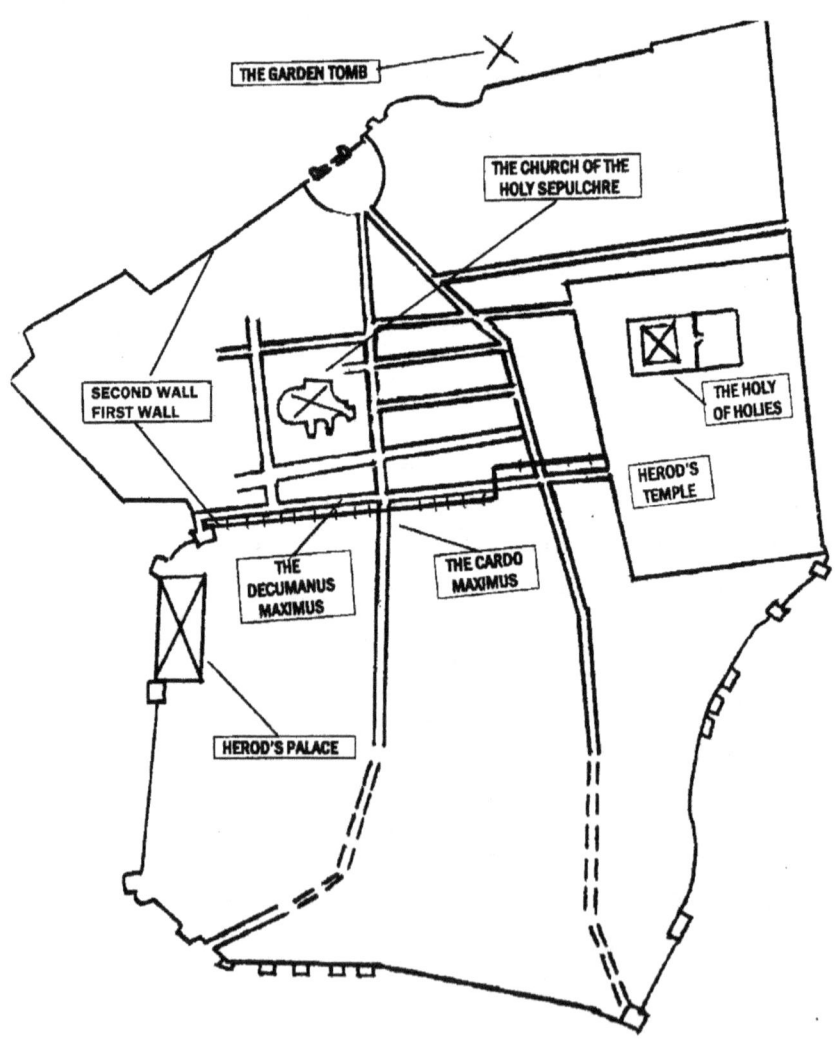

The Killing Field of Jerusalem

The Second Wall (ca. 50–51 BC?)

This wall, Josephus notes, began at the Gennath Gate of the first wall and encompassed the northern quarter of the city, reaching as far as the Antonia Fortress.

The Third Wall (41–44 AD)

The third wall was more expansive than the first two. It began at the Hippicus Tower, stretching around the north quarter of the city to the monuments of Helena, then passed by the sepulchral caverns of the kings, and bent at the corner tower, which is the "Monument of the Fuller," and finally joined the "old wall" at the Kidron Valley (*Wars* 5.4.2).[114] From this map, we can easily see that the Church of the Holy Sepulchre is located outside Josephus' Second Wall, which extends southward across the Tyropoean Valley to the First Wall. Excavations inside the Old City have shown that the Second Wall did not enclose the Holy Sepulchre Church.

Thus, the question of inside or outside the wall is settled. The Church of the Holy Sepulchre cannot be disqualified as a potential location for Jesus' crucifixion due to the position of the wall.

A PLACE CALLED GOLGOTHA

One would think that a location as necessary to the Passion narratives would be mentioned dozens of times by the Gospels. However, Golgotha is found in only three verses in the New Testament (Matt 27:33; Mark 15:22; and John 19:17). So, what do we know about it?

The meaning of Golgotha

According to John's account, we learn that Golgotha is an Aramaic word. We know it as a Greek transliteration (Aramaic: גֻּלְגָּלְתָּא; English: *gulgultha*' and Hebrew: גֻּלְגֹּלֶת; English: *gulgolet*) that comes from the root consonants (Hebrew: גלגל; English: *glgl*) that mean "round things," such as a wheel or a human skull.

One has to wonder why the site of Jesus' crucifixion is not mentioned in the Gospel of Luke. Why didn't he also name the site where Jesus was executed? The fact is, he did. "And when they came to the place that is called

The Skull, there they crucified him, and the criminals, one on his right and one on his left" (Luke 23:33). Golgotha means "skull." In all four Gospels, the word in the Greek text is κρανίον (English: *kraníon*). It sounds a lot like our English word "cranium."

So why did Luke not use the word κρανίον like the other Gospel authors? He did. He just translated the word as "The Skull" or "Calvary." The word "Calvaria" is the Latin equivalent of κρανίον, and this name for Golgotha became popular because the translators of the King James Bible chose to use "Calvaria" or "Calvary" instead of "Golgotha" in Luke 23:33 (see also the NKJV and AKJV).

These translators were not alone,[115] but most Bible translations today have opted for the Aramaic over the Greek meaning of "the Skull" (CEV, ESV, GNT, HCSB, JBP, TLB, NASB, NIV, NRSEV, NRES (Catholic Edition), RSV, and more).[116]

The reason behind the name

For many centuries, the reason this site is called Golgotha, "the Place of the Skull" or "Skull Hill" (see MSG) has been vigorously debated. Several theories present themselves with varying degrees of plausibility.

Topography. The first view pertains to the site's topography. Golgotha, the Place of the Skull, could refer to a geological formation resembling a skull at this execution site. The first stop on every guided tour of the Garden Tomb in Jerusalem is an overlook from where the visitor sees a rock formation that resembles the face of a skull. Garden Tomb guides acknowledge that the face of this rock outcropping would have changed over the centuries.

However, there are no references in the Bible to a skull-like rock formation, only to the fact that the site was called "the Place of the Skull." In fact, the Bible does not record that this was an elevated place or that it was called Mount Calvary, and neither do any Greek, Jewish, or Roman writers.

Cecil Frances Alexander, a nineteenth-century Anglo-Irish hymn writer, composed these words: "There is a green hill far away, Without a city wall, Where the dear Lord was crucified, Who died to save us all." Unfortunately, these wishful words may not reflect reality. The romantic notion that Jesus climbed a mountain to be crucified does not appear in any of the Gospel accounts.[117]

Nevertheless, the Scripture references are not irreconcilable, with the suggestion that the site resembled a skull. It is a rounded knoll that rises above the surrounding surface.

Pilgrims in the fourth century spoke of Calvary as a monticulus or small hill.[118] What remains today of such a hill within the Church of the Holy Sepulchre stands about 16 feet high.[119] Execution on a raised area above the surrounding roads would certainly have facilitated the Roman goal of making the punishment a public warning.

> "Calv'ry's mournful mountain climb; there, adoring at His feet, Mark that miracle of time, God's own sacrifice complete. 'It is finished!' hear him cry; learn from Jesus Christ to die."
> —James Montgomery

Boneyard -- The second view holds that Golgotha, the Place of the Skull, may refer to the remains of skulls left from previous Roman executions. The site where Jesus was crucified was the customary killing field of the Romans, and as such, the area may have been littered with the skulls of the condemned.[120] The preeminent Christian scholar and Bible translator Jerome (347–420 AD) held this view, as did the English historian and monk Venerable Bede (673–735 AD).

"Boneyard" is the English word for a place of this type. My favorite historic location in London is a four-minute walk south of the Old Street Underground Station. It is Bunhill Fields, directly across City Road from Wesley's Chapel. Because it was a dissenters' cemetery, those who refused to join the Church of England are buried here.

That would include such English notables as authors Daniel Defoe (*Robinson Crusoe*), John Bunyan (*The Pilgrim's Progress*), and William Blake (the famous English poet and artist), plus English hymnists Isaac Watts and John Rippon. George Fox, founder of the Quaker movement, and Susanna Wesley, known as the "Mother of Methodism," are buried here. The word "Bunhill" is a colloquial pronunciation of "Bone Hill." This is what Golgotha was like in the first century: a boneyard.

Adam's skull -- Another tradition claims that when David returned from the battle with Goliath, he carried the giant's bloody head to Jerusalem and buried it at the place of the skull.[121] First Samuel 17:54 informs us, "And

David took the head of the Philistine and brought it to Jerusalem, but he put his armor in his tent." From the text, we know David brought the giant's giant head to Jerusalem, but it does not tell us what he did with it. There is no indication he buried it at the place called Golgotha.

Although this story has not gained much traction, another Christian tradition dating back to the third century AD suggests that Golgotha was Adam's burial site. This tradition had a profound impact on the early Church. Origen (185–254 AD) speaks of it as well-known in his time (*Tractate 35* in *Matthew*). So does Ambrose (340–397 AD) (*Epistle 71*), Athanasius (296–373 AD), (*Sermons de Passione Opera* ii.⁹⁰), and Epiphanies of Salamis (312–403 AD) (*Panarion 46.5*).

Augustine notes, "The ancients hold that because Adam was the first man and was buried there, it was called Calvary because it holds the head of the human race" (*De Civitate Dei*, chapter 32). The fourth-century AD Greek bishop Basil the Great remarks, "Probably Noah was not ignorant of the sepulcher of our forefather and that of the firstborn of all mortals, and in that place, Calvary, the Lord suffered, the origin of death there being destroyed" (Sermon 38 *Patrologia Graeca* 85.409).

St. John Chrysostom (349–407 AD), the Bishop of Constantinople, also wrote:

> 'And He came to the place of a skull.' Some say that Adam died there, and there lieth; and that Jesus in this place where death had reigned, there also set up the trophy. For He went forth bearing the cross as a trophy over the tyranny of death; and as conquerors do, so He bear upon His shoulders the symbol of victory.[122]

Although this is merely a tradition, it remains a strong one.

The seventeenth-century English poet and cleric John Donne wrote a hymn that demonstrates the strength of this belief in his day. The "Hymn to God my God in my Sickness" says:

> We think that Paradise and Calvarie,
> Christ's cross and Adam's tree stood in one place,
> Look Lord, and find both Adams met in me;
> As the first Adam's sweat surrounds my face,
> May the last Adam's blood my soul embrace.

Donne was expressing the widespread belief that Adam was buried at the spot where Jesus was crucified, and this was done intentionally by the Sovereign God.

THE KILLING FIELD OF JERUSALEM

Visitors to the Church of the Holy Sepulcher, below the site of Jesus' crucifixion, are shown a large rock streaked with red. The priest will tell you that this small cave was Adam's tomb, and the blood of Christ dripped from above onto Adam's bones so he, too, could be redeemed from his sins.

> "Even those scholars and critics who have been moved to depart from almost everything else within the historical content of Christ's presence on earth have found it impossible to think away the factuality of the death of Christ." —John McIntyre

Everyone around Jerusalem knew that Golgotha was the place you go to die. Thomas Schmidt commented:

> Crucifixion was common enough in the Roman world that major cities set aside areas for multiple and prolonged executions. Crucified bodies, some still living, others in various stages of decomposition, would there be displayed as a warning to others. In Rome, the site was called the *Campus Esquilinus*, the "place of vultures." In Jerusalem, it was given a Hebrew name that people in Rome would not understand without a translation: *Golgotha*, "the place of a skull," or more literally, "the place of the [death's] head."[123]

We must now turn our examination to the central question of this chapter. Where was Golgotha, the place where the Savior was crucified? Can the location of the most momentous event in history be identified? First, let's explore some of the possibilities.

CRUCIFIXION AT QUMRAN

The most implausible thesis comes from Barbara Thiering. It is available to the public in her book *Jesus and the Secret of the Dead Sea Scrolls*.[124] Thiering claims to have discovered the interpretive key to the Dead Sea Scrolls and the New Testament. To understand the Gospels, Thiering said, the reader must recognize two levels of meaning. First, a symbolic surface level of miracle and mystery designed to inspire awe and fear in the "babes in Christ." Second, a purely historical level that tells the true story of Jesus' life as a man.

The caves at Qumran

Thiering believes the Dead Sea Scrolls, which include manuscripts of various Old Testament books, are the key to understanding the location of Jesus' crucifixion. The Dead Sea Scrolls contain previously unknown writings believed to be from the Essene community, many of which relate to a struggle between the "good guy," the Teacher of Righteousness, and his "bad guy" opponent, known as the Wicked Priest or the Man of a Lie. The twist Thiering brings to interpreting the Dead Sea Scrolls is that she believes the events recorded in the Gospels and the life of Jesus prove that Jesus is the Wicked Priest or the Man of a Lie.

She arrives at her conclusion by understanding the Gospels to be "pesher" stories that have two levels of meaning. Pesher is a Hebrew word meaning "interpretation." The authors of pesharim (plural of pesher) understand Scripture to have been written on two levels: the surface level for ordinary readers with limited knowledge and the concealed or deeper level for specialists with a higher consciousness. The pesher's literary form became known with the discovery of the Dead Sea Scrolls.

The Killing Field of Jerusalem

The author photographing the floor of Cave #4 in 1964

On the surface, to the uninitiated reader, the Gospels recount stories of an itinerant teacher and miracle worker who died for his followers and then rose from the dead. Thiering claims this simplistic, surface understanding is what is understood by the Christian Church. For Jesus' inner circle and those who have the interpretative key of the Scrolls today, there is a second, coded meaning. This is accessible only to those who have the code.

Somewhere along the way, Barbara Thiering lost her way, wandering far from Christian orthodoxy. This is evident in that she came to believe the following:

- Jesus married Mary Magdalene for the second time on Wednesday evening before Good Friday;
- Jesus and Mary Magdalene had children;
- The Gospels do not take place in Galilee or Judea; all Gospel events occur in the Qumran community;
- Jesus' crucifixion was real, but it took place at Qumran as well;
- Jesus did not die on the cross but was drugged to make it appear he had died;
- When Jesus was taken down from the cross, he was placed in a cave where he was revived. Thiering claimed she could even identify the cave;

- Jesus' disciples were not bumbling fools as they sometimes are portrayed, but they understood the deceptive plan and carried it out completely and efficiently.

If some of these things sound familiar to you, it likely means you have read Dan Brown's blockbuster book and/or viewed the subsequent movie *The DaVinci Code*. Brown relied heavily on Michael Biagent's book *Holy Blood and the Holy Grail*. Biagent, in turn, relied heavily on Barbara Thiering's book *Jesus the Man* and the theories she proposed. Jewish scholar Géza Vermes reflected the attitude of almost all biblical scholars with his review of Thiering's book in the December 1, 1994, edition of *The New York Review of Books*. Vermes wrote:

> Professor Barbara Thiering's reinterpretation of the New Testament, in which the married, divorced, and remarried Jesus, father of four, becomes the "Wicked Priest" of the Dead Sea Scrolls, has made no impact on learned opinion. Scroll scholars and New Testament experts alike have found the basis of the new theory, Thiering's use of the so-called "pesher technique," without substance.

These are harsh but truthful words, which Thiering's theory is not. To find the truth, we must move on.

THE MOUNT OF OLIVES

The second theory of the location of Golgotha comes from Ernest L. Martin. Martin lived a fascinating life. He was a meteorologist, a minister in the Worldwide Church of God, and author of a dozen books on biblical topics. While he is perhaps best known for his controversial works on the *Star of Bethlehem* and the location of the *Temple in Jerusalem*, it is his book *Secrets of Golgotha* (1987) that propagated his theory that the site of Jesus' crucifixion was on the Mount of Olives.

Martin virtuously announced at the beginning of *Secrets of Golgotha* that he would use no evidence except that which comes from the Bible. While the Gospel accounts are the only Spirit-inspired narratives of the life and death of Jesus of Nazareth, and while they are the primary resources of Jesus' life, death, and resurrection, plenty of non-biblical evidence exists that corroborates the Gospels' accounts. We must also take that into account. Martin, on the other hand, claimed to appeal only to the evidence found within the pages of Scripture.

"Outside the gate" and "outside the camp."

Rather than basing his case on the Gospel's narratives, Martin appealed mainly to the book of Hebrews to make his case. His theory on the location of Jesus' crucifixion is based on Hebrews 13:10–13:

> We have an altar from which those who serve the tent have no right to eat. For the bodies of those animals whose blood is brought into the holy places by the High Priest as a sacrifice for sin are burned outside the camp. So Jesus also suffered outside the gate in order to sanctify the people through his own blood. Therefore let us go to him outside the camp and bear the reproach he endured.

Martin maintained that the two phrases "outside the gate "and "outside the camp" were not simple expressions but referred to a "specific place in the area of Jerusalem . . . to the author of the book of Hebrews, it was a specific 'gate' of Jerusalem that he emphasized. Only one area in the vicinity of Jerusalem was being referred to by the two geographical expressions mentioned above, and that was in the *eastern* region outside the city limits of Jerusalem."[125]

> "The geographical parameters mentioned in the book of Hebrews are of themselves sufficient proof to show that Golgotha was located at the southern summit of the Mount of Olives."   —Ernest L. Martin

Claiming that most twenty-first-century people, including scholars and Christian clergy, do not understand the geographical features associated with the Temple and its ritualistic ceremonies, Martin symbolically interpreted the book of Hebrews. He embraced the idea that "the Temple at Jerusalem was patterned after the Tabernacle that Moses . . . which in turn was patterned after the geographical features of the Garden in Eden . . . The Temple and its environs were further patterned after God's heavenly palace and its celestial surroundings" (Heb 8:5; 9:23).

Ernest L. Martin claimed that just as the location of Jesus' crucifixion was not an accident, the location being on the Mount of Olives, neither was the orientation of the Temple in Jerusalem. In fact, he claims that the Temple was patterned after the Tabernacle that Moses built and had the same orientation. This is believable and probably correct. However, he then claims that the location of Jesus' crucifixion must be the Mount of Olives because the Tabernacle in the wilderness was patterned after the topography of the Garden of Eden. Since the Bible does not provide any information about the topographical features of Eden, I am not certain where Martin would have gleaned this information. Furthermore, just as the site of the crucifixion was connected to the position of the Temple, which was patterned after the Tabernacle, which was in turn was patterned after the Garden of Eden, which, finally, was patterned after God's "celestial surroundings," [one's head begins to spin], the site of Golgotha is the final stop in God's grand design of holy places.

Appealing to the three divisions of the Temple, the Holy of Holies (the innermost portion on the west), the Holy Place (just east of the Holy of Holies), and the Court of the Gentiles (surrounding the enclosed structures), Martin believed the divisions were lined up in such a way as to point through the Eastern Gate to the Mount of Olives.

In Jesus' day, the Temple area was connected to the Mount of Olives by a double-tiered arched bridge spanning the Kidron Valley. The Mishnah indicates that the priests constructed this bridge to facilitate the sacrifice of the red heifer. "They made a ramp from the Temple Mount to the Mount of Olives, being constructed of arches above arches."[126]

Focusing on the sacrifice of the red heifer and the requirement that this must occur "outside the camp" and "outside the tent," Martin saw the bridge between the Temple and the Mount of Olives as the key to understanding where the red heifer would be sacrificed.

The third altar of the Temple

Only two altars are mentioned in the Tabernacle and later in the Temple. One was in the outer court, and the other was in the Holy Place. One was without, and the other within. They are the Altar of Burnt Offering and the Altar of Incense. The Altar of Burnt Offering (Exod 30:28) is also called the Brazen Altar (Exod 39:39), the Outer Altar, the Earthen Altar, the Great Altar, and the Table of the Lord (Mal 1:7). The Altar of Burnt Offering was located inside the Court of the Priests, between the Chamber of Hewn Stone and the outer curtain before the Holy of Holies (see Table 2).

The second altar was the Altar of Incense (Exod 30:1–10). It was also called the Golden Altar (Exod 39:38; Num. 4:11) and the Inner Altar. It was the altar from which, once a year on the day of Atonement, the High Priest would remove hot coals in a fire pan and, along with incense, would carry them into the Holy of Holies (Lev 16:12) to make atonement for Israel.[127]

TABLE 2

The Temple of Jerusalem

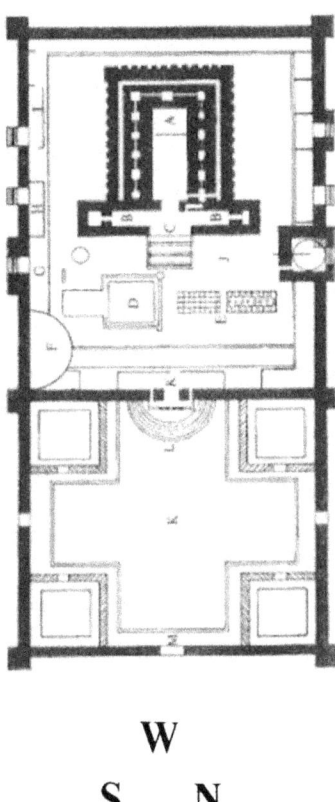

W

S   N

E

The Jerusalem Temple at the time of Jesus Christ. East is at the bottom, and West is at the top. (A) Holy of Holies, (B) Outer Holy Place, (C) Outer Curtain, (D) Altar of Burnt Offering, (E) Slaughter Areas, (F) Chamber of Hewn Stone (Sanhedrin Hall), (G) Counselor's Chamber, (H) House of Abtinas, (I) Chamber of Wood, (J) Court of Priests, (K) Court of Israel, (L) Steps to Nicanor Gate, (M) Eastern Gate. Credit: *Diagram by Norman Tenedora.*

Martin believed the altar being discussed in the book of Hebrews was the third altar of the Temple. "This important Third Altar was located near the summit of the Mount of Olives, where the Red Heifer was killed and burnt to ashes, and where special sin offerings were burnt according to the Law of Moses" (Lev 4:12).

This outer altar, which the King James translators rendered as 'the appointed place' (Ezek 43:21), "In the words of Ezekiel, was located 'without the sanctuary,' positioned outside the sanctified area of Jerusalem. That is why it was located on the summit of the Mount of Olives," claimed Martin.[128]

In Martin's approach, much is made about the altar being on the east. In the time of Moses, the holiest location within Israel's encampment was in front of the entrance on the east side of the sanctuary. The eastern region was also the side of the sanctuary administered by the tribe of Judah, from which would arise both King David and the Messiah (Num 2:3).[129]

Martin considered the region east of the Temple and on the slopes of the Mount of Olives to be the holiest part of the area that surrounds the Temple. He assumed there was a third altar there, a permanent altar upon which the red heifer was sacrificed.

> " I am now prepared with further reasons for believing that our Lord was crucified (and, necessarily, buried) to the east of the city."
> —R. F. Hutchinson

Middoth 1:3 confirms the red heifer was taken out of the city on the east side but says nothing about the existence of a third altar on the Mount of Olives.

Martin claimed:

> There can actually be no doubt that the "clean place" for burning the sin offerings on the day of Atonement as well as performing the Red Heifer sacrifice was located directly east of the Temple. It was a permanent site called the Beth ha-Deshen or the House of the Ashes (Lev 4:12). It was located on a slope of a hill.[130]

Problems with the Mount of Olives site

Since Martin claimed to use only the Bible as his source, one would think the third altar would be prominently mentioned in the Old Testament. However, there is no mention of a third altar anywhere in the Bible. None! That is a problem for a theory based solely on the text of Scripture. So, where did Ernest Martin find a third altar in the Temple? From his interpretation of Hebrews 13:10, 11.

Parah is the Mishnah tractate that discusses the laws of the red heifer. The problem this creates for Martin's approach is that no altar is mentioned in Parah. In the entire tractate about the red heifer, the word "altar" (Hebrew: מִזְבֵּחַ; English: *mizbêach*) never occurs. Not once!

Martin also claimed that all the locals were aware of this place on the mountain. However, I have an Arab friend whose family has lived on the Mount of Olives for many, many generations. His house is a multi-generational home, with his father living on the first level, his brother and family on the second, and his family on the fourth. The third level was empty until the marriage of his oldest son in 2020.

From my friend's balcony facing west across the Kidron Valley toward the Temple Mount, you get the absolute best view of Jerusalem, especially at night. Nevertheless, when I asked him to show me the altar on the mountain where his family had lived for centuries, he knew nothing about it. Apparently, Martin did not include this Arab family among those locals who were aware of the Mount of Olives altar.

The critical importance of the torn curtain

Since geographical positioning is the crux of Martin's theory, he advanced one more facet of the geography he believed proved the Mount of Olives was the location of Golgotha. In *Secrets of Golgotha,* he quoted from Luke 23:47, "But the centurion having seen THE THING having occurred glorified God saying: Surely this man was righteous (Luke 23:47)." Martin emphasized the word "THING" [which he placed in all capital letters] and then explained, "It should carefully be noted that not only the centurion but also those standing beside him witnessed the effects of the earthquake."

Martin claimed it was not the unnatural things the centurion witnessed that caused him to praise God but a single thing, the tearing of the curtain. He asserted that since "the King James renderings are a little archaic to us moderns," he quoted Luke 23:47 in what he called a modern translation. However, he failed to identify the translation he was quoting. I searched no less than sixty translations of Luke 23:47 and did not find Martin's rendering in any of them.[131]

Martin made his own translation of Luke 23:47 and included the word "THING" in all caps to emphasize something seminal to his case but something not found in the text of Scripture. It is odd how Martin claims to use nothing but the Bible in his arguments, but he "invents" Scripture to bolster his case.

Nonetheless, Martin's point was simple. Only from the eastern side of the Temple could this curtain be seen by spectators located outside the walls of Jerusalem. It would have been a physical impossibility for anyone to have seen the curtain from the south, the north, or the west. This means that anyone near the Church of the Holy Sepulchre or the Garden Tomb would have only seen the back walls of the Temple and not the tearing of the curtain.[132]

Did the centurion see the veil being torn from top to bottom? Even though Ernest Martin claimed to use no evidence but the Bible in presenting his case, there is no biblical evidence that the centurion personally witnessed the tearing of the Temple curtain.

In fact, the Gospel of Matthew does not link the centurion to the tearing of the curtain at all. Matthew 27:54 says, "When the centurion and those who were with him, keeping watch over Jesus, saw the earthquake and what took place, they were filled with awe and said, 'Truly this was the Son of God!'" If any unnatural phenomena were singled out in the narrative, Matthew says it was the earthquake, not the curtain.

Mark's reference seems to contradict what Martin earlier claimed — that it was not Jesus' death, but the tearing of the curtain that caused awe among the witnesses. "And the curtain of the Temple was torn in two, from top to bottom. And when the centurion, who stood facing him, saw that in this way he breathed his last, he said, 'Truly this man was the Son of God!'" (Mark 15:38–39).

Mark says the centurion was facing Jesus, not the Temple curtain. Mark also clearly maintains that when the centurion saw Jesus take his last breath, he uttered his statement of faith regarding the deity of Jesus Christ. This had nothing to do with the Temple veil.

In the third and final Gospel account of this event, Luke mentions the curtain of the Temple was torn in two and says, "Then Jesus, calling out with a loud voice, said, 'Father, into your hands I commit my spirit!' And having said this he breathed his last. Now when the centurion saw what had taken place, he praised God, saying, 'Certainly this man was innocent!'" (Luke 23:46–47). Luke appears to parallel the account of Mark but not that of Matthew.

In none of the Synoptic accounts do the authors link the sole event of the torn curtain to the centurion's expression of faith. Nevertheless, Martin's theory requires the centurion to be able to see the tearing of the curtain as proof that Jesus' crucifixion must have occurred on the Mount of Olives.

Artist's rendering of the Temple's Veil being torn

While Ernest Martin's observations are intriguing, they are not rooted in fact, and therefore, his identification of Golgotha with the Mount of Olives must be dismissed.

In our examination of the site of Jesus' crucifixion, we now come to a more plausible location, one dear to millions.

GORDON'S CALVARY

Israeli archaeologist Gabriel Barkay describes the *Sitz im Leben* into which modern archaeology took shape. It was the beginning of the nineteenth century. Europeans, especially the British and Germans, fostered an interest in the Middle East. At the same time, the science of archaeology became more sophisticated. Protestants began to join Roman Catholics in their interest of exploring biblical sites.

The Archbishop of York founded the Palestine Exploration Fund (now the Palestine Exploration Society, or PES) in 1865 to study the Holy Land from a scientific perspective, as opposed to that of the traveler. The society sponsored military engineers Sir Charles Wilson (of Wilson's Arch) and Sir Charles Warren (of Warren's Shaft) to map and record details in and around Jerusalem. It was into this climate that General Charles ("Chinese") Gordon came.[133]

General Charles Gordon

In 1883, British General Gordon took a hiatus from his celebrated military career and spent the months of January to December in the Holy Land. During that time, he wrote *Reflections on Palestine* in which he argued that a skull-like outcrop and a nearby tomb discovered a few years earlier were the authentic crucifixion and burial sites of Jesus of Nazareth.[134] General Gordon was a national hero in Great Britain, embodying the perfect blend of military heroics, fervent Christian faith, and Victorian Romanticism. Consequently, his argument won immediate approval, especially among Protestants in the British Isles.

The idea that Skull Hill was Golgotha did not originate with "Chinese" Gordon. Several earlier travelers and writers proposed the same identification as early as the 1840s. Among them was Claude Conder, a Palestine

Exploration Society explorer and surveyor who was sent to Palestine in 1872 and recorded his findings in two books: *Tent Work in Palestine* (1878)[135] and *The City of Jerusalem* (1909).[136]

Other early proponents of this site as Golgotha included the English scholar and clergyman Canon Henry Baker Tristram, the German archaeologist Conrad Schick, the German theologian Otto Thenius, the German scholar and traveler Jonas Kortens, and the Protestant Bishop of Jerusalem Samuel Gobat.

> "In my opinion, the recent excavations in the neighborhood of 'Jeremiah's Grotto,' ... all tend to confirm the view that this spot is without doubt the site of the crucifixion and of the Holy Sepulchre."
> —Edward Hull

Physical features

Just as the direction from the Temple was essential to Ernest Martin's argument that Golgotha had to be east of the Temple, so too, Charles Gordon based his argument in part on topography. He believed that, according to the Mishnah, because sacrificial animals were slaughtered in ancient Jewish holy sites north of the altar, Jesus must have been crucified north of the city. Among the contenders for the location of Golgotha, only Gordon's Calvary is north of Jerusalem and its Temple. It was located outside the city wall in Jesus' day and was situated well over 25 meters (82 feet or 55 cubits) to the north of the city.

The grounds adjacent to Gordon's Calvary, in which the Garden Tomb is located, were purchased in 1894 by The Garden Tomb (Jerusalem) Association, a Charitable Trust based in the United Kingdom. Today, visitors by the thousands visit the Garden Tomb and are first taken to a platform that's an overlook to view the rocky outcropping of Gordon's Calvary.

There, a friendly volunteer guide will relate the story of Jesus' crucifixion with the heart of a true believer. He will point out the general outline of a face, which features two deep eye sockets that, with a bit of imagination, make the face look freakishly like the face of a skull.

From the Upper Room to Joseph's Tomb

Gordon's Calvary 100 years ago and today

The skull-like feature is a naturally occurring rock formation located on the southern scarp of a hill called El-Edhemieh by local Arabs. This is located just west of the stone quarry that has traditionally been known as "Jeremiah's Grotto." On top of the hill, a Muslim cemetery has existed for approximately two centuries.

There used to be a slightly distended piece of stone sloping downward from between the two easternmost caves, giving the impression of a bridge on a skeletal nose. However, on February 20, 2015, the bridge of the skull's nose collapsed during a strong storm. Indeed, in times past, this formation made a perfect skull's head, complete with eye sockets, a crushed nose, and a gaping mouth.

Some argue, "This natural formation has probably not changed significantly in the last three thousand years."[137] However, while the eye sockets were even more impressive a hundred years ago, they likely were not there in Jesus' day.

In 1610, George Sandys, an Oxford-educated English traveler, undertook a two-year journey from Italy to Syria and Egypt. Sandys visited Jerusalem and drew pictures of some of the area's outstanding geographical features. His drawings prominently featured the site of Jeremiah's Grotto near the Garden Tomb. However, they displayed no caves in the escarpment that looked like eye sockets. Possibly, they were not there in the seventeenth century. Perhaps natural erosion formed the skull-like face 150 to 250 years ago, just as it is now destroying it. We just don't know. Having visited this site each year for over fifty years, I have watched the face of the rock deteriorate so that each year, it looks less and less like a skull. In the natural world, erosion is a fact of life and rarely a friend.

> "Erosion is nothing new, and the rock face [of Gordon's Calvary] likely did not have the same skull appearance 2,000 years ago."
> —Ted Bolen

The location of crucifixions

As interesting as the physical features of Gordon's Calvary are, the real question is whether any crucifixions were known to have been carried out in this area north of Jerusalem. We know that the Romans were accustomed to crucifying their criminals in conspicuous places, just outside the city walls, but still near cities and towns. Perhaps the most prominent place outside the Jerusalem wall was the road north from the Damascus Gate, over the spine of the Judean and Samaritan mountains, to Nablus, Capernaum, and then on to Damascus. It was known as the Nablus Road and still is today. The Nablus Road ran right past Gordon's Calvary. It would give the most exceptional opportunity for travelers to see the horror of crucifixion and be so frightened they would be deterred from any criminal activity.

As popular as the Garden Tomb is, there is a site that is even more popular. We are now left with the final potential site for Jesus' crucifixion, the traditional location, the Church of the Holy Sepulchre. Eusebius said in the *Onomasticon* that Golgotha was to the north of the Mount of Sion (πρὸς τοῖς βορείοις τοῦ Σιὼν ὄπους).[138] Let's examine this location as the potential site of Jesus death and resurrection.

THE CHURCH OF THE HOLY SEPULCHRE

Many visitors to the Church of the Holy Sepulchre find it aesthetically distasteful. If you were looking for a quiet garden, an empty tomb, and a skull-like hill, you must go to the Garden Tomb. If you do not mind incense, icons, and priests scurrying from place to place, often being rude to visitors, you have come to the right place. The Church of the Holy Sepulchre is a shrine with all the trappings accumulated through years of "religion."

A brief overview of the church

The modern pilgrim to Jerusalem can freely enter the church, but to see the site of Calvary, you must climb an awkward set of rock-cut stairs, ascending sixteen feet above street level. Visitors may also see the Altar of the Cross, an outcropping of rock with a fissure in it, which tradition claims was made by the great earthquake at the time of Jesus' death. Under the Altar of the Cross is a silver disk with a hole in the center, which the priests of the church will tell you is the exact spot where Jesus' cross was planted in the ground of Golgotha.

One hundred fifty feet to the northwest stands the ancient Rotunda and within it the traditional tomb of Jesus, hence the name—The Church of the Holy Sepulchre. This ornate enclosure is a free-standing structure within the church. While this somewhat gaudy edifice reflects the zenith of history and tradition, it poorly reflects the tomb of Joseph of Arimathea or the miracle of the resurrection. Only the most devout find it refreshing.

Still, they come, especially at Easter. During Holy Week celebrations, thousands upon thousands of people ascend the mountains to Jerusalem and descend on the Church of the Holy Sepulchre. The crowds in the church are jam-packed, chock-a-block as the British would say, so tightly squeezed in that you cannot move with ease. The pilgrims recite prayers, chant songs, and burn candles, filling the air with the heavy aroma of incense.

For the Eastern Orthodox Church, especially the Greek Orthodox, the burning of candles takes on new meaning on "Holy Saturday," the day before Easter. The Holy Fire ceremony in Jerusalem is an annual event held at the Church of the Holy Sepulchre. It involves the belief that a divine spark descends from heaven to light candles, known as the Holy Fire, symbolizing the resurrection of Jesus Christ. Everyone packed into the church will eventually receive light from a single candle within the tomb.

The Church of the Holy Sepulchre is known to Orthodox Christians as the Church of the Resurrection or the Church of the Anastasis. Located within the Christian Quarter of Old Jerusalem, it is the largest and most important church in Jerusalem. According to tradition, within the church are the 10th through the 14th stations of the Via Dolorosa. This would include the traditional locations of Golgotha and the tomb of Jesus.[139]

The Killing Field of Jerusalem

In 1757 AD, the Ottoman Sultan Osman III forced a compromise between the religious orders that came to be known as the *Status Quo* agreement. It is designed to maintain order within the church. The Status Quo began with a decree (known as a *firman*) from the sultan that preserved the division of ownership and responsibilities of various Christian holy places, including the Church of the Holy Sepulchre. Additional *firmans* released in 1852 and 1853 affirmed that no changes could be made without consensus from all the Christian communities.[140]

Today, the Church of the Holy Sepulchre is jointly administered by six Christian denominations. The church is the headquarters for the Greek Orthodox, the Roman Catholic (represented by the Franciscan Order), and the Armenian Apostolic Church. In the nineteenth century, these denominations were joined by the Syrian Orthodox Church of Antioch, the Coptic Church of Egypt, and the Ethiopian Orthodox Tewahedo Church.

Unfortunately, the addition of religious groups claiming a slice of the Church of the Holy Sepulchre fostered huge resentment and anger among the groups who were the original guardians of the church. They regularly fight over turf and influence, and police are occasionally forced to intervene.

The Church of the Holy Sepulchre, Jerusalem

In 2004, a door to the Franciscan chapel was inadvertently left open. The Greek Orthodox interpreted this as a sign of disrespect, and a fistfight broke out. No one was seriously injured, but some religious leaders were arrested.[141] On Palm Sunday in 2008, police were called to stop the fisticuffs, but they were immediately attacked by those engaged in the brawl.[142] On Sunday, November 9, 2008, another altercation broke out between

Armenian and Greek monks.[143] It appears Golgotha is still a place of brutality and bloodshed.

Before you enter, visitors to the church should look up between the two windows on the second floor. There, they will see a ladder standing that has been dubbed "the immovable ladder." Almost 150 years ago, a man placed a ladder on a ledge, leaning it against the exterior wall of the church. Due to the imposition of the *Status Quo* and the fear of inciting violence, no one has dared touch it since. There it sits, for a century and a half.

Because of the tensions between the religious groups, almost nothing gets done quickly within the church. In 1995, the six religious traditions finally agreed on painting a section of the central dome, but only after seventeen years of debate. As a result of the lack of trust between them, no one religious group controls the security of the church. The Hashemite noble family Joudeh Al Husseini (Al Ghodayya), descendants of the Prophet Mohammad, are the keepers of the keys, the gatekeepers of the church. Although Joudeh is in charge of holding the key, another Muslim family is responsible for opening the door. That responsibility currently falls to Wajeeh Nuseibeh.

When Nuseibeh arrives at the church early in the morning, he takes the key from Joudeh, climbs a small wooden ladder to unlock the top lock, then steps off the ladder to unlock the lower lock. The doors are swung open, and the church is accessible to all visitors. These two Muslim families have shared this responsibility since the seventh century, protecting the holy site and keeping it open to the Christian faithful. Unlocking the church door requires strong fingers because the key is 30 centimeters (12 inches) long and weighs 250 grams or half a pound.[144]

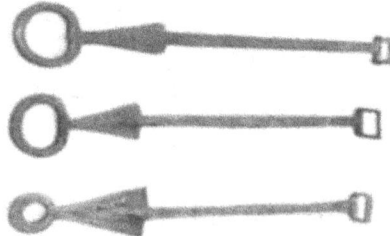

Keys to the door of the Church of the Holy Sepulchre

The history of the church

The history of the Church of the Holy Sepulchre roughly parallels the history of Jerusalem; it is tumultuous. Just as the city has been destroyed and rebuilt, so too, the Church of the Holy Sepulchre has been destroyed and rebuilt.

Roman Period (70–324 AD). After the Roman general Titus Flavius reduced Jerusalem to ruins during the siege of 70 AD, the Holy City remained primarily in ruins until 130 AD. In that year, the Roman Emperor Hadrian began to implement his vision of a new Roman colony on the site he called Aelia Capitolina. Hadrian built a pagan temple on the destroyed site venerated by the first-century church as the site of Jesus' crucifixion. This temple remained until the fourth century.

Byzantine Period (324–638 AD). After seeing a vision of a cross in the sky in 312 AD, Emperor Constantine the Great converted to Christianity. He signed the Edict of Milan, making Christianity legal, and sent his mother, Queen Helena, to Jerusalem to find the authentic tomb of Jesus. When three crosses were found near a tomb, leading Helena to believe she had discovered the location of Golgotha, Constantine ordered the Temple of Jupiter and Venus on that site to be replaced by a church. The dirt and debris were removed from the cave beneath, revealing a rock-cut tomb that both Helena and Bishop Macarius of Jerusalem identified as the burial site of Jesus. In 335 AD, construction was begun on the Church of the Holy Sepulchre.[145]

First Muslim Period (638–1099 AD). The Sassanid Empire was the last kingdom of the Persian Empire before the Islamization of Iran. In May of 614 AD, under Khosrau II, the Sasanians invaded Jerusalem, capturing the "True Cross." In 630 AD, Heraclius, emperor of the Byzantine Empire (610–641 AD), rebuilt the Church of the Holy Sepulchre after recapturing the city. When Jerusalem came under Arab rule, the early Muslim rulers protected the city's Christian sites. However, the church was severely damaged by an earthquake in 746 AD and by fire in 841, 938, and 966 AD.[146] On October 18, 1009, Fatimid caliph Al-Hakim bi-Amr Allah ordered the total destruction of the church as part of his campaign against Christian places of worship in Palestine and Egypt.

Crusader Period (1099–1187 AD). An agreement was made between the Fatimids and the Byzantines (1027–1028 AD), whereby the new caliph, Ali az-Zahir (Al-Hakim's son), would permit the rebuilding of the Church of the Holy Sepulchre. However, Pope Urban II called for the First Crusade in 1095 AD. The idea of recapturing Jerusalem was the primary focus of the Crusade, which, in 1099, became a reality. Emperor Constantine IX Monomachos spent vast sums of money to restore the church. The rebuilt church site consisted of "a court open to the sky, with five small chapels attached to it."[147] Control of Jerusalem and the Church of the Holy Sepulchre changed hands several times between the Fatimids and the Seljuk Turks until the arrival of the Crusaders.[148]

Ayyubid Period (1187–1259 AD). The rebuilt Church of the Holy Sepulchre was taken from the Fatimids by the Crusader knights on July 15, 1099. However, the church was lost to Saladin, along with the rest of the city, in 1187 AD. Under Saladin's leadership, the Ayyubid army defeated the Crusaders at the decisive Battle of Hattin just west of the Sea of Galilee. From that point, Saladin wrestled control of Palestine from the Crusaders, who had conquered the area eighty-eight years earlier. As a result, in succession, Jerusalem was ruled by the Ayyubid dynasty [a Muslim dynasty of Kurdish origin founded by Saladin, centered in Egypt], the Bahri Mamluk dynasty [Mamluk dynasty that ruled the Egyptian Mamluk Sultanate from 1250 to 1382 AD], and the Burji Mamluk dynasty [another Mamluk dynasty that ruled Egypt from 1382 until 1517 AD].[149]

Mamluk Period (1250–1516 AD). The Muslim Caliph dismantled the walls of Jerusalem. As a result, the population of the Holy City declined rapidly. This was a period of deterioration throughout the city. The Mamluks are widely credited with a defeat over the invading Mongol forces in Syria, as well as cleansing Jerusalem and Israel of a Crusader presence. Still, Pope Nicholas IV negotiated an agreement with the Mamluk sultan to allow Latin clergy to serve in the Church of the Holy Sepulchre. With the sultan's agreement, Pope Nicholas, a Franciscan, sent a group of friars to keep the Latin liturgy going in Jerusalem. The Mamluk control over Palestine and Jerusalem ended with the Ottoman takeover in 1517 AD.

Ottoman Period (1517–1917 AD). In 1517, the same year Martin Luther tacked his 95 Theses on the church door at Wittenberg, Germany, Jerusalem fell to Suleiman the Magnificent [also spelled Suleyman]. Fortunately, Jerusalem experienced a period of renewal and peace under Suleiman, marked by the construction of the present walls of the Old City. Jews, Christians, and Muslims enjoyed freedom of religion as the city remained open to all faiths. Suleiman was considered a very gracious and fair ruler.[150]

British Mandate (1917–1948 AD). After World War I, the British were granted control of Jerusalem, and worship at the Holy Sepulchre experienced a resurgence. This mandate continued for some thirty-one years until Israel became a nation.

Divided City (1948–1967 AD). In 1948, the State of Israel was established. Jerusalem was divided between Israel and Jordan by the armistice lines. The entire Old City, including the Church of the Holy Sepulchre, was located in Jordanian Jerusalem.

United Jerusalem (1967 AD–present). After the "Six-Day War" in 1967, Israel claimed all of Jerusalem and reunited the city once more. While tensions still exist between East Jerusalem and the Israeli government, at least most can travel somewhat freely throughout the city. The Church of the Holy Sepulchre is located near the Muristan in the Old City of Jerusalem. Under the Roman Emperor Hadrian, the Muristan was the religious and political center of the Roman city of Aelia Capitolina. So, from antiquity, this has been a significant area of Jerusalem to many people.

Archaeologists have discovered the remnants of walls built by the Roman Emperor Hadrian in the second century. On one of the walls is a stone with a drawing of a merchant ship inscribed with the words DOMINE IVIMVS, "Lord, we shall go." It's believed this drawing likely dates from before the completion of Constantine's church.

An early tradition maintains that the site of Jesus' crucifixion and resurrection is the center of the world. By the tenth century, Jerusalem was marked by an omphalos, a rounded stone representing the navel of the earth in ancient Greek mythology. For adherents of the three major religions—Judaism, Christianity, and Islam—Jerusalem is, indeed, the center of the world.

The author (left) receiving an award from the Israeli government, with the Tri-leaf Globe showing Jerusalem as the Center of the World.

The Tri-leaf Globe showing Europe (NW), Asia (NE), and Africa (S). Jerusalem is at the Center.

Is the Church of the Holy Sepulchre outside the wall of Jerusalem?

One of the reasons people have questioned the Holy Sepulchre Church as the site of Golgotha is that it is inside the city walls of present-day Old Jerusalem. Nevertheless, Golgotha would have to be located outside the city, following the Roman and Jewish customs of the time. Besides, the Gospels suggest that Jesus was crucified outside the city. John 19:17, "He went out, bearing his own cross, to the place called The Place of a Skull, which in Aramaic is called Golgotha." Matthew 27:31 and Mark 15:20 both state the same thing.

It is essential to note that the current Old City walls are not the same as those from Jesus' Jerusalem. As Serr and Vieweger note below, finding the so-called Second Wall of Jerusalem, which would have been the northern wall during Jesus' time, has proven to be challenging. Several archaeological digs have been undertaken with unsatisfactory results. Josephus mentions this Second Wall (*Wars* 5.4.2), but its discovery has proven to be terribly elusive.

Renowned archaeologists Conrad Schick and Père Louis-Hugues Vincent thought they had found the Second Wall in 1893. A wall was uncovered during the construction of the Church of the Redeemer, which is just south of the Church of the Holy Sepulchre. This appeared to answer the question; it placed the church outside the city wall in Jesus' day. However, in the 1970s, German archaeologist Ute Wagner-Lux of the German Protestant Institute of Archaeology in Jerusalem excavated under the Church of the Redeemer and determined that this wall could not have been the Second Wall. "This wall was only five feet thick—far too narrow to be a city wall," reported Serr and Vieweger.[151] From the excavations at the Church of the Redeemer, there are clues that the Church of the Holy Sepulchre is located outside that elusive Second Wall. Indeed, this church has history and tradition on its side.

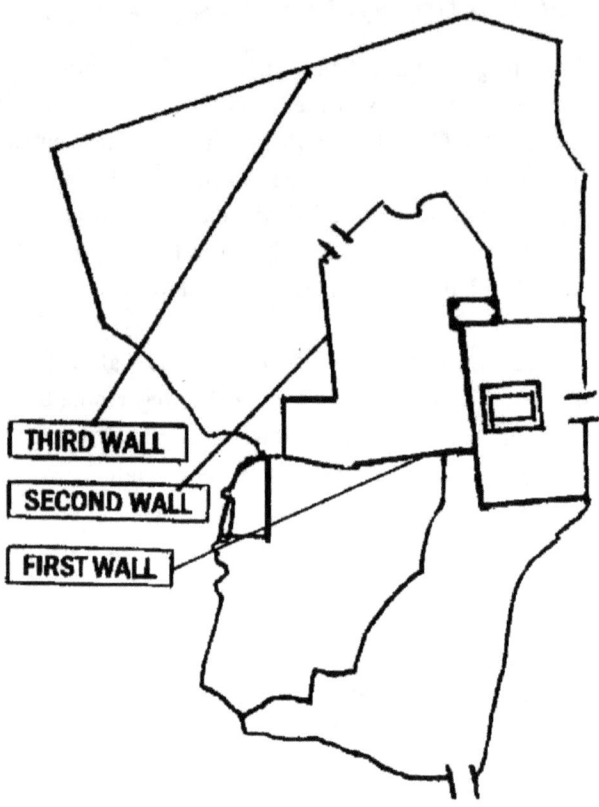

The Three Walls of Jerusalem

While careful scholars will not and cannot say with absolute certainty that the Church of the Holy Sepulchre is the site of Golgotha and the tomb of Jesus of Nazareth, the evidence strongly favors this location. The bottom line is this. The Garden Tomb is appreciated for feelings; the Church of the Holy Sepulchre for facts. Most of the convincing facts point to this church, but most of the comfort from Jesus' resurrection comes from the Garden Tomb. If you're visiting Jerusalem, be sure to stop by both sites to experience the best of both worlds.

> "One will never be able to prove beyond doubt where Golgotha stood, but no candidate more credible than the traditional site is likely to emerge."
> —Raymond E. Brown

Much more will be said about the Garden Tomb and the Church of the Holy Sepulchre in the next chapter, *The Tomb of Joseph: Jesus' Temporary Resting Place.*

Chapter 8

The Tomb of Joseph

Jesus' Temporary Resting Place

Visit the Church of the Holy Sepulchre for information; visit the Garden Tomb for inspiration. Go to the Church of the Holy Sepulchre for the evidence; go to the Garden Tomb for the experience.

Tomb Essentials
Lesser Contenders for the Tomb
The Garden Tomb
Evidence for the Authenticity of the Garden Tomb
The Church of the Holy Sepulchre
Evidence for the Authenticity of the Church of the Holy Sepulchre
Conclusion

One of the most controversial issues related to Jesus' crucifixion is the location of his tomb. Where was the most famous person in history buried after the most famous crucifixion in history? With so much speculation surrounding the authentic tomb of Jesus, is there anything we can say for sure? This chapter will elaborate on the arguments for and against both the Garden Tomb and the Church of the Holy Sepulchre. The last chapter served as an introduction to these two competing sites. In this chapter, we will nail down the facts. The chapter begins with a few essentials for the tomb of Jesus and then explores locations claiming to hold the most important tomb in the history of humankind.

TOMB ESSENTIALS

There are certain requirements that the historical record imposes on any location claiming to be the tomb of Jesus. By historical record, I mean the Gospel narratives, the account against everything else must be judged. If these five tomb essentials are not met, the contender for Jesus' tomb, regardless of veneration, history, or speculation, cannot be the tomb of Joseph of Arimathea, in which Jesus of Nazareth was buried. What are these essentials?

Essential #1: The tomb was near Jerusalem

The references in the Gospels are numerous that Jesus' death and burial are associated with the Holy City.

- At his transfiguration, Moses and Elijah spoke of Jesus' death, which would occur in Jerusalem (Luke 9:31).
- As the Passion Week approached, Jesus "set his face to go to Jerusalem" (Luke 9:51, 53; 13:22).
- Jesus declared that "it cannot be that a prophet should perish away from Jerusalem" (Luke 13:33).
- The Savior revealed to his disciples that he must go to Jerusalem and be crucified, buried, and raised from the dead (Matt 16:21; 20:17–18; Mark 10:32–33; Luke 18:31–33).
- Jesus triumphantly entered Jerusalem at the beginning of Passion Week (Matt 21:1, 10; Mark 11:1, 11; Luke 19:28ff; John 12:12ff).
- Herod Agrippa was in Jerusalem when Pilate sent Jesus to him for trial (Luke 23:7).
- On the Via Dolorosa, as Jesus carried his cross to Golgotha, he addressed some women in the crowd as "Daughters of Jerusalem" (Luke 23:28–31).

- After betraying Jesus, Judas hanged himself in what became known as Akeldama, the "Field of Blood," which was in Jerusalem, and everyone was familiar with it (Acts 1:19).
- On the road to Emmaus, Cleopas questioned whether Jesus was a stranger to Jerusalem because he seemed unaware of the day's events (Luke 24:13, 18).
- Cleopas and his friend returned to Jerusalem after meeting Jesus (Luke 24:33).

The historical accounts of the Gospels require that Jesus was crucified and buried near the Holy City of Jerusalem. Saviors go to Jerusalem to die; politicians go to Washington D.C.

Essential #2: The tomb was outside the city walls

In almost every society of antiquity, burials took place outside the city, beyond the city walls. The Necropolis of Cairo, also known as the "City of the Dead," is a series of vast cemeteries and tombs located on the outskirts of historic Cairo, Egypt. They are located outside the old city walls, north and south of the Cairo Citadel. The *Kerameikos* of ancient Athens is another example of a complex for the dead, as is the Mayan cemetery near Campeche, Mexico.

Before the Romans, the Etruscan site known as *Cerveteri* Necropoli della Banditaccia dates back to the ninth century BC. It is a necropolis that contains thousands of tombs, demonstrating that burial places were not just a field outside the city but a complex in their own right. Perhaps this is why they got the name "City of the Dead."

In ancient Rome, everyone was buried beyond the city's limits or *pomerium*. The *Campus Martius*, although an essential part of Rome, was beyond the *pomerium* during the Republic and part of the Empire. It was the place for those buried at public expense. Private burial spots were along the roads leading into Rome, especially the Via Appia. Because these were considered sacred places, violation of a sepulcher was punishable by exile, deportation to the mines, or death.

Jews living within the Empire followed both their Halacha law and Roman law. Some of the earliest mural paintings in Rome's Late Antiquity catacombs are on the grounds of the present Villa Torlonia where Jewish families buried their dead beginning in the second century AD.

The Tomb of Joseph

In Jewish thought, because God dwells with his people inside the camp, all practices that would defile his holiness were to be conducted outside the city or the camp. When a Sabbath-breaker was punished, the LORD said to Moses, "The man shall be put to death; all the congregation shall stone him with stones outside the camp. And all the congregation brought him outside the camp and stoned him to death with stones, as the LORD commanded Moses" (Num 15:35–36). Executions were always conducted outside the city. This is why Stephen was stoned outside the city of Jerusalem (Acts 7:58).

Burials were always undertaken outside the city walls. Jewish law strictly forbade burial within the city. When Nadab and Abihu, the sons of Aaron, died as a result of their sin, Leviticus 10:4 tells us, "Moses called Mishael and Elzaphan, the sons of Uzziel the uncle of Aaron, and said to them, 'Come near; carry your brothers away from the front of the sanctuary and out of the camp.'"

The practice was the same in the New Testament. After he healed the centurion's servant, Jesus "went to a town called Nain, and his disciples and a great crowd went with him. As he drew near to the gate of the town, behold, a man who had died was being carried out, the only son of his mother, and she was a widow, and a considerable crowd from the town was with her" (Luke 7:11–12).

This practice was also evident in the case of Ananias and his wife, Sapphira. Acts 5 records that the couple lied to the Holy Spirit. As a result, Ananias fell down dead. "The young men rose and wrapped him up and carried him out and buried him" (vv. 5, 6). When Sapphira heard her husband was dead, "Immediately she fell down at his feet and breathed her last. When the young men came in, they found her dead, and they carried her out and buried her beside her husband" (v. 10).

In each of these biblical examples, the offender who died was immediately transported outside of the city to be buried. This was both Jewish custom and Jewish law. The Gospels suggest that Jesus was also crucified outside the city. John 19:17 notes, "He went out, bearing his own cross, to the place called The Place of a Skull, which in Aramaic is called Golgotha." Matthew 27:31 and Mark 15:20 both state the same thing. If Golgotha was outside the walls of Jerusalem, so was the tomb in which Jesus was buried.

Essential #3: The tomb was in a garden near Golgotha

John 19:41, 42 reads, "Now in the place where he was crucified there was a garden, and in the garden a new tomb in which no one had yet been laid. So because of the Jewish day of Preparation, since the tomb was close at hand, they laid Jesus there." This represents the best clue provided in Scripture to pinpoint the location of Joseph of Arimathea's tomb. John is not saying that the crucifixions took place in a garden, but that not far from where they took place, there was a garden (Greek: κῆπος; English: *kēpos*). This same word was used to identify the place called Gethsemane (John 18:1, 26).

Judah's King Amon "was buried in his tomb in the garden of Uzza" (2 Kgs 21:26). A garden implies greenery. It implies peace and quiet. From the chaos of Calvary, Jesus' body was taken to the tranquility of a garden. As a wealthy man, Joseph of Arimathea could afford a choice spot for his family tomb, a spot in a garden, just as the Gospels describe.

Essential #4: The tomb was a rock-cut tomb

Matthew 27:59, 60 says, "And Joseph took the body and wrapped it in a clean linen shroud and laid it in his own new tomb, which he had cut in the rock." Mark 15:46 indicates the same. "And Joseph bought a linen shroud, and taking him down, wrapped him in the linen shroud and laid him in a tomb that had been cut out of the rock."

Tombs cut out of solid rock were not uncommon in the Middle East. There was plenty of rock from which to cut them. Sometimes, caves were used or even enlarged to accommodate family tombs. "Abraham breathed his last and died in a good old age, an old man and full of years, and was gathered to his people. His sons, Isaac and Ishmael, buried him in the cave of Machpelah" (Gen 25:8-9; see 23:7-9; 49:29, 30; 2 Chr 16:13, 14). In a divine oracle against the city of Jerusalem, the Prophet Isaiah reveals, "You have cut out here a tomb for yourself, you who cut out a tomb on the height and carve a dwelling for yourself in the rock"? (Isa 22:16).

Within a chamber cut into a rock, you would experience a significant difference in temperature from the hot sun outside. This was always a comfort to the mourners who came to visit the grave. It also helped slow the rate of decomposition of the body. Thus, a tomb in a garden helped keep the smell of the decomposing body to a minimum as it was being prepared for burial.

The Tomb of Joseph

Essential #5: The tomb was a new tomb

Luke 23:52–53 notes, "This man went to Pilate and asked for the body of Jesus. Then he took it down and wrapped it in a linen shroud and laid him in a tomb cut in stone, where no one had ever yet been laid." Matthew 27:60 also confirms that Jesus was buried in a new tomb.

The fact that Joseph's tomb was "a new tomb" and "where no one had ever yet been laid" likely means the tomb was not yet complete when Jesus was laid in it. From the primary choices for this tomb, in either case, one or more arcosolia were complete, but it appears more were yet to be carved out of the rock.

Jesus' life was wrapped in virtue. It was bookended in purity. His life began in a virgin womb and ended in a virgin tomb.

LESSER CONTENDERS FOR THE TOMB

All this being said, do we know the location of Jesus' grave? There is some evidence, although it is not conclusive. There are five leading contenders for the location of the tomb owned by Joseph of Arimathea. Three of these are lesser contenders and can be dismissed easily. Those three contenders are the following.

Roza Bal, Srinagar, India

The Roza Bal (also known as Rouza Bal or Rozabal) is a shrine situated in downtown Srinagar, India. Srinagar lies in the Kashmir Valley on a tributary of the Indus River. You may never have heard of Srinagar, but it is the northernmost city of India and has a current population of over one million people.

The word *roza* means tomb; the word *bal* mean place. Locals believe two Muslim holy men are buried there. The shrine is housed in a small, unlikely-looking building. It was relatively unknown until Mirza Ghulam Ahmad espoused the theory that Jesus was buried there. Ahmad claimed both to be the promised Mahdi (Guided One) and the Messiah expected by Muslims to appear in the end times, bringing Islam its final triumph. It is reported that on May 8, 2010, "One of the caretakers of the tomb, Mohammad Amin, closed the door and padlocked the shrine, believing the theory that 'Jesus is buried anywhere on the face of the Earth is blasphemous to Islam.'"

According to Fida Mohammad Hassnain, a Sufi mystic, Kashmiri writer, and supporter of Ahmadi beliefs, the tomb contains a rock carving that is said to show feet bearing crucifixion wounds. He contends the body inside was buried according to Jewish customs, not according to Islamic tradition.[152]

American religious scholar and founding director of the Institute for the Study of American Religion, J. Gordon Melton, writes in his *Religions of the World: A Comprehensive Encyclopedia of Beliefs and Practices,* that Ghulam Ahmad, having declared himself the promised Messiah for the Christians, commandeered the legend that Jesus had visited India to increase his self-identification with Jesus.[153]

Religious writer Simon Ross Valentine classifies this location as the burial tomb of Jesus and Ahmad's identification with Jesus as a legend and a myth.[154] There is no reason to believe Jesus was buried in India. So, how about Japan?

The tomb of Jesus in Shingo, Japan

Shingō is a small village in northern Japan, with a population of about 2,500. The village would pass without notice if it were not purported to be the location of the tomb of Jesus (*Kirisuto no haka*), as well as the town where Jesus' last descendants reportedly still live. The family of Sajiro Sawaguchi claims that Jesus did not die on the cross at Golgotha, as both the Gospels and historical records generally indicate. Instead, Jesus' brother, Isukiri, took his place on the cross while Jesus fled across Siberia to northern Japan. Once he arrived in Japan, according to legend, he changed his name to Torai Tora Daitenku and became a rice farmer. The story claims Jesus married a twenty-one-year-old Japanese girl named Miyuko and raised three daughters in Shingō.

Mark 6 records the story of Jesus' return to the town where he grew up, Nazareth. He entered the synagogue there as he often did elsewhere and began to teach. Nevertheless, whoever said you cannot go home again probably had this incident in mind when he said it. The Jews of Nazareth did not receive Jesus well. They did not recognize Jesus' authority because they remembered him as a mason and a carpenter. The proud Jews asked, "Is not this the carpenter, the son of Mary and brother of James and Joses

The Tomb of Joseph

and Judas and Simon? And are not his sisters here with us?" (v. 3). I see his brothers listed here: James, Joses, Judas, and Simon. One person I do not see is Brother Isukiri. Maybe he was a foreign exchange student living in Joseph and Mary's house.

The world took notice of the claims of the Sawaguchi family in 1933 after the discovery of supposed "ancient Hebrew documents detailing Jesus' life and death in Japan."[155] The locals refer to these documents as the Testament of Jesus or Jesus' Last Will. The documents are claimed to be ancient, having been passed down through the Takeuchi Kiyomaro family for generations.

Allegedly, the documents were seized by Japanese authorities shortly before World War II and taken to Tokyo but have not been seen since.[156] There is no reason to believe Jesus was buried in Japan.

The Talpiot Tomb, Jerusalem, Israel

Coming closer geographically to the biblical account of Jesus' burial, the Talpiot Tomb is a rock-cut tomb that was discovered in 1980. It is in the East Talpiot neighborhood of Jerusalem, about 5 kilometers (3 miles) south of the Old City. Talpiot (Hebrew: תלפיות) translates as "turrets" or "magnificently built." It comes from the love story of Solomon. "Your neck is like the tower of David, constructed in layers." (Song 4:4, HCSB) The neighborhood was established in 1922 by Zionist pioneers.

The Talpiot tomb was first unearthed on March 28, 1980, as the result of a construction project. The Israel Antiquities Authority promptly recorded the tomb as IAA-80, and its ten ossuaries were cataloged with the numbers 500–509. The tomb is carved from the solid limestone bedrock. Inside the tomb were located six *kokhim* and two *arcosolia*. Also found were ten ossuaries, of which six were inscribed. The six inscriptions bear the names of seven individuals:

- Jesus ("Jesus, son of Joseph")
- Joseph
- Mary (there are two)
- Judah
- Yose (or Joses to a Greek speaker)
- Matthew

These are eminent names in the Gospel story. The question is, do they refer to the figures in the Gospel story? To that question, there is no definitive answer.

In 2007, a highly controversial documentary film, "The Lost Tomb of Jesus," directed by James Cameron and produced by Simcha Jacobovici, was released in conjunction with a book titled "The Jesus Family Tomb," written by Jacobovici and Charles Pellegrino. The storyline of both the book and the film is that the Talpiot Tomb was the burial place of Jesus of Nazareth and his extended family.

The inference is that this is actually where Jesus was buried, and thus, the Gospel accounts are frivolous failures at recording history. While biblical and archaeological scholarship is divided on whether this is indeed Jesus' tomb, with the vast majority of scholars rejecting it, the discovery does shed light on popular New Testament names of the first century, and that is the problem. Each of the names represented on the ossuaries was a common name in the late Second Temple Period. They could refer to anyone at that time.

> "If Jesus already had a family tomb in Talpiot, there would be no need to bury him in a temporary tomb, despite the onset of the Sabbath. It's little more than a half-hour's walk from Golgotha to Talpiot."
> —Hershel Shanks

The pros and cons of the Talpiot Tomb do not need to be presented here, as they have been well-documented elsewhere.[157] Suffice it to say that the scholarly community has all but unanimously rejected this tomb as the tomb of Jesus. Academia has also dismissed the idea that Mary Magdalene was buried there because, as Jacobovici falsely claimed, they were a "couple."

In fact, a statement condemning Jacobovici's claim was signed by Shimon Gibson, Amos Kloner, Jodi Magness, Eric M. Meyers, Stephen Pfann, Jonathan Price, and Joe Zias, among many other competent archaeologists. There is no reason to believe Jesus was buried in the Jerusalem suburb of Talpiot.

That leaves our investigation with the two top contenders for the location of Jesus' burial—the Garden Tomb and the Church of the Holy Sepulchre.

THE TOMB OF JOSEPH

THE GARDEN TOMB

All four Gospels help to identify the location and appearance of the tomb in which Jesus was buried. As noted above, the tomb was near Golgotha, a new tomb carved out of sheer rock, and located in a garden. In Jesus' day, a garden did not mean a place where you grew carrots, lettuce, and chili peppers. It usually indicated a working vineyard, orchard, or olive grove.

A description of the Garden Tomb

In 1874, a brief report on the tomb was prepared by the German architect and archaeologist Conrad Schick. This was the earliest detailed investigation of the tomb itself. In the late twentieth century, Gabriel Barkay, a professor of biblical archaeology at the Hebrew University of Jerusalem, conducted the most comprehensive archaeological study of the area to date.

When you enter the Garden Tomb, you immediately find yourself in the first of two chambers. This is the vestibule, also known as the "weeping chamber," with a bench against the back wall. This chamber is roughly rectangular, approximately ten feet long, almost seven feet wide, and about six feet high. Initially, below an obvious horizontal line on the back wall, a rock-hewn burial bench appears to have extended out from the wall. This burial bench is no longer there.

To the right (south) of the entry chamber was an entryway to the burial chamber measuring six and a half feet high and two feet wide. Today, most of the wall separating these two chambers is missing. Now, an iron gate separates the two chambers. The floor of this inner chamber is about eight and a half inches lower than that of the outer chamber. The inner chamber is nearly eight feet long by eleven feet wide, with a seven-foot ceiling.

Along each wall of the inner room, except for the entry wall, are burial places carved out of the rock. They resemble sarcophagi in that they are carved as a box, but with the front wall missing. The trough-shaped burial spot opposite the inner chamber entranceway is only four and three-quarters feet long, whereas the other two burial spots each are seven and a half feet long.[158]

Most interesting is that distinct Christian symbols are painted on the east and south inner chamber walls. They are crosses painted in dark red. Above the horizontal crossbeam of the Greek crosses are the letters "IS" and "CS" in Greek. These letters are *iota sigma* and *chi sigma*. *Iota* is the initial letter of the Greek word for Jesus (Ἰησοῦς), and *sigma* is the last Greek letter in Jesus' name. The *chi* stands for the first Greek letter Christos (Χριστός), and the *sigma* is the last letter. Beneath the horizontal crossbeam of the crosses are the letters A and Ω. *Alpha* and *Omega*, the first and last letters of the Greek alphabet, were used to designate the Alpha and Omega of Revelation 21:6, "I am the Alpha and the Omega, the beginning and the end." Significantly, the cross is not among the Christian symbols discovered in the Garden Tomb.

The history of the Garden Tomb

The Garden Tomb was first discovered in 1867 by a Greek peasant. He was attempting to cultivate the land at the site, and to make the land fertile, he needed to cut a cistern into the rock. While doing so, he accidentally came upon a cave. Soon after its discovery, Conrad Schick, a Jerusalem correspondent for several European academic societies, visited the cave. He continued to log information about the site and, in 1874, filed a report. According to Schick's account, the cave was half filled with dirt and human bones. At the cave's entrance, there was an iron bar and hinge. After Schick's initial visit to the cave, the owner cleared it for use.

In 1892, Schick published a second report.[159] Because of an early suggestion that this might be the tomb of Jesus, Schick's second report was much more detailed than the first. Charles Warren and Claude Regnier Conder also published a description of the tomb in the Jerusalem volume of the *Survey of Western Palestine* on behalf of the London-based Palestine Exploration Fund.

Perhaps the key figure in the history of the Garden Tomb and the adjacent hill thought to be Golgotha is General Charles Gordon, also known as "Chinese" Gordon. General Gordon, who had served with distinction in the Crimean War and later successfully suppressed the Taiping Rebellion in China, arrived in Jerusalem in 1883. He stayed in Palestine for less than a year. In January 1884, he was dispatched to Khartoum, where he was killed.

At the same time, Horatio Spafford was a prominent nineteenth-century American lawyer and devout Christian. Spafford is best known for writing the words to the hymn, *It is Well With My Soul*, following a family tragedy in which his four daughters died aboard the *S.S. Ville du Havre* on a transatlantic voyage. After this, Spafford, his wife, Anna, eleven other adults, and three children settled in Jerusalem and established the American Colony on Nablus Road, just north of the Old City. The colony

The Tomb of Joseph

engaged in philanthropic work among the people of Jerusalem regardless of religious preferences, gaining the trust of the local Muslim, Jewish, and Christian communities.[160] The American Colony remains at the exact location today as an exquisite boutique hotel.

General Charles Gordon was not only a military hero but also an adventurer. When he arrived in Jerusalem, Gordon, himself a Christian, stayed with the Spaffords at the American Colony. Just a thousand meters (3,281 feet) south on Nablus Road was a hill with a rock escarpment that caught Gordon's eye. Because of its physical characteristics, he immediately identified it as Golgotha.

The Garden Tomb is cut into the vertical escarpment on the western slope of that hill, just 250 meters (820 feet) north of Damascus Gate. On the southern side of the hill was the former central bus station of East Jerusalem, directly across from the Old City wall.

It would be incorrect to say that General Gordon "discovered" Gordon's Calvary and the location of the Garden Tomb because even before he identified the adjacent hill as Golgotha, other scholars had already mentioned this possibility. It appears that the first to suggest this was Otto Thenius, a German scholar, who proposed that this site was Golgotha in 1842. In 1881, English soldier, explorer, and antiquarian Claude Regnier Conder suggested the tomb of Jesus was another burial cave cut into a rocky outcrop just west of the Garden Tomb. Today, the grounds of the Franciscan White Sisters Convent on Nablus Road cover Conder's suggested cave.

In 1894, the area of the cave and the surrounding garden were purchased by the British Garden Tomb Association for £2,000 sterling ($1,263.00). The money was raised by an influential group of Englishmen that included the Archbishop of Canterbury. This association still owns, operates, and maintains the site today. After the purchase, the association members cleared the entire facade of the cave, removing debris and ruins that had accumulated over the years in front of it. If you have visited the Garden Tomb, you know that the Garden Tomb Association has made this truly one of the "greenest areas" of Jerusalem. Today, it is a lovely garden with well-maintained paths and benches for visitors to sit and meditate.

In 1904, Karl Beckholt, both the Danish consul in Jerusalem and the warden of the Garden Tomb, conducted a small excavation in the yard of the Garden Tomb. He discovered some objects that were not published until 1924. In 1955, the Garden Tomb Association sponsored a small excavation in the garden area; however, no record of this dig was ever published.

EVIDENCE FOR THE AUTHENTICITY OF THE GARDEN TOMB

With this background, what evidence can be presented in favor of the authenticity of the Garden Tomb? Is there any archaeological or literary evidence? What about the biblical evidence from the gospels' description of the tomb? It is to this that our attention is now turned.

Evidence #1. Location, location, location

There is no question about the location of Jerusalem's wall and the Garden Tomb. It is located outside the walls of Jerusalem today. Sultan Suleiman I of the Ottoman Empire built the existing wall between 1537 and 1541 AD. Some Christians erroneously point to this wall as evidence that the Garden Tomb is outside the wall of Jerusalem. However, this wall was not built until 1500 years after Christ's death, so it has no bearing on the location of the tomb.

What does bear on the tomb's location is the first wall of Jerusalem. This was the wall around Jerusalem in the days of Jesus. Originally built by King Hezekiah of Judah in the late 8th century BC, it was later rebuilt by the Hasmoneans in the 2nd century BC. Until the first century BC, the northern limit of Jerusalem's residential district was the east-west line of this first wall. The Garden Tomb's location lies beyond this wall, making it a strong candidate for the burial site of Jesus.

Josephus refers to three fortified walls around Jerusalem in his day, the first century AD. They are described more fully in Chapter 7.

The question that has divided many scholars is not whether the Garden Tomb is outside the first and second walls but whether the Church of the Holy Sepulchre is.

Evidence #2. The date of the Garden Tomb

Over the years, various shifts in the dating and interpretation of the tomb have emerged with the discovery of new archaeological evidence. What was once held as fact is now deemed fiction. What was once dated in one century is now dated in centuries distant. Hopefully, with each revision, we are getting closer to the truth.

The Tomb of Joseph

This has been true with the dating of the Garden Tomb. In my lifetime, the prevailing opinion has shifted from the Byzantine era, which followed the collapse of the Roman Empire, to the seventh or eighth century BC, with a brief stop in the first century AD along the way.

Claude Reignier Conder was a nineteenth-century English soldier, explorer, and surveyor. As a member of the Corps of Royal Engineers, he worked surveying Palestine from 1872 to 1873. Later, he was twice seconded to the Palestine Exploration Fund to survey the land. Conder was an early proponent of the authenticity of the Garden Tomb area without explicitly naming the tomb. Among the twenty-seven or so publications of his survey work, his best-known is *Tentwork in Palestine*, first published in 1879.

> We have yet another indication—namely, that Calvary should be near the cemetery in which was the tomb of Joseph of Arimathea, in the garden beyond the city. Now the great cemetery of Jewish times lies north of Jerusalem, on either side of the main north road; here we have the sepulchre of Simon the Just, preserved by Jewish tradition; here is the magnificent monument of Helena, Queen of Adiabene, fitted with a rolling-stone, such as closed the mouth of the Holy Sepulchre. The first of these tombs dates from three centuries before Christ; the second was cut in the first century of his era. Thus the northern cemetery was probably that which was in use in his time.[161]

Conder also argues that the Church of the Holy Sepulchre cannot have been the tomb of Jesus of Nazareth because it features *kokh* tombs. Initially used by the Jews, with this type of tomb, the whole body was slid into a niche in the wall of the burial chamber. Conder points out that a *kokh* tomb would afford no place for two angels to sit, "one at the head and one at the feet" (John 20:12). A *kokh* (plural *kokhîm*) tomb would be somewhat similar to the corpse racks in a morgue, without the refrigeration and with a different purpose.

Conder remarks, "It must have been one of the later kinds of tombs, in which the body lay in a rock sarcophagus under a rock arch parallel with the side of the chamber. This is the kind of tomb which throughout Palestine we find closed by a rolling-stone; it is the kind in use in the late Jewish times, and the kind, moreover, which is found north of Jerusalem."[162]

He concluded:

> These considerations would lead us to fix Calvary, the place of execution, north of Jerusalem, near the main road to Shechem, and near the northern cemetery. Now, close to this road, on the east, is a rounded knoll, with a precipice on the south side, containing a cave known to Christians as Jeremiah's Grotto. The knoll is called by the natives El Heidhemiyeh ("the rent"), being severed from the Bezetha Hill by a deep trench.[163]

He was describing the area of the Garden Tomb, which he dated to the "late Jewish times," first century AD.

Several older archaeologists who examined the Garden Tomb believed it to be a Jewish tomb from the Herodian Period, spanning from the first century BC to the first century AD. These included Dame Kathleen Kenyon, Sir Charles Marston, Sir Flinders Petrie, and others (see the London *Daily Telegraph Magazine* of March 27, 1970).

They pointed out that the type of chiseling on the face of the cliff both outside and inside the tomb resembles that found in the "Sanhedrin Tombs," the tombs of the Kidron and Hinnom valleys, also the so-called "Tomb of the Kings," and the "family tomb of Herod," all of which are Jewish tombs dating to the Herodian Period.

While Conder's dating has been accepted by many over the years, it is essential to remember that he was writing almost 150 years ago, and much new information has come to light during those decades.

In March 1986, *Biblical Archaeology Review* published a then-controversial article by Gabriel Barkay, a Hungarian-born Israeli archaeologist who has taught at various universities in Israel, including Bar-Ilan University, the University of the Holy Land, and the Hebrew University. In 1974–1975, Amos Kloner, the District Archaeologist of Jerusalem, and Barkay conducted an archaeological investigation of two large complexes of burial chambers in the courtyard of the Monastery of St. Étienne, just north of and adjacent to the Garden Tomb.

Because the Garden Tomb is at the exact location as these burial chambers, Barkay wrote, "I have concluded that the cave of the Garden Tomb was originally hewn in the Iron Age II, sometime in the eighth or seventh century B.C. It was reused for burial purposes in the Byzantine Period (fifth to seventh centuries AD), so it could not have been the tomb of Jesus."[164]

Professor Barkay advanced three fundamental propositions to support his dating conclusion.

1. The Garden Tomb could not have been a "new tomb" (Matt 27:60) "wherein never man before was laid" (Luke 23:53) in Jesus' day if it was originally an Iron Age II triple-bench sepulcher.

2. Four to six hundred years after Jesus' death, the tomb's benches were carved into fixed sarcophagi for the burial of Byzantine Christians. This would never have occurred if the site were venerated as the tomb of Jesus.

3. The features in the garden outside the Garden Tomb, which have been misinterpreted, do not lend themselves to corroborating the site as the first-century tomb of a rich man like Joseph of Arimathea.

While these reflect Barkay's determination that the Garden Tomb could not have been a Second Temple tomb, other considerations should be noted when dating the tomb.

First, there is no long history of identifying the site as Jesus' tomb. While the earliest recorded tradition about the Holy Sepulchre being the place of Jesus' burial is only three centuries after the crucifixion, there is no such history for the Garden Tomb. The identification of the Garden Tomb as the tomb of Jesus did not become a consideration until the nineteenth century. Thus, its identification is relatively new, with no tradition behind it.

Second, the Garden Tomb is situated amid tombs dating back to the Iron Age. North of the Damascus Gate, there are numerous burial caves, most of which were excavated when archaeology was in its infancy—about 150 years ago. This area gives evidence of many tombs from the Iron Age. The Garden Tomb is located between the St. Étienne tombs to the north and two Iron Age tombs to the south.[165] The link between St. Etienne's tombs and the other Iron Age tombs suggests both a geographical and chronological relationship between them.

Third, there appears to be a link between the Garden Tomb and the St. Etienne tombs. In 1974–1975, Amos Kloner and Gabriel Barkay conducted an archaeological survey of two massive complexes of burial chambers in the courtyard of the Monastery of St. Étienne. This is just north of the Garden Tomb. Kloner and Barkay have dated the St. Etienne tombs to the Iron Age B (1000–539 BC). The Garden Tomb appears to be part of the same cemetery as the St. Étienne tomb complexes. This conclusion arises from the fact that the Garden Tomb is only a few feet from St. Etienne's Cave

Complex Number 1 and is hewn out of the very same cliff. This would appear to date the Garden Tomb to the Iron Age as well.

And fourth, not a single Second Temple tomb has been found in the area of the Garden Tomb. Jesus of Nazareth lived in the late Second Temple Period. The Romans destroyed the Second Temple in 70 AD when General Titus led the siege of the city. It appears that by the Second Temple Period, the people of Jerusalem relocated their cemeteries to a location further north. The southernmost burial cave of the Second Temple Period is the so-called "Tombs of the Kings," about 600 meters (1,970 feet) north of the Garden Tomb.

Since a large number of tombs from the Second Temple Period have been discovered in other areas of Jerusalem, if the Garden Tomb dates back to Jesus' era, it would be entirely out of place.

Will this estimate of the date of the Garden Tomb remain accurate over the next 150 years, as it has over the last 150 years? Probably, well, maybe. As of this decade, however, the prevailing view is that this tomb predates Jesus by 700–800 years and thus cannot have been the "new" tomb of the risen Savior.

Evidence #3. The schema of the burial chamber

If you look closely at the inner chamber of the Garden Tomb, there is a visible location for a body in the area on the eastern wall. This provides further evidence of the Garden Tomb's authenticity. Its area also gives the impression that the south end was extended from the original space allocated. It has been suggested that this represents a hurried elongation of the burial site. Those who have made this suggestion believe this area was enlarged to accommodate the height of Jesus Christ. One person even wrote, "[Jesus] must have been taller than Joseph of Arimathea, who had the tomb constructed for himself and was approximately five feet and eight inches tall. The cutting of the stone was hastily completed to accomplish the task of burial before the Sabbath hours, Friday at sunset" (https://arkdiscovery.com/aoc-1.htm).

The Tomb of Joseph

The Interior of the Garden Tomb

Unfortunately, as evidence for the Garden Tomb, these calculations of Joseph and Jesus' height are unfounded and unsupported in biblical, literary, or archaeological records. They are the speculations of an adventurer and amateur archaeologist, not a biblical scholar or a professional. The Garden Tomb Association would not endorse these conjectures.[166] This anomaly in the length of the burial location cannot, therefore, reasonably contribute to the evidence for the Garden Tomb as the location of Jesus' burial. There was barely enough time to get Jesus' body to the tomb and leave before sundown, let alone to chisel away at lengthening the rock-cut tomb.

However, the essential arrangement of the two chambers in the Garden Tomb may provide a clue to its date. This tomb consists of two adjoining rooms situated side by side. The entrance from the outside to this two-chamber burial cave is through the northern weeping chamber. To the right of the first room is the second, where the bodies of the deceased would have been placed. However, this is not the typical configuration of a two-chamber burial tomb. Ordinarily, the inner chamber would be cut further into the rock behind the weeping chamber. This would provide added safety against grave robbers.

Typical of a Second Temple Period burial cave are burial niches called *kokhim* cut vertically into the cave wall. Caves of this period typically feature an *arcosolia,* an arch hewn into the wall of the cave, forming the ceiling of a resting place or a shelf for stone coffins and ossuaries. They also have low burial benches carved around sunken floors. The Garden Tomb has none of the features you would expect to find in a Second Temple burial cave.

Also, Second Temple tombs give evidence of a so-called comb chisel. The comb chisel had a toothed edge that left small parallel lines, called combing, on the rock surfaces. The Garden Tomb displays no sign of comb chiseling. This makes a Second Temple Period dating for the tomb unlikely.

There are First Temple tombs in the Jerusalem area that are cut to the same pattern as the Garden Tomb, with one room adjacent to another. For example, there is the burial chamber of the "Royal Steward" in the Siloam Village, southeast of the Temple Mount. Professor Nahman Avigad identified it as the tomb of the Royal Steward based on two inscriptions found on the facade of the cave. One of the inscriptions refers to the plan of the cave, with "a room at the side of the monument." This information was designed to keep someone from chiseling out another burial chamber beside the visible one.[167]

Burial caves from the First Temple Period with this same plan have been discovered in places other than Jerusalem. An example is Cave Number 9 in the Iron Age II cemetery at Beth Shemesh, as well as an Iron Age II burial cave at Sobah, located west of Jerusalem.[168]

As more discoveries are made, the evidence mounts that the schematic plan of the Garden Tomb appears to be more in line with the seventh or eighth century BC than it is with the first century AD. To date, no Second Temple-era tombs have been found anywhere in the vicinity of the Garden Tomb.[169]

Evidence #4. The great cistern

When searching for physical evidence that the Garden Tomb may have been the tomb of Jesus, advocates point to an underground cistern, a reservoir used to store rainwater in the garden. Cisterns were quite common in the ancient Near East. There are two of them beneath the grounds of the Garden Tomb. The smaller one lies beneath the rock floor, very close to the tomb, to the left of the entrance. In 1921, this was filled in because it was no longer needed.

The Tomb of Joseph

The Great Cistern of the Garden Tomb

The larger one, which is further back but still not far from the tomb, measures 10.16 meters (33'4") wide x 17.27 meters (56'8") long x 10.97 meters (36') tall.

Growing up on a farm and helping my father build a cistern for our house, I have some knowledge of cisterns. I thought ours was huge; it held 11,221 gallons of water. However, the great cistern under the Garden Tomb grounds holds 200,000 gallons of water (some say 250,000 gallons). That is almost 18 times larger than our tiny cistern on the farm. This is one of the largest cisterns in Israel and the third-largest in Jerusalem.

It is claimed that there is evidence to show this cistern was built before the time of Christ and would, therefore, have been in service when Jesus was crucified and buried. The whole chamber is roofed over by durable masonry, vaulted, and reminiscent of a church. The walls and ceilings were lined throughout with a double layer of fine Roman cement. The first layer applied directly to the natural rock, consisted of lime and ashes, approximately three-quarters of an inch thick. The second layer, applied directly over the first, consisted of lime mixed with broken pottery. It measured about three inches thick. The entire lining of cement was just under four inches in depth.

Gabriel Barkay concluded that the waterproofing on the cistern is of the type used by the Crusaders, and therefore, the cistern must date to that era.[170] Nevertheless, this theory does not appear to hold water any more than a leaky cistern. Suppose the waterproofing and two Crusader-style crosses found in the cistern give evidence of later activity. In that case, that does not necessarily mean the cistern itself was constructed in a later period.

To use the cistern in Crusader times, it would need some repair. The major crusades took place during the eleventh and twelfth centuries. Those repairs would reflect Crusader craftsmanship but could very well hide original Herodian craftsmanship. Thus, the cistern cannot be ruled out as in use during Jesus' time, according to the plaster repairs at least.

Evidence #5. The winepress

As you enter the Garden Tomb compound, directly ahead of you and slightly below ground level, there is a nicely restored winepress. It is somewhat shaped like a giant keyhole or a baby grand piano and is lined with stone. This press was excavated in 1924, and it, too, is one of the largest in Israel. Believed to be of pre-Christian origin, it is often cited as evidence that a wealthy individual owned the garden, the tomb, and an extensive vineyard at this location.

While archaeologists have uncovered numerous winepresses around Israel, most of them, such as those at Mt. Gerizim, Apollonia (Arsuf), and Hippos (Sussita), are Byzantine presses. There are some Roman presses at Shiloh (Early Roman), Achziv (Late Roman), Usha (Roman), and Manot (Roman), all of which show both the essentials of a press and the variety of shapes that depict those essentials.

Typically, winepresses consisted of a complex structure that included a treading floor and a channel allowing the grape juice to flow through a filter down to a collecting pool. There would be steps down to this pool to access the juice, jars to transport it, and a storage area to keep it. The Garden Tomb winepress shows only the collection area; the rest is presumably underground in the tomb area.

Nevertheless, does this reflect a wealthy man's vineyard? Was there even a vineyard at this location?

The Tomb of Joseph

The Garden Tomb Winepress

John 19:41 says, "Now in the place where he was crucified there was a garden, and in the garden a new tomb in which no one had yet been laid." The word for "garden" (Greek: κῆπος; English: *kēpos*) is used only five times in the New Testament, once in the parable of the mustard seed (Luke 13:19), twice about the Garden of Gethsemane (John 18:1, 26) and twice referring to the garden where Joseph's tomb was located (John 19:41). Also, when Mary Magdalene first saw the risen Christ, she mistook him for the gardener (John 20:15), which comes from the same root word, *kēpos*. Does the presence of a winepress indicate this was the garden of a rich man? Unfortunately, the word *kēpos* bears no relationship to a vineyard. It relates to an orchard or garden of trees, like olive trees.

There is a word that means vineyard (Greek: ἀμπελών; English: *ampelṓn*). Jesus used it frequently in his parables, such as the laborers in the vineyard (Matt 20:1–8), the parable of the two sons (Matt 21:28), and the parable of the wicked tenants (Matt 21:33–41; Mark 12:1–9; Luke 20:9–16).

Had John wanted to use a winepress to identify the garden in which Joseph's tomb was located, he more likely would have used the word for vineyard (*ampelṓn*), not the word for garden (*kēpos*).

The fact that no winepress or vineyard is mentioned concerning the burial of Jesus moots any evidence the winepress might provide for the authenticity of the Garden Tomb. It is not likely that both an olive orchard and grapevines were planted in the same location. This would be a violation of Mosaic Law: "You shall not sow your vineyard with two kinds of seed, lest the whole yield be forfeited, the crop that you have sown and the yield of the vineyard" (Deut 22:9). Besides, grapes need full sun to grow and mature, and the leaves of the olive trees would hide them from the sun. I have a twenty-foot-tall Russian Olive tree in my backyard, and it casts quite a shadow.

Additionally, the term John 20:15 uses for the caretaker of this garden is "gardener" (Greek: κηπουρός; English: *kēpourós*). When Jesus was talking about a vineyard, he used the word vinedresser (Greek: γεωργός; English: *geōrgós*) ("husbandman" in KJV). There does not seem to be sufficient linguistic evidence to support the notion that this location had a vineyard in Jesus' day.

Evidence #6. The great stone

Matthew says: "And Joseph took the body and wrapped it in a clean linen shroud and laid it in his own new tomb, which he had cut in the rock. And he rolled a great stone to the entrance of the tomb and went away" (Matt 27:59, 60). Mark says: "And they were saying to one another, 'Who will roll away the stone for us from the entrance of the tomb?' And looking up, they saw that the stone had been rolled back—it was very large" (Mark 16:3, 4). Luke says: "And they found the stone rolled away from the tomb, but when they went in they did not find the body of the Lord Jesus" (Luke 24:2, 3).

All three Synoptic Gospels mention that a large stone was rolled in front of the doorway of the tomb, sealing Jesus inside. All three comment that when the women arrived at the tomb early Sunday morning, the stone was already rolled back from the door. Matthew 28:2 informs us, "There was a great earthquake, for an angel of the Lord descended from heaven and came and rolled back the stone and sat on it." Although this was the second earthquake within forty-eight hours (it could have been an aftershock), Matthew is careful to tell us that it was an angel who rolled back the great stone, not Jesus, not his disciples, not even the earthquake.

The fact that the stone was huge is supported by the words used to describe it. It was a "great stone" (Greek: μέγας λίθος; English: *mégas líthos*) (Matt 27:60) and "it was very great." (Greek: σφόδρα μέγας; English: *sphódra mégas*) (Mark 16:4 KJV).

Mégas is a word that we should be familiar with. It is used to describe many things, but it always means great or large, exceeding what is normal. Here are some examples of the ways *mégas* is used in the Bible.

TABLE 1

Use of the Greek mégas in the New Testament

Scripture	Citation
Matt 5:35	"Jerusalem, the city of the *mégas* king."
Matt 8:24, 26	"There arose a *mégas* storm . . . there was a *mégas* calm."
Matt 22:38	"This is the *mégas* and first commandment."
Mark 4:37–41	"A *mégas* windstorm arose . . . and there was a *mégas* calm."
Mark 5:11–13	"A *mégas* herd of swine ran down the steep bank into the sea."
Mark 14:15	"He will show you a *mégas* upper room."
Luke 1:32	"He will be *mégas* and will be called the Son of the Most High."
Luke 22:12	"He will show you a *mégas* upper room."
John 11:43	"He cried out with a *mégas* voice, 'Lazarus, come out.'"
Acts 8:1	"There arose a *mégas* persecution against the church."
Acts 10:11; 11:5	"A *mégas* sheet descending, being let down by its four corners."
1 Cor 16:9	"A *mégas* door for effective work has opened to me."
Heb 4:14; 10:21	"We have a *mégas* High Priest . . . Jesus, the Son of God"
Heb 13:20	"Our Lord Jesus, the *mégas* shepherd of the sheep."
Titus 2:13	"The appearing . . . of our *mégas* God and Savior Jesus Christ."
Revelation	The book of Revelation uses *mégas* more than eighty times.

As is evident from this table, the word *mégas* has multiple applications and is used to describe many types of people and things. Nevertheless, its meaning never deviates from "superior" or "more than usual."

The word *mégas* is frequently used in the Gospel narratives of Jesus' crucifixion.

- Jesus cried out with a loud (*mégas*) voice, saying, "*Eli, Eli, lema sabachthani*" (Matt 27:46; Mark 15:34)
- "Jesus cried out again with a loud (*mégas*) voice and yielded up his spirit" (Matt 27:50)
- "And Jesus uttered a loud (*mégas*) cry and breathed his last" (Mark 15:37).
- "Then Jesus, calling out with a loud (*mégas*) voice, said, 'Father, into your hands I commit my spirit!'" (Luke 23:46).

- "And behold, there was a great (*mégas*) earthquake, for an angel of the Lord descended from heaven and came and rolled back the stone and sat on it" (Matt 28:2).
- "So they departed quickly from the tomb with fear and great (*mégas*) joy, and ran to tell his disciples" (Matt 28:8; see also Luke 2:10 and Acts 15:3).

There can be no doubt that the stone rolled in front of Joseph's tomb was a *mégas* stone. It was larger than the normal stones of the time. However, there is no such *mégas* stone at the Garden Tomb today. It has been missing for centuries.

Over the last few years, there has been considerable buzz about the discovery of a remarkable stone in Jordan. The Abu Badd stone is a large stone used as a fortified door for a sixteenth-century Byzantine monastery in the old village of Faisaliyah, Jordan. Some believe it is the stone rolled in front of Jesus' tomb in Jerusalem. They point to these considerations:

- The stone is the perfect thickness for the fifteen-inch-channel in front of the Garden Tomb;
- The diameter of the stone is large enough (9 feet, 8 Inches) to cover both the doorway and the "spirit" window of the Garden Tomb, essentially covering much of the tomb face;
- The stone is carved from the same color, same texture, and same kind of rock as the Garden Tomb;
- The chisel marks on the stone are like those found on the face of the Garden Tomb.

The Abu Badd Stone

The Tomb of Joseph

There is, of course, no way presently to prove beyond question that this stone was the rolling stone that sealed Jesus' tomb. The arguments for its genuineness are reasonable but circumstantial. Many questions remain unanswered, such as why the stone was removed from Joseph's garden and why it was taken down into the Jordan Valley, across the river, and up to the mountains of Moab. Surely, if someone had wanted to safeguard this stone, they could have done so in the Jerusalem area, where its transport would have been much easier.

Some who believe this to be the rolling stone of Joseph's tomb suggest a theological reason for removing it to Mount Nebo. They assert that the top of Mount Nebo is where Moses lifted up the serpent in the wilderness, which relates to Jesus' words, "As Moses lifted up the serpent in the wilderness, so must the Son of Man be lifted up" (John 3:14).

There are at least two problems with a theological identification of Mount Nebo and the Garden Tomb. First, this connection may be appropriate for Golgotha, but not for the tomb. Jesus was "lifted up" at Golgotha, but Joseph, "laid it [Jesus' body] in his own new tomb" (Matt 27:59, 60). "Up" on the cross; "down" in the tomb.

There is no correspondence between the actions of Moses and the tomb of Jesus. Gordon's Calvary, maybe, but not the tomb. However, more importantly, Moses did not lift the serpent on Mount Nebo. He did it in the wilderness. Numbers 21 indicates the Israelites were at Mount Hor, more than 200 kilometers (125 miles) south of Mount Nebo, when Moses raised the bronze serpent into the air. Location is important when drawing a conclusion, but the Abu Badd stone and Moses do not relate to each other.

Was the stone that sealed Jesus' tomb round? Even the shape of the stone has been questioned by some.

Each of the Synoptics (Matt 27:60; 28:2; Mark 15:46; 16:3, 4; and Luke 24:2) reference the stone as being "rolled" (Greek: ἀποκυλίω; English: *apokyliō*) to and from the door to Joseph's tomb.

Such rolling stones for tomb entrances are known from other Jewish tombs of the time. Examples would be the so-called Herod's Family Tomb adjacent to the King David Hotel; the so-called "Tomb of the Kings" across from St. George's Cathedral; the Nicophoria tomb, east of Herod's family tomb; the church at Bethphage on the Mount of Olives, approaching Bethany; the Hinnom Valley tomb; the Kidron Valley tomb; and the tomb on the road from Mount Carmel to Megiddo near the Jezreel Valley. Each of these tombs, featuring rolling stones, is located either in or near Jerusalem. Other similar tombs have been discovered at Horvat Midras, the cemetery of Hesban, near Kiriath Jearim (Abu Gosh), Michmash (Mukmas), and Megiddo.[171]

Rolling stone at "Herod's Family Tomb"

Example of a rolling stone and sepulcher

In a controversial article in *Biblical Archaeology Review*, Israeli archaeologist Amos Kloner suggested that Jesus' tomb was not sealed with a disk-like "rolling stone" of the type generally imagined. Kloner claimed that "98 percent of the Jewish tombs from this period . . . were closed with square blocking stones." He asserts that the Synoptic accounts of Jesus' burial and resurrection likely refer to a square stone approximately a meter wide. "Of the more than 900 burial caves from the Second Temple Period found in and around Jerusalem, only four are known to have used round (disk-shaped) blocking stones."[172]

Still, there were four, and that is a diputed number. The odds of winning the Lottery are infinitesimally small, yet someone wins every time. Ninety-eight percent of the global population does not have green eyes, but you should not discount the two percent that do.

The Tomb of Joseph

Kloner concludes: "Matthew, Mark, and Luke all describe the stone being 'rolled' (in John it is 'taken away'), and thus it is only natural to assume that the stone was round. But we must remember that 'rolled' is a translation of the Greek word *kulio*, which can also mean 'dislodge,' 'move back,' or simply 'move.'"[173]

However, Kloner's interpretation of kulio as meaning "dislodge" is misleading.

While "dislodge" is a possible translation of the Greek, it is not the usual or preferred translation.

The word *kulio* [which is part of the word προσκυλίω above] comes from the root word (Greek: κῦμα; English: *kŷma*) meaning "to bend" or "curve" like a wave of the sea (see Matt 8:24; 14:24; Mark 4:37; Acts 27:41; and Jude 1:13). This would imply roundness, not a square block.

Another word of the exact derivation (Greek: κύκλῳ; English: *kýklōi*) in the dative case means a "ring" or "cycle." That certainly implies roundness.

Archaeology positively impacts our understanding of Scripture. It provides valuable insights into the milieu in which the Testaments transpire. It has been the Bible scholar's friend for over 100 years. However, it is not the sole contributor to our understanding of the Sacred Text. Every reference using the words "rolling" or "roll" must be viewed in light of their context. Also, the words in their original language must be compared with those exact words in other Scriptures.

Since the word occurs in only four New Testament verses (Matt 28:2, Mark 16:3–4, and Luke 24:2), we must look for help in related words that convey the same meaning.

The corresponding Hebrew word (Hebrew: גָּלַל; English: *gâlal*) to the Koine Greek word *kulio* contributes to our understanding of "roll." Consider Genesis 29:8, "When all the flocks were gathered there, the shepherds would *roll* the stone from the mouth of the well and water the sheep," or Genesis 29:10, "Jacob came near and *rolled* the stone from the well's mouth and watered the flock," or even Joshua 10:18, "*Roll* large stones against the mouth of the cave and set men by it to guard them." In each case, the word "roll" could conceivably be translated as "dislodge," but this is highly unlikely and makes better sense translated as "roll."

Think of other verses where *gâlal* is used, especially when the meaning is symbolic or metaphorical.

> Joshua 5:9, "And the Lord said to Joshua, 'Today I have *rolled away* the reproach of Egypt from you.'"

1 Samuel 14:33, "All the host of heaven shall rot away, and the skies *roll up* like a scroll."

2 Samuel 20:12, "And Amasa lay *wallowing* in his blood in the highway" (see Mark 9:20).

Proverbs 26:27, "Whoever digs a pit will fall into it, and a stone will come back on him who starts it *rolling*."

Isaiah 9:5, "For every boot of the tramping warrior in battle tumult and every garment *rolled* in blood will be burned as fuel for the fire."

Isaiah 34:4, "All the host of heaven shall rot away, and the skies *roll up* like a scroll."

Amos 5:24, "But let justice *roll down* like waters, and righteousness like an ever-flowing stream."

These verses do not appear to mean "dislodge" or anything close to it. Clearly, they mean "to roll." You would never say, *Let justice 'dislodge down' like waters*. Let it roll down like waters. We must never allow the science of archaeology to be the sole interpreter of the Bible.

Evidence #7   The stone channel

Every person who has ever visited the Garden Tomb has taken notice of a stone channel running parallel to the face of the tomb. You had to step over it to enter the small doorway to the tomb. This channel runs the full 8.5 meters (27 feet 7 inches) of the tomb's face. It measures 15 inches wide and has often been thought of as a track, which would have enabled the rolling stone to hug the face of the tomb. However, while that explanation is plausible and the great stone of Abu Badd fits this track perfectly, other considerations would give us pause before understanding this as a rolling stone track.

For one, if the Garden Tomb channel were actually the track for a *mégas* stone disk, you would expect the low point of the channel—the resting point of the stone in the channel—to be directly in front of the cave opening. Nevertheless, the channel continuously slopes downward to the west all the way to the end. This, of course, would require a stop-stone to be put in place to hold the rolling stone in front of the doorway, and such a stone exists. The earliest photographs of the Garden Tomb show a stop-stone at a location that would be in the correct position for a *mégas* stone. So, the pitch of the channel is no detriment to the authenticity of the Garden Tomb.

In his oft-quoted article in *Biblical Archaeology Review*, archaeologist Gabriel Barkay observed that the groove outside the tomb has a diagonal edge. This means the inside face of the channel's outer edge was not cut straight up and down like the façade of the tomb, but was cut at a 45-degree angle leaning away from the tomb's face. As a result, the channel is 37 centimeters wide (15 inches) at the bottom but a full 50 centimeters wide (19 inches) at the top. This configuration reduces contact with the rolling stone, thereby reducing the stability of the great stone in the track. It also diminishes the possibility that this is a channel for the rolling stone.

The other rolling stone tombs, such as the Tomb of the Kings and the tomb at Midras in the Shephelah (*Shfelah*), place the stone between a higher wall and the façade of the tomb. This wall, often several meters high, is built straight up, mirroring the façade of the tomb. In reality, because the outside support for the rolling stone is a wall itself, the rolling stone actually rolls between two walls, the façade of the tomb and the outer, shorter support wall. Barkay claims, "There is no archaeological precedent for a low-cut track for a stone-disk door, particularly a track with a slanted outer edge as we see at the Garden Tomb."[174]

If a higher wall would give more stability to the stone, and this smaller outside edge of the track would be insufficient to hold such a *mégas* stone, what was the purpose of the track? Again, Barkay contends it was not for drainage (there is no outlet for water), nor was it the channel of a rolling stone. He says it was more likely used as a trough for watering animals. Barkay suggests Crusader workers cut it as a water trough for an eleventh-century donkey stable, which was built directly in front of the Garden Tomb. Since a watering trough would not need a higher outside wall, and since the outside edge of this channel was well below the opening of the door (so water would not flow through the open door), Barkay is convinced that at that time, the cave was probably used as a storage room for fodder.

If this were the case, do the dimensions and configuration of the trough fit the needs of a watering trough? In fact, they do. The trough was raised above the bedrock floor in front of the tomb so the donkeys could comfortably drink from the water. However, what is the reason for the channel's outer edge being tapered at a 45-degree angle away from the cave's façade? It would provide a more comfortable angle for the donkeys' heads and throats as they drank from the trough. It is entirely possible, however, that the current channel of the eleventh century was cut down from its original wall to be repurposed as a watering trough. In Jesus' day, the wall could have been much higher.

However, if this were a Crusader-era watering trough for animals, is there any evidence of a stable at the site? There is an arched feature on the face of the cave that is 6 meters (19 feet 7 inches) wide and some 5.5 meters (19 feet) high. It appears to be the beginning of a vaulted roof that extended outward from the tomb façade and covered the bedrock floor in front of the tomb.

There is a similar arrangement at a stable at Nebi Samuel (the tomb of the Prophet Samuel). There, you can see higher stone-cut troughs, which were used for horses, as well as a flat, finished bedrock floor. The Nebi Samuel's stone floors had a shallow drainage channel about 10 centimeters (nearly 4 inches) in width that allowed liquid waste from the animals to flow to the outside of the stable, where the workers could wash it away. There is a similar arrangement at the Garden Tomb. Barkay claims that the archaeological parallels between the Nebi Samuel stables and the Garden Tomb exterior are too significant to be ignored.

However, we must remember that the theory that the Garden Tomb area was later used as a stable is just one of many theories for the use of this space. It is a plausible one, but it is just one of many.

Evidence #8. Traditional execution site

Significant support for the authenticity of the Garden Tomb comes from the claim that this site has long been known as an execution site. If this claim can be substantiated, it definitely helps the Garden Tomb's case. In 1874–1875, the British surveyor Major Claude Conder was examining the site, and he was told of a Jewish tradition that the site was where, for centuries, the Jews stoned those who broke their law.[175] One of those Jewish traditions is that it was here, at this execution site, the prophet Jeremiah died.

Jeremiah's early prophecies were not welcomed by the Jews of Jerusalem because, as a faithful voice for YHWH, he prophesied the downfall and destruction of the Holy City. Some Jews, fearing reprisal, took Jeremiah against his will to Egypt. There, he continued to speak out against false worship and social injustice. Several ancient authors, including Jerome, Epiphanius, Tertullian, Abulpharagius, and Elmacin, were quoted by later historians as indicating that Jeremiah was stoned by his countrymen in the

Egyptian city of Tahpanhes. If this established tradition is correct, Jeremiah could not have died at the Garden Tomb.

There is another old tradition that this was the site of the martyrdom of Stephen, the deacon of the Jerusalem church mentioned in Acts 7:54–60.[176] The Crusaders originally called the main eastern gate of Jerusalem "St. Stephen's Gate" (Latin: *Porta Sancti Stephani*). This was because of the proximity of the site to the location of the stoning of Stephen. Acts 7:58 says, "They cast him (Stephen) out of the city and stoned him."

Death by stoning was not accomplished just by people throwing rocks at you. When someone was stoned, he was first thrown from a high building or a cliff. If the guilty person survived the fall, the executioners would then drop a huge rock onto his chest from the building or cliff. If the person still survived, as unlikely as that would be, the guilty person would be pelted with rocks by his accusers until he was dead.

It is argued that the cliff out of which Joseph's tomb had been carved would have served well the Jewish method of stoning from Christ's time. Described in the Mishnah (*Sanhedrin* 6, 1–4) are the very curious restrictions and rituals the Jews followed for killing someone. The tradition about Stephen is strong enough that some say it began as early as the fifth century AD and continued until at least Crusader times, when even the Damascus Gate was reportedly called "St. Stephen's Gate."

A Christian pilgrim named Luciana, writing in 415 AD, notes that the northern gate of Jerusalem was called the "Gate of St. Stephen." From the end of the Crusader Period, after the disappearance of the Byzantine Church, the name "Saint Stephen's Gate" was applied to a still-accessible gate located just north of the Eastern Gate. Today, this gate is also called the "Lions Gate."[177]

If this is where Stephen was stoned and were the recognized place of execution, this would also be the place where Jesus was crucified. It, too, was a known place of execution. The question would be if the Jews stoned their offenders in the same place where the Romans crucified theirs. This is unlikely. Given the general revulsion of the Jews toward crucifixion and their equal distaste for the Romans, it does not seem reasonable that Jews would be pushing other Jews off cliffs where the Romans were crucifying people below. It does not seem likely that stoning would take place anywhere near a bloody crucifixion site.

Just a few hundred feet to the north, adjacent to the Garden Tomb, lies the Church of Saint-Étienne (St. Stephen's Church), a part of the same rock escarpment. It was built in 460 AD by Empress Eudocia, the highly cultured wife of the fifth-century AD Eastern Roman Emperor Theodosius II. The church and an accompanying monastery commemorate Stephen's death.[178] The site on top of the cliff also houses the famous *École Biblique et Archéologique Française de Jérusalem*, more commonly known as the *École Biblique*, a French academic center specializing in archaeology and biblical exegesis. The discovery of the fifth-century St. Stephen's Church in 1882 provided further evidence in support of the early tradition of placing Stephen's execution near here.

When excavations were done in the late nineteenth century, the area around the ruins of Saint-Étienne revealed numerous Christian burial vaults and in-ground gravesites. Two tombstones were discovered in one of the underground burial vaults, situated so close to the Garden Tomb that they almost touch it. One displayed the inscription: "*To Nonnus Onesimus deacon* [or Nonnus and Onesimus Deacons – the inscription was somewhat marred] *of the church of the* [witness] *of the resurrection.*"

This strongly suggests that Jesus' resurrection was nearby; otherwise, why would you build the church there? The second inscription is even more direct. It read, "buried near his Lord." This may be one of the most compelling arguments for the authenticity of the Garden Tomb as the burial site of Jesus.

Wheaton College Professor of New Testament Emeritus, the late John McRay, however, says these two tomb inscriptions were misused as supporting evidence for this as the site of Jesus' tomb. On its own, the 1889 inscription marked the site of "Deacon Nonnus Onesimus of the Holy Resurrection of Christ and of this monastery."[179]

The late Professor Jerome Murphy-O'Connor, at the *École Biblique*, examined this inscription and its confusing application as proof of the authenticity of the Garden Tomb site. A full accounting of why this inscription cannot be used to authenticate the Garden Tomb is provided in his 1986 BAR article.[180]

Thus, while there is evidence for the Garden Tomb being the authentic location of Jesus' crucifixion and resurrection, that evidence is inconclusive. Some of the evidence presented in the past has since been disqualified. That means we must investigate the alternative site further to verify its authenticity.

The Tomb of Joseph
THE CHURCH OF THE HOLY SEPULCHRE

For many Christians, the most venerated site in Jerusalem is the Church of the Holy Sepluchre. Just as a visit to the Garden Tomb is essential, so too is this site, the preferred location for Roman Catholics and Eastern Orthodox pilgrims to Jerusalem.

It is now to the Church of the Holy Sepulchre as the possible location of the tomb of Jesus that our investigation turns.[181] Before we launch into that investigation, however, we must deal with the elephant in the room. The Church of the Holy Sepulchre has been revered as the site of Jesus' tomb since the third century AD. So, why did so many people latch onto the Garden Tomb as the location of Jesus' tomb in the nineteenth century? That is a fair question.

Why do some pilgrims to Jerusalem avoid the Church of the Holy Sepulchre?

Visitors to the church today are in for a shock. Frankly, for many, the church is aesthetically repulsive. If you enjoy incense and icons, you will be pleased with the Church of the Holy Sepulchre. If, however, you are looking for a quiet garden, an empty tomb, and a skull-like location, you must look elsewhere.

The Church of the Holy Sepulchre is noisy, busy, and the scene of recurrent fights between priests of the Latin (Roman Catholic), Greek Orthodox, Armenian Orthodox, Syriac Orthodox, Ethiopian Orthodox, and Coptic Orthodox churches. All of them have laid claim to their corner of the church. Six denominations, six church traditions–you can imagine the chaos.

> "There is very little as entertaining as watching monks hitching up their cassocks and laying into each other." —Rabbi Cohen

For those who belong to a brand of Christianity that is not given to ritual, formalism, and hierarchy, the Church of the Holy Sepulchre is often not on their list of places to visit in Jerusalem. While I fully understand their feelings, this is a mistake. This church may be the authentic location of Jesus' crucifixion and resurrection. However, unless you are a devout Catholic or

From the Upper Room to Joseph's Tomb

Orthodox Christian, you are likely going to come away from your visit with an empty feeling. The place is so unlike what your spirit longs for.

This church is the poster child for divisions within the Christian faith. It is a territorial battlefield. Nevertheless, it somehow emerges as the winner in the contest for authentic sites of Jesus' Passover Weekend. Therefore, we will set aside the hostilities in the church and slice through the crusty trappings of religion to look for truth. After all, while our focus in this book is on the places in Jerusalem where Jesus stopped on his journey to Calvary, ultimately, we are not so much interested in the place as in the Person who was crucified there.

The location of the tomb vis-à-vis Golgotha

As you enter the church, immediately ahead of you is the Stone of Anointing (also known as the Stone of Unction). Tradition says this is where Jesus' body was laid and prepared for burial by Joseph of Arimathea. This tradition, however, does not date back to the first century but originates from 1288 AD, when an Italian Dominican friar, travel writer, and Christian apologist named Riccoldo da Monte di Croce traveled. The present stone is of Italian pink marble and was added during the 1810 reconstruction of the church; therefore, it is not original.[182]

*The Stone of Anointing, in
the Church of the Holy Sepulchre*

The Tomb of Joseph

To the left is the rotunda, located under the dome on the far west side of the church. In the center of the rotunda is a small, box-like structure, known as the Edicule or Aedicula in Latin, which serves as a chapel. In ancient Roman religion, an *aedicula* was a small shrine, often a household shrine with an altar. The word *aedicula* is the diminutive of the Latin *aedes*, meaning a temple building. In English, this small temple is referred to as an edicule. The Edicule in this significant church encloses the Holy Sepulchre, believed to be the burial place of Jesus. There are approximately 23 meters (75 feet) between the Rock of Golgotha and the tomb of Jesus.

The Edicule consists of two tiny rooms. As you enter the Edicule, the first room is called the Chapel of the Angel. Here is a stone that tradition claims to be a fragment of the large stone that sealed the tomb. After the resurrection earthquake, "An angel of the Lord descended from heaven and came and rolled back the stone and sat on it" (Matt 28:2). This is allegedly that stone.

The second chamber, situated further within the Edicule, is believed to be the presumed site of Jesus' tomb. You cannot see the tomb because, in the fourteenth century, a marble slab was placed over it to prevent damage from pilgrims eager to take home a piece of the authentic tomb of Jesus.[183]

Restoration of the Edicule

If you visited the Church of the Holy Sepulchre before 2016, you would recall the unappealing-looking supports and iron beams on the exterior of the Edicule. These beams were the definition of hideous, but they were keeping the Edicule from crumbling to the ground. Finally, the Israel Antiquities Authority declared the structure unsafe because it was on the verge of collapse. Something had to be done.

Unsightly supports held up the Edicule for decades

From May 2016 to March 2017, the Edicule underwent restoration and repairs. It was a $3,000,000 project, much of which was funded by the World Monuments Fund, a private, international, non-profit organization dedicated to preserving historic architecture and cultural heritage sites around the world.[184]

The delicate restoration was carried out by a team of about fifty experts from the National Technical University of Athens, which had previously worked on the Acropolis in Athens and the Hagia Sophia in Istanbul. These Greek experts worked mainly at night, so visiting pilgrims could access the church during daylight hours.

Perhaps the most exciting moment was one night in October when the marble slab covering the rock-cut tomb was raised. It was the first time in more than two centuries anyone had seen beneath the slab of marble. The workers, archaeologists, and priest watchdogs were afforded the first opportunity to examine the original rock shelf on which Jesus's body is thought to have rested.

The Tomb of Joseph

Using radar, laser scanners, and drones, the Greek team repaired and stabilized the shrine with titanium bolts and mortar. They also cleared away thick layers of candle soot and pigeon droppings.

> "Scientists have discovered that there is a 'very real risk' that the holiest site in Christianity may collapse if nothing is done to shore up its unstable foundations." —Kristin Romey

The Edicule has been rebuilt four times in its history, the last time being in 1810 after a fire. To understand how badly in need of repair the Edicule was, the British governor who ruled Palestine during the British Mandate, which ended in 1948, issued the order to brace the sides with iron girders. Do the math!

Is the tomb of Jesus located within the church?

After Constantine the Great signed the Edict of Milan, which legalized the Christian religion, he sent his mother, Queen Helena, to Jerusalem to look for holy sites. With the help of Eusebius, Bishop of Caesarea, and Macarius, Bishop of Jerusalem, legend has it that Helena and the team she accompanied discovered three crosses at the site now occupied by the Church of the Holy Sepulchre. This led the queen to believe she had found Golgotha, the place where Jesus died.

As a result, in 326 AD, Constantine ordered the Temple of Jupiter/Venus, which Hadrian had built on that site, to be removed and a colossal church built in its place. The temple was demolished, and its ruins removed. The soil and debris were removed from the cave, revealing a rock-cut tomb that Helena and Macarius identified as the burial site of Jesus.[185]

The Church of the Holy Sepulchre was built as separate buildings over the two holy sites: the grand Basilica (the *Martyrium* which was visited by Egeria in the 380s AD), the Triportico (an enclosed colonnaded atrium with the traditional site of Golgotha in one corner), and across a courtyard the *Anastasis* (a rotunda housing the tomb).[186]

The new church was consecrated on September 13, 335 AD. It is certain from archaeological excavations in the seventies that the construction of this church complex covered almost the entire site of Hadrian's earlier temple enclosure. Archaeologist Dan Bahat points out that, "the *Triportico* and *Rotunda* roughly overlapped with the temple building itself; the excavations indicate that the temple extended at least as far back as the Aedicule, and the temple enclosure would have reached back slightly further."[187]

Since the presumed site of Golgotha and the tomb of Jesus are nearby, both housed under the roof of the Church of the Holy Sepulchre, if there is proof for the authenticity of one, it is reasonable to assume there is likewise proof of the authenticity of the other. Thus, the evidence for the tomb also applies to the Place of the Skull.

Inside the Edicule

Archaeologist John Wilkinson comments:

> The Garden Tomb and Gordon's Calvary have been shown to people as the place of Jesus' death and burial for more than a century, but the location where the Church of the Holy Sepulchre stands has been shown to people since before 135 AD and has been regarded as the place of Jesus' burial since its recovery by the Emperor Constantine in about AD 325.[188]

EVIDENCE FOR THE AUTHENTICITY OF THE CHURCH OF THE HOLY SEPULCHRE

So, what is the evidence for the authenticity of the tomb in the Church of the Holy Sepulchre? Does it "cut the mustard"? Are the scholars right? How strong is the case for this old church? The evidence is quite substantial vis-à-vis the other possible locations for Calvary. The following arguments are presented.

Evidence #1. The presence of a quarry

The Muristan (derived from the Persian word meaning "hospital") is a complex of shops, churches, and other buildings located within the Christian Quarter of the Old City of Jerusalem. Adjacent to the Church of the Holy Sepulchre, it was the location of the first hospital of the Knights Hospitaller. The bedrock under the Muristan, the Church of the Holy Sepulchre, and the Lutheran Church of the Redeemer exhibited traces of a quarry that had been used until the first century BC. This is what British archaeologist Dame Kathleen Kenyon discovered in the nineteen seventies.

Present-day archaeologists have confirmed that the 198.12 x 144.78 meter (650 x 475 feet) area known as Golgotha was a quarry for building materials.[189] When the quarrying ended, the next higher (later) stratum of soil washed into the area, making it suitable for gardens or fields in the first century AD.

The discovery of a first-century BC quarry at this location supports the argument that it was located outside the city wall during Jesus' time. This also means the Second Wall was somewhere east of today's Church of the Redeemer, making it east of the Church of the Holy Sepulchre as well.

John 19:41 tells us, "Now in the place where he was crucified there was a garden, and in the garden a new tomb." The stratum above the quarry, which shows traces of fields or gardens, can be dated to the first century AD. This is possible evidence of the church's authenticity.

Around my rural and rustic hometown of Ashland, Nebraska, there are many quarries, the most famous being the Quarry Oaks Golf Course. If there were ever two words that did not belong together, they are "quarry" and "golf." Nevertheless, after quarrying was finished, dirt was brought in to landscape the area and create the premier golf course in Nebraska, which *Golf Digest* named as one of "America's 100 Greatest Golf Courses."

When you visit the Holy Sepulchre Church, you must ascend those eighteen stone steps on the right to get to the height of Golgotha. It is believed by many that this was a raised hill in the ancient quarry. This identification comes from three similar verses: "There were also women looking on from a distance" (Mark 15:40); "The women who had followed him from Galilee stood at a distance watching these things" (Luke 23:49);

and Matthew 27:55, "There were also many women there, looking on from a distance."

It is assumed that if the women could see Jesus dying on the cross from a distance, he must have been at a higher elevation. However, this is not necessarily so. The women could have been at a higher elevation, which enabled them to see the cross. Alternatively, being a filled-in quarry, the area may have been quite level, allowing the women to see from a distance. Assumptions are dangerous only when they are taken as fact.

Evidence #2. Hadrian's Temple foundation

Born January 24, 76 AD near Naples in 117 AD, Publius Aelius Hadrianus became Caesar Traianus Hadrianus Augustus, or just Hadrian. He was educated to be an admirer of Greek civilization, an admiration that remained with him for life. Hadrian did not share the expansionist goals of his predecessor, Trajan. Instead, he invested in developing defensible borders and unifying the dissimilar peoples of the empire. It was in this pursuit that he built his most famous namesake, Hadrian's Wall, which marked the northern limit of Britannia.

In Palestine, the Jewish people stood in the way of Hadrian's plan for the unification of the empire. As a result, he suppressed the Bar Kochba revolt. In 135 AD, Emperor Hadrian conquered Jerusalem, razed much of it, and constructed a Roman city in its place, which he renamed Aelia Capitolina. *Aelia* came from Hadrian's *nomen gentile*.[190] *Capitolina* meant the new city was dedicated to the chief Roman deity, Jupiter, whose monument, the Temple of Jupiter Capitolinus, is the most famous temple in ancient Rome. It was located on the Capitoline Hill.

Aelia Capitolina was built according to the plan of a typical Roman town. Hadrian also renamed Judaea Province as Syria Palaestina so he could eliminate the name Judea.[191] While Hadrian viewed the Bar Kokhba Revolt as a failure of his Pan-Hellenic ideal, there was an even more troubling threat to unifying the disparate peoples of the Roman Empire. This was the new start-up religion of the Christians. His followers saw Jesus Christ as the great unifier of peoples, where in his church "there is neither Jew nor Greek, there is neither slave nor free, there is no male and female, for you are all one in Christ Jesus" (Gal 3:28).

To thwart the rapid growth of this new religion in the second century AD, Hadrian was prepared to suppress the message and eradicate any reminders of it. The veneration of the spot thought to be where Jesus was crucified and where he rose from the dead became a prime target for Hadrian's campaign of eradication. He removed anything "Christian" from these locations and attempted to wipe them from memory. When he razed this district, the area of Golgotha and the tomb were filled with dirt and debris. Terraces were built for the construction of Hadrian's Forum.

On top of this reconstructed site, Hadrian built a temple to Venus (also variously identified as Jupiter, Juno, or Minerva) to prevent Christians from worshiping there (Eusebius, *Life of Constantine* 3.26). Archaeologists have uncovered remains from this temple. John Wilkinson describes the situation. "Eighty or ninety years after this official Roman Temple was built, practically no Christians were left who had known it (Golgotha and the tomb) as it was before. Two centuries later, or to be exact, in AD 325, no living eye had seen what was beneath the (Venus) temple."[192] It seemed the site where first-century Christians remembered Jesus' death and burial would be gone forever by the second century AD.

Coins were found in the debris of the beaten-earth floor that came after the quarry was abandoned. They have been dated to the First Jewish Rebellion against Rome (66–70 AD). This would confirm both traces of Hadrian's rebuilding of Jerusalem as Aelia Capitolina and his suppression of the Second Jewish Revolt. It would also lend credence to the claim that within the Church of the Holy Sepulchre is a tomb from the time of Jesus of Nazareth.

Evidence #3. Beneath the Lutheran Church of the Redeemer

In an article entitled, "Site-Seeing: Archaeological Remains in Holy Sepulchre's Shadow," Boston University's Professor of Religion, Jonathan Klawans, implores his readers not to miss taking in the Lutheran Church of the Redeemer on their visits to Jerusalem. This is the church adjacent to the Church of the Holy Sepulchre, featuring a tall bell tower. Climb the 177 steps, and from here, you get the best photos of Jerusalem from deep within the Old City itself. (I only did this when I was much younger.)

The Redeemer Church is strategically located. On the north side, the traditional route of the Via Dolorosa runs. To the west lies Muristan Street, the thoroughfare to the Muristan, a gathering place of sorts. To the south, Muristan Street connects to David Street, which runs west past Herod's

Jerusalem palace and out the Jaffa Gate. Adjacent to the Muristan and the Church of the Redeemer is the Holy Sepulchre Church itself.

Today, this is a busy, thriving area with shops, restaurants, residences, and more; however, it was not so in the first century AD. This area was just outside the city. It was formerly a rock quarry, now it's a mix of grass and shops. There was only hustle and bustle on the day of Jesus' crucifixion. These two churches are inexorably connected, not by time, but by location. They both sit over the site formerly occupied by Hadrian's forum and temple.

When Jerusalem expanded in the seventh century BC, this area was inhabited for the first time. Excavations beneath the floor of the Lutheran Church revealed that the area was covered with a beaten-earth floor in which seventh-century BC pottery was found. The dating was confirmed by carbon-14 tests of the ashes beneath the floor.

Today's Church of the Redeemer was built on the site of an old Crusader church. That earlier church was known as Santa Maria Latina. While some ruins are visible in the yard north of the church, the most interesting ruins lie beneath the church. Before the church was constructed, excavations were undertaken underneath it.[193] You may access these ruins by descending a staircase near the entrance to the bell tower. Here, you will find remnants of walls built by Hadrian (117–138 AD), as well as those from later periods.[194]

The archaeological evidence of Hadrian's Temple wall, which was discovered beneath the Lutheran Church of the Redeemer, is significant due to its proximity to the Church of the Holy Sepulchre. They are both located in the area filled in by Hadrian with dirt and debris to erase any memory of Jesus and his tomb.

Evidence #4. Beneath the Alexander Nevsky Church

Alexander Yaroulavitz was a thirteenth-century Russian warrior prince who expelled Swedish and German invaders from Russia in 1242 AD at the "Battle of the Ice." The name "Nevsky" comes from the Narva River, where the Swedish army was defeated. The prince became a Russian saint, known as Alexander Nevsky.

There are cathedrals dedicated to and named after Alexander Nevsky all over the world. I have visited the cathedrals in Tallinn (Estonia), Sophia (Bulgaria), Paris (France), and elsewhere.[195] The entrance to the Alexander

Nevsky Church in Jerusalem is about 70 meters (230 feet) from the entrance to the Church of the Holy Sepulchre. It is just north, across the street from the Lutheran Church of the Redeemer. As such, it is situated in the same area as the original quarry of Jerusalem, the Forum, and the Temple built by Emperor Hadrian.

This location, at 25 Souq al-Dabbagha, was intended to be a Russian consulate and a hostel for Russian immigrants to Israel who were arriving by boatloads at the port of Jaffa. However, in 1883, work on the foundation was halted due to significant archaeological discoveries. Work never resumed. The Russian consulate was built elsewhere.

The Archimandrite Antonin Kapoustin, Chief of the Russian Ecclesiastical Mission in Jerusalem, led the excavations. Since the church is Russian Orthodox, as you would expect, there is an iconostasis replete with icons and crosses. Behind the iconostasis are stairs with a huge cross standing inside the arcade, marking the place where Jesus used to enter and exit the city during his time. Remnants of a Hadrianic triple arch that opened onto the forum of *Aelia Capitolina* and part of the retaining wall of the Temple precinct are visible above ground in the basement of the church.

As you enter the excavated area in the basement of the church, you descend a set of stairs to an archway. The right-hand column dates back to the eleventh century AD, but the stonework on the left-hand column is part of an entrance to the main forum, built by Emperor Hadrian in the second century. This arch is one of four arches Hadrian built in Jerusalem. Another, more famous one, is the *Ecce Homo* Arch at the beginning of the traditional Via Dolorosa.

Passing through the underground arch, to the left is a reconstruction of the broad stairway that led to the original Church of the Holy Sepulchre. New Testament scholar Jerome Murphy-O'Connor noted that this corresponds precisely to the eastern end of Constantine's fourth-century Holy Sepulchre Church, as it is depicted in the sixth-century Madaba Map.

From the Upper Room to Joseph's Tomb

The Madaba Map

Straight ahead, under a glass covering, is the gate threshold once thought to have been where Jesus left the city on the way to Golgotha. Today, archaeologists think the gate probably dates to the second century AD. Next to the threshold is a large piece of the rock of Calvary, purchased by the Russians when the church was built. Above it stands a crucifix.

Initially, the main entrance to the Basilica of the Holy Sepulchre was located on the Roman Cardo Maximus, the primary road constructed by the Romans that cut directly across Jerusalem. This is clearly evident on the Madaba map. In the Jewish Quarter of Jerusalem today, you can still see some of the columns of the ancient Roman Cardo.

Those who believe the Church of the Holy Sepulchre is the authentic location of Golgotha and the tomb of Joseph of Arimathea find sufficient evidence beneath the Alexander Nevsky Church to confirm their belief.

Evidence #5. *The Indiana Jones of the fourth century AD*

Tradition is just that—tradition. Sometimes it is based on fact; sometimes not. However, regardless of the origin of the tradition, the fact that it has endured for centuries must be taken into account. With the Church of the Holy Sepulchre, there is more than enough tradition to go around.

The Tomb of Joseph

Tradition claims that in the days of Constantine the Great, the cross on which Jesus died was "rediscovered" in Jerusalem by Constantine's mother, Queen Helena. Whether this occurred or not is not the point here. The point is that, due to the tradition surrounding this alleged discovery, Helena was canonized as a saint by both the Roman Catholic and Eastern Orthodox Churches. In recent decades, she has been hailed as the first biblical archaeologist. Perhaps she should be better remembered as the female Indiana Jones.[196]

Constantine the Great

It appears Helena converted to Christianity after 312 AD, when her son began to protect and favor the Christian Church. Eusebius reports that Constantine converted Helena, and he is responsible for making her a devoted servant of God.[197] Whether Constantine is responsible for her conversion or not, we do have evidence of her early faith. Sometime after she became a Christian, Helena transformed part of the *Palatium Sessorianum*, her palace in Rome, into a chapel or church called the *Basilica Heleniana*, now known as *Santa Croce in Gerusalemme*.[198]

Helena is best known for her journey to the eastern provinces of the Roman Empire, particularly to the region of Palestine. This journey occurred about 326–327 AD. Her adventures are lavishly expressed by the

Church Father Eusebius in his *Life of Constantine* (3.41–47). Eusebius describes her religious enthusiasm, her desire to pray at places where Christ had been present, and her care for the poor and the needy. Eusebius also ascribes to her the construction of the Constantinian churches in Bethlehem and on the Mount of Olives. Most importantly, he connects her with the construction of the Church of the Holy Sepulchre in Jerusalem.

In his definitive work on Helena, Jan Willem Drijvers claims her greatest fame was acquired by an act for which she was credited but probably did not accomplish, *i.e.*, the finding of the "True Cross."[199] The origin of this legend dates back to Jerusalem during the second half of the fourth century. Beloved as she was, the legend of Helena and the cross spread quickly throughout the empire.

Drijvers, from the Department of History and Classics at the University of Groningen in the Netherlands, maintains that Helena's presence in Jerusalem and Eusebius's detailed account of her visit ultimately led to connecting Helena with the discovery of the cross. After 351 AD, Cyril of Jerusalem wrote to the new Emperor Constantius II that the cross was discovered during the reign of his father, Constantine I. However, the bishop carefully refrained from identifying who had discovered it.[200]

The remains of the cross were reportedly already venerated in the Church of the Holy Sepulchre by the end of the 340s AD. This is verified in the sermons of Cyril.[201] The Roman Emperor Julian believed the discovery of the relic to be authentic, but he rebuked Christians for worshipping the cross.[202]

Ambrose's Latin account of the discovery of the cross was long thought to be the most original version of the legend. However, there is a slightly earlier Greek text, recorded in a *Church History* written in 390 by Gelasius, Bishop of Caesarea. The preface of this account suggested that it was written about 350–387 AD at the request of Gelasius' influential uncle Cyril, Bishop of Jerusalem.[203] This Greek text brings us even closer to the men who first recorded the legend of Helena.

Does Helena's visit to Jerusalem and her alleged discovery of the "True Cross" prove the Church of the Holy Sepulchre is the authentic location of Golgotha and Joseph of Arimathea's tomb? No, it does not. Nevertheless, the enduring legacy of the legend and the numerous historical references to Helen's pilgrimage to Jerusalem somehow connect her to the site of the tomb, lending secondary credibility to the church. However, the literary evidence undergirds the legend of Helena even more.

The Tomb of Joseph

Evidence #6. *The confirmation by Eusebius*

Perhaps the most prolific literary source confirming much of the story of the discovery of the Church of the Holy Sepulchre is Eusebius. "Eusebius seems to have been present at its discovery when a boy; he speaks as an eyewitness."[204] Consider the following corroborations.

- *That the Holy Sepulchre had been covered with debris and idols.* "For it had been in time past the endeavor of impious men (or rather let me say of the whole race of evil spirits through their means), to consign to the darkness of oblivion that divine monument of immortality to which the radiant angel had descended from heaven, and rolled away the stone for those who still had stony hearts, and who supposed that the living One still lay among the dead" (Book 3, Chapter 26).

- *How Constantine commanded the debris from the idol Temple and the soil itself to be removed at a considerable distance from the sacred area.* "Nor did the emperor's zeal stop here, but he gave further orders that the materials of what was thus destroyed, both stone and timber, should be removed and thrown as far from the spot as possible; and this command also was speedily executed. The emperor, however, was not satisfied with having proceeded thus far: once more, fired with holy ardor, he directed that the ground itself should be dug up to a considerable depth, and the soil which had been polluted by the foul impurities of demon worship transported to a far distant place" (Book 3, Chapter 27).

- *The discovery of the tomb of Jesus.* "But as soon as the original surface of the ground, beneath the covering of earth, appeared, immediately, and contrary to all expectation, the venerable and hollowed monument of our Saviour's resurrection was discovered. Then indeed did this most holy cave present a faithful similitude of his return to life, in that, after lying buried in darkness, it again emerged to light, and afforded to all who came to witness the sight, a clear and visible proof of the wonders of which that spot had once been the scene, a testimony to the resurrection of the Saviour clearer than any voice could give" (Book 3, Chapter 28).

- *Constantine comments about the preservation of the holy sites.* "Such is our Saviour's grace, that no power of language seems adequate to describe the wondrous circumstance to which I am about to refer. For, that the monument of his most holy Passion, so long ago buried beneath the ground, should have remained unknown for so long a series of years until its reappearance to his servants now set free through the removal of him who was the common enemy of all, is a fact which truly surpasses all admiration" (Book 3, Chapter 30).

- *Constantine commissions an unsurpassed church to be built on the site.* "It will be well, therefore, for your sagacity to make such arrangements and provision of all things needful for the work, that not only the church itself as a whole may surpass all others whatsoever in beauty, but that the details of the building may be of such a kind that the fairest structures in any city of the empire may be excelled by this. That whatever quantity or sort of materials we shall esteem from your letter to be needful, may be procured from every quarter, as required . . . for it is fitting that the most marvelous place in the world should be worthily decorated" (Book 3, Chapter 31).

- *Constantine builds a "New Jerusalem" from the site of Golgotha.* "This was the emperor's letter, and his directions were at once carried into effect. Accordingly, on the very spot which witnessed the Saviour's sufferings, a new Jerusalem was constructed . . . It was opposite this city that the emperor now began to rear a monument to the Saviour's victory over death, with rich and lavish magnificence" (Book 3, Chapter 33).

- *The splendor of Constantine's church.* "This temple, then, the emperor erected as a conspicuous monument of the Saviour's resurrection, and embellished it throughout on an imperial scale of magnificence. He further enriched it with numberless offerings of inexpressible beauty and various materials,—gold, silver, and precious stones, the skillful and elaborate arrangement of which, in regard to their magnitude, number, and variety, we have not leisure at present to describe particularly" (Book 3, Chapter 40).

- *The three gates to the church.* "Three gates, placed exactly east, were intended to receive the multitudes who entered the church. Opposite these gates, the crowning part of the whole was the hemisphere, which rose to the very summit of the church. This was encircled by twelve columns (according to the number of the apostles of our Saviour), having their capitals embellished with silver bowls of great size, which the emperor himself presented as a splendid offering to his God" (Book 3. Chapter 37).

Eusebius of Caesarea was a first-rate historian of Christianity. He was also an exegete, Bible scholar, and Christian polemicist. He was a scholar of the biblical canon and is regarded as an extremely learned Christian of his time.[205] Eusebius came to see himself as a spiritual advisor to Constantine. This relationship led to the famous posthumous biography, Eusebius's *Life of Constantine.*

However, did Eusebius's close friendship and evident admiration for Constantine blind his eyes when it came to writing about Helena and her escapades in Jerusalem? His panegyric eulogy of Constantine I paints the emperor in the most favorable light. However, does that nullify the facts? No, it does not.

The truth is, Helena did make a journey to Palestine and did determine the location she believed was the site of Golgotha and the tomb. That location is where the Church of the Holy Sepulchre stands. Eusebius, the historian, attests to that regardless of his personal feelings and admiration for the emperor.

Evidence #7. Additional literary corroboration

While Eusebius was the most famous and prolific historian to describe the Church of the Holy Sepulchre in antiquity, he was not alone. Others describe the church or the discovery of the "True Cross" as well. Among them are these.

Egeria–fourth century

About half a century after Helena made her famous trip to the Holy Land, another female pilgrim headed there. Egeria was a fearless woman who lived in the western part of the Roman Empire. She may have hailed from Galicia in Spain or the southern region of France. The original Egeria was a legendary nymph in the early history of Rome, a divine counselor and consort to Numa Pompilius, the second king of Rome, who hailed from the Sabine people. Her name is used as an eponym for a female advisor, and thus, the Egeria who wrote this travelogue may not be using her given name.

The fourth-century Egeria visited most of the known sites of interest to Christian pilgrims in her day. What we know of her travel itinerary comes from those pieces of her travelogue that have survived, as well as the accounts of other travelers such as the Pilgrim of Bordeaux and some later writers who quote Egeria's words.

Egeria described her travels in one of two letters she addressed to her *sorores*, which is Latin for "sisters." Some believe the references to her *sorores* indicate Egeria belonged to a religious society and may have been a nun. On the other hand, she may have been merely referring to her "sisters" in the faith, e.g., "brothers and sisters in Christ." Nonetheless, Egeria demonstrates a remarkably high level of understanding of the details of the Christian liturgy.

> "The Church of the Holy Sepulcher is 1,700 years of religion wrapped around a rock." —Max Lucado

Having arrived in Jerusalem just before Easter, Egeria gave a day-by-day description of the Holy Week festivities at the Church of the Holy Sepulchre. Significantly, Egeria, like our other early sources, never mentioned Helena in connection with the church. She did, however, emphasize the importance of the relics of the cross to the Jerusalem church. Egeria's most significant contribution to our understanding stems from her descriptions of church services she attended in the Church of the Holy Sepulchre, her conversations with monks, and her observations of the "Jerusalem liturgy" which has greatly influenced the expression of the Christian liturgy today.[206]

Unfortunately, the text of Egeria's travels was lost for almost 700 years. In 1884, the Italian scholar Gian Francesco Garmurrini discovered the *Codex Aretinus* in the monastic library of Santa Maria in Arezzo, Italy. Known today as *Itinerarium Egeriae* or *The Travels of Egeria*, this manuscript is part of the *Codex Aretinus* 6, 3, the script of which indicates the text was copied between the ninth and twelfth centuries AD.[207] Only about a third of her text remains, which means we lack some fundamental information about Egeria herself, including her origin and the year she began her pilgrimage. What we do have is a remarkably detailed account of her three-year stay in Jerusalem and her trips to Egypt, Syria, Turkey, and beyond.

The Tomb of Joseph

Abbot Daniel—twelfth century

The travels of a Russian abbot named Daniel are usually dated to 1125 AD during the reign of Baldwin II, King of Jerusalem. Abbot Daniel described the ruins of the place where Helena found the Holy Cross. "It was a very large church with a wooden roof; now, however, there is nothing but a small chapel. Towards the east is the large doorway to which Mary the Egyptian came, desiring to enter the church . . . She passed out of this door on the way to the desert of Jordan. Near this door is the place where St. Helena recognized the True Cross."

Daniel then described the Holy Sepulchre. He tells us that at the beginning of the twelfth century, the Church of the Holy Sepulchre was protected by a wall enclosing it. This wall was cased with marble.

> The Holy Sepulchre—this as the chief part of the whole monument, the Emperor [Constantine I] caused to be decorated with the greatest care, and with magnificent columns. Outside was a vast court, open to the sky, paved with polished stone, and with long porticoes on three of its sides. Towards the east, opposite the tomb, was joined a basilica, an admirable work of immense proportions.[208]

The abbot described that in the interior of the chapel, on the northern side, there was a bench upon which Jesus' body was laid. This bench was cut into the rock of the cave and covered with marble slabs. The stone that was rolled away, upon which the angel sat, was shown to the abbot three feet in front of the entrance to the sepulchral chamber. And then comes his description of the "holy rock." "Approached by a little door through which a man can scarcely get by going on bended knees. The sacred rock was visible through a covering of marble slabs by three small round openings on one side."[209]

Abbot Daniel's description of the Church of the Holy Sepulchre is significant because he saw the church before the Crusaders renovated it into its present form. He mentioned "The Navel of the Earth" in a small oratory just outside the wall of the eastern apse, as well as a "Golgotha" and "Calvary" in a small building outside the church.[210] He also alluded to the "place of the descent from the cross" and the locations of "the parting of the vestments," "the crowning with thorns," "the mocking," "the striking of Jesus," and "the prison," all under a single roof not far to the north of Golgotha.

Finally, the abbot described the site where Saint Helena discovered the Holy Cross called "the Invention of the Cross," located east of the place of crucifixion. At the time of Abbot Daniel's visit, there was only a small church at the location of the crucifixion and resurrection, but a huge one had previously stood there, which Sæwulf said was built in honor of St. Helena. The Infidels utterly destroyed this large church. It is likely that the large church, mentioned both by Daniel and Sæwulf, was the Basilica of Constantine itself. The small church must then have been the Chapel of St. Helena.

Sæwulf–twelfth century

During the First Crusade, Christian knights from Europe captured Jerusalem after a seven-week siege. When the Holy City fell to the Christian forces, traveling to Jerusalem for European Christians became feasible. Sæwulf was an English pilgrim who is known mostly from the *Relatio*, or written account he left of his pilgrimage to Jerusalem in 1102 AD. This was just a few years after the Crusaders recaptured the city in 1099 AD.

In the *Relatio*, Sæwulf describes how he traveled to the Apulia region of southeastern Italy on the coast of the Adriatic Sea. There, he began his account of sailing from July 13, 1102 AD, to Jerusalem. As this was late in the season, Sæwulf embarked on the only type of vessel available, a trading ship. Via multiple ports, he eventually docked at Jaffa and began a tour of Palestine. Sæwulf's description of the Lord's Sepulchre, "surrounded by a very strong wall and roof, lest the rain should fall upon it," squares with Abbot Daniels' description of the same. The Chapel of the Holy Sepulchre is, and has always been, a small building.

Thus, having investigated both the physical and the literary evidence for the Church of the Holy Sepulchre being the authentic site of Golgotha and the tomb of Jesus, we must conclude that the evidence is quite strong. Nevertheless, there is more scientific evidence.

Evidence #8. Optically Stimulated Luminescence

An exciting scientific discovery resulting from the refurbishment of the Edicule in 2016–2017 relates to the mortar found between the limestone surface of the tomb and the marble slab that covered it. Experiments conducted on the mortar indicate that it dates to 345 AD.

The chief scientific supervisor for the restoration project was Antonia Moropoulou, who led an interdisciplinary team from the National Technical University of Athens (NTUA). Moropoulou tested the mortar with a technique called Optically Stimulated Luminescence (OSL). In physics, OSL is a method for measuring ionizing radiation. It is used in luminescence dating of ancient materials, primarily geological sediments, as well as occasionally in fired pottery, bricks, and other similar materials. The difference between radiocarbon dating and OSL is that the former is used to date organic materials, while the latter dates minerals.[211]

The energy within mineral grains, such as quartz, builds up when they are not exposed to sunlight. Through the OSL technique, scientists can measure this energy to determine how long the mineral has been exposed to light. In turn, this enabled the NTUA team at the Church of the Holy Sepulchre to date the burial associated with the mortar they tested.

The fact that the quartz mineral in the mortar from this tomb, which the NTUA team discovered, dates from the fourth century AD, strengthens the case for the authenticity of the Church of the Holy Sepulchre.[212] It also provides the first piece of non-literary, non-traditional evidence related to dating the church Constantine built to venerate the alleged tomb of Jesus.

Evidence #9. The Holy Sepulchre ring

During 1974, excavations south of the Temple Mount in Jerusalem, directed by Professor Benjamin Mazar of the Hebrew University, a gold ring was discovered in a Byzantine house near the Triple Gate. It was the mid-nineteenth century, and, at the time, considerable skepticism existed among scholars regarding the suggestion that the ring depicted the Holy Sepulchre, the tomb of Jesus.

Positively dating the ring was fraught with difficulty. Rings are often best dated by their style. Unfortunately, the style of this ring did not pinpoint any date within multiple centuries. It is likely to be dated anywhere from the twelfth to the sixteenth century AD, when rings of this type, featuring the Holy Sepulchre as it was rebuilt during the Crusader Period, were sold in Jerusalem as souvenirs and carried back to Europe.

There are, however, rings similar to this one found in several other collections. In the Benaki Museum in Athens, for example, a very similar ring is displayed. Another is a sixth- or seventh-century gold ring found near Milan, now in the British Museum. It presents itself in the same manner as the Holy Sepulchre ring.

The band encircling the finger is made of ornamented wire. The head or bezel (the part that protrudes upward from the band) is in the form of a square structure with a pyramidal roof. The walls of the building are pierced with rounded arches. The sides of the roof are decorated with pellets arranged in triangles.[213]

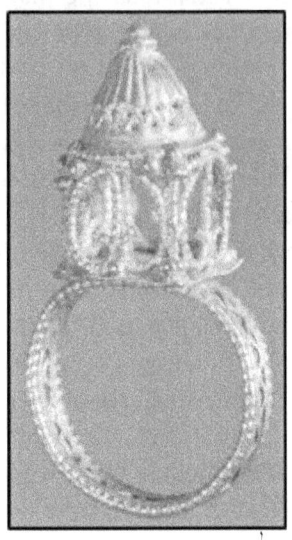

Ring featuring the Holy Sepulchre

The bezel of the ring itself is shaped like the structure of a square building with a cone-shaped cupola on top. Each side of the bezel features a large round vault composed of gold granulation. In the center of each round vault is a shaft with two branches at the bottom. The cupola on top of the ring is composed of long golden strips, joined at the top by a ring. Near the bottom of the roof are two rows of holes alternating one row above the other. The hoop or band (the part through which you put your finger) features two parallel rings with golden granulated edges. There is a line that ambles around the band in a zig-zag manner. The ring is the product of a master jeweler or craftsman.

Yaakov Meshorer was the Chief Curator for Archaeology at the Israel Museum in Jerusalem. After studying the ring, he gave this assessment:

> It is my impression that the ring is Christian because of the design of the vaults: The shaft with two branches resembles a stylized lily with a long central petal reaching the top of the vault . . . The lily was a well-known Christian symbol during the Crusader Period.

We should, therefore, look for an important building from the Christian world to identify the structure [214]

We do not have to look far. There is a remarkable similarity between the building on the ring and the Crusader Holy Sepulchre Church. The Crusader Holy Sepulchre Church is depicted on marble screens, which were part of the Crusader lintels on the facade of the Holy Sepulchre Church before it was damaged in a fire. These screens, now housed in the Rockefeller Museum in Jerusalem, represent the Church of the Holy Sepulchre as a cone-shaped cupola with a knob at its apex. This is the same as the building on the gold Holy Sepulchre ring.

In the fourth century AD, the emperor Constantine built the Anastasis over Jesus' tomb. It was a circular, pillared, open structure with a dome. Inside the present Church of the Holy Sepulchre, original parts of Constantine's Anastasis still survive, although many parts have had to be reconstructed.[215] The Byzantine parallels between the church and the ring provide strong evidence that the Holy Sepulchre gold ring from Jerusalem dates to the earlier Byzantine Period. The date is not entirely settled among academics.

While the evidence for the Church of the Holy Sepulchre being the authentic site of Jesus' death and resurrection is robust, the site is not without hindrances to its authenticity. Hence, we must honestly examine why some question the site as the genuine location of Golgotha and the tomb of Jesus.

Problems with the Church of the Holy Sepulchre

As with the Garden Tomb, the Church of the Holy Sepulchre has difficulties with the evidence. Some of those difficulties are examined here.

Since the Church of the Holy Sepulchre features *kokhim*-type tombs, where the body was slid into a niche cut out of the rock wall, how is it when Mary Magdalene looked into the tomb "she saw two angels in white, sitting where the body of Jesus had lain, one at the head and one at the feet" (John 20:12). *Kokhim* would not permit an angel to sit in a cramped niche in the wall.

This is not an objection to trifle with. If the Gospels suggest that the tomb of Joseph of Arimathea was constructed with arcosolia-type graves, and the Church of the Holy Sepulchre does not feature them but rather a different design, we are compelled to question the identification of the church with the events of Jesus' Passion weekend.

While this difficulty is often overlooked in scholarly publications, I consider it a significant issue for the Church of the Holy Sepulchre. It is not an insurmountable difficulty, but it is a significant one.

Burial kokhim in the Church of the Holy Sepluchre

And then there is the issue of the Church of the Holy Sepulchre's location. It has been established that the church was outside the wall of Jerusalem in Jesus' day. However, there may be a problem with the church's location outside the wall.

From the tenth century BC through the first century AD, which corresponds to the archaeological Iron Age through the Herodian Period, no tombs were constructed west of the inhabited areas of Jerusalem. The only exceptions were tombs located more than 1,000 meters (3,280 feet) west of the city walls. West of the wall was avoided as a burial area, and the reason appears to be geographic and meteorological factors.

Jerusalem sits high on the ridge of mountains that run north to south down the spine of the country of Israel. If you walked down the mountainside from Jerusalem west toward Ashdod on the Mediterranean Sea, you would walk approximately 68 kilometers (42 miles). Except on those occasions when a haboob or sirocco blows from the deserts toward the east, Jerusalem enjoys westerly breezes coming right off the Mediterranean. More than 350 days a year, the wind is from the west, from the sea.

Because of these prevailing westerly winds, the Jews did not bury their dead on the west side of Jerusalem. They had tombs and cemeteries to the east, north, and south of the city, but archaeological research has shown that west of the city was off-limits for the dead.

The Tomb of Joseph

A map in the *New Encyclopedia of Archaeological Excavations in the Holy Land* indicates the locations of Jerusalem's *necropoli* (burial grounds). It shows hundreds of tombs on the Mount of Olives, located east of Jerusalem, as well as large cemeteries to the north and south, but none within a kilometer of ancient Jerusalem's western wall.[216]

If tombs were located to the west of Jerusalem, that presented two problems for the Jews. First, the stench of decomposing corpses would wash over the city, forced along by the sea breezes from the west. Second, Jews believed ritual impurity from the "city of the dead" could cause the inhabitants of Jerusalem, or any Jewish town, to become defiled or unclean. The first reason is practical: not permitting a cemetery on the western side of the city. The second is a religious reason.

The Mishnah says:

> One must distance animal carcasses, and graves, and a tannery [*haburseki*], a place where hides are processed, fifty cubits from the city. One may establish a tannery only on the east side of the city, because winds usually blow from the west and the foul smells would therefore be blown away from the residential area. Rabbi Akiva says: One may establish a tannery on any side of a city except for the west, as the winds blowing from that direction will bring the odors into the city, and one must distance it fifty cubits from the city.

While the Jews of Jerusalem made every effort to bury their dead before sundown on the day a person died, it did not always happen for various legitimate and excusable reasons. Jesus is a prime example. Although Joseph and Nicodemus attempted to place Jesus' body in the tomb with all the burial preparations complete, they were unable to do so because of the approaching sunset. They left him in the tomb, dead, but not entirely prepared for the long term.

The stench of a dead carcass, even that of a dead human, causes an unbearable smell. Anyone who has passed "roadkill" day after day before the highway department removed it knows how true this is. It was merely a matter of practicality not to put a cemetery on the western side of the city.

However, more to the point was the religious reason why cemeteries were not placed west of the city. The Jews were super careful about being defiled by death. "There were certain men who were unclean through touching a dead body so that they could not keep the Passover on that day" (see Num 9:6–10). Ritual impurity removed a Jew from the reasonable requirements of Jewish life, as well as the usual social interactions of that life.

This presents a problem for the Church of the Holy Sepulchre's location. It is to the west of the Temple area. University of Haifa archaeologist Rami Arav and researcher John Rousseau have asserted that Pharisaic tradition would not have allowed a cemetery or killing ground anywhere west of the expanded Temple Mount, as the wind from the Mediterranean would pass over the cemetery before reaching the Temple Mount, thereby defiling everyone who breathed it in.[217]

Arav and Rousseau argue that "tombs found in this area (west of the city) are either older than the first century C.E. or are located more than a distance of 2,000 cubits (3,000 feet) from the Temple Mount."[218] The archaeologists concluded that since "burial customs in the first half of the first century C.E. preclude burials and their attendant impurities west (windward) of the Temple, then the crucifixion and burial of Jesus could not have taken place at the site of the Church of the Holy Sepulchre, which is almost exactly due west of the Holy of Holies."[219]

This appears to be another devastating blow to the Church of the Holy Sepulchre's claim to be the site of Jesus' crucifixion and resurrection. You can see why there is such a debate about the location of these two events.

Here's what we know for sure.

With so much speculation and tradition surrounding the Church of the Holy Sepulchre, what do we know for certain?

- Until the first century BC, there was a functioning quarry at the location of the present Church of the Holy Sepulchre.
- In the early Roman Period, this quarry was covered with soil, and the area was cultivated. This corresponds with what John 19:41 says: "Now in the place where he was crucified there was a garden, and in the garden a new tomb in which no one had yet been laid."
- In about 135 AD, according to the historian Eusebius, Emperor Hadrian built a temple to Venus over the presumed site of Golgotha and Jesus' tomb to prevent Christians from worshiping there.[220]
- Archaeologists have uncovered the remains of Hadrian's Temple. This pagan temple stood on the presumed site of Golgotha from the second to the third centuries. In the fourth century AD, both archaeological and historical sources corroborate that Emperor Constantine ordered the pagan temple to be destroyed and a church to be built on the site.

The Church of the Holy Sepulchre, rebuilt several times, still stands in the Christian Quarter of the walled Old City of Jerusalem.

- When layer after layer was excavated, Eusebius writes, "The testimony of the Savior's resurrection [that is, Jesus' empty tomb], was against all expectation revealed," and "the cave, the holy of holies, took on the appearance of a representation of the Savior's return to life"[221]

- In multiple sources from the early to mid-fourth century AD, such as the pilgrim Egeria and the Abbot Daniel, it is recorded that in the church there were relics, including the "True Cross."

- None of these earliest sources, including Eusebius, associates Helena with the actual construction of the Holy Sepulchre Church. Constantine, in letters describing the construction of the church, does not. The Bordeaux pilgrim who visited Jerusalem in 333 AD describes the building of the Holy Sepulchre but does not mention Helena or the discovery of the cross. Gregory of Nyssa (died c. 385), St. Jerome (c. 340–420), John Chrysostom (c. 347–407) and the female pilgrim Egeria (380s) all mention the relics of the cross in the Holy Sepulchre, but none credits Helena with their discovery.

Unfortunately, she did not live long enough to hear the stories that would make her famous. Within a year or two after her journey to the East, and several decades before her name came to be associated with the cross, Helena died in the presence of her son Constantine.[222]

CONCLUSION

So, where does that leave us in determining the location of Calvary, where Jesus died, and the tomb from which he rose to life? Perhaps with more questions than answers. The truth is, there is no "smoking gun" that forces you to say, "This is definitely the site." The Church of the Holy Sepulchre has more archaeological evidence in its favor than the Garden Tomb. It also has literary evidence dating back to the fourth century; however, the Garden Tomb has no such literary evidence. The Church of the Holy Sepulchre has more hard evidence for authenticity than does the Garden Tomb. It also has seventeen hundred years of tradition behind it.

From the Upper Room to Joseph's Tomb

> "We may not be absolutely certain that the site of the Holy Sepulchre Church is the site of Jesus' burial, but we certainly have no other site that can lay a claim nearly as weighty, and we really have no reason to reject the authenticity of the site." —Dan Bahat

Nevertheless, the Garden Tomb remains a viable option, especially for Protestants who are repulsed by the cacophony of smells, sounds, sights, and fights that are part of the atmosphere of the Church of the Holy Sepulchre. In 2016, Kristin Romey wrote for National Geographic and traveled to the Holy Land, speaking with numerous scholars about the location of Jesus' tomb. She also witnessed the opening of Christ's tomb at the Church of the Holy Sepulchre. There, she experienced an epiphany.

"At this moment, I realize that to sincere believers, the scholars' quest for the historical, non-supernatural Jesus is of little consequence," Romey wrote. "That quest will be endless, full of shifting theories, unanswerable questions, irreconcilable facts. But for true believers, their faith in the life, death, and resurrection of the Son of God will be evidence enough."

That being the case, on your pilgrimage to the Holy City, you may wish to visit both locations. Visit the Church of the Holy Sepulchre for information; visit the Garden Tomb for inspiration. Go to the Church of the Holy Sepulchre for the evidence; go to the Garden Tomb for the experience.[223]

The final stopover along Jesus' journey ends at Calvary itself. In the previous chapters, we have focused on the tangible, archaeological, traditional, and literary evidence for those sites that pilgrims making the journey to Jerusalem love to visit. The concept of "walking where Jesus walked" or following his footsteps along the Via Dolorosa has captured the imagination of millions. It seems that wars, conflicts, or threats are insufficient to keep pilgrims from following their hearts to these sacred sites.

In the chapters of this book, we have joined Jesus on his "dead man walking" journey from the Upper Room to Joseph's tomb. Along the way, we have stopped at the places where the Gospel narratives tell us Jesus stopped—Gethsemane, the High Priest's compound, Pilate's Judgment Hall, Herod Antipas' palace, and Calvary, to name a few. Each stopover is filled with meaning and often scoffing, scourging, and shame in the abuse of the Savior. The final stopover is the tomb itself. Many Evangelical Christians rush through the gore of Golgotha to get to the open tomb. But to get to the tomb you must go through Calvary and the cross.

Lead my steps to where He died,

> In the shadow of His cross I hide;
> There Jesus suffered for my sin;
> There God's family took me in.
> There the Savior died for me,
> LORD, lead my steps to Calvary.
>   WMK

In the long term, it does not really matter whether Jesus' grave is located at the Garden Tomb or the Church of the Holy Sepulchre. In the future, we may discover evidence that proves neither of them is the authentic site of Jesus' crucifixion and resurrection. There is, however, one thing both sites have in common, one fact they share. In both the Garden Tomb and the Church of the Holy Sepulchre, the tombs are empty. There is no one there.

"Do not be afraid, for I know that you seek Jesus who was crucified. He is not here, for he has risen, as he said. Come, see the place where he lay. Then go quickly and tell his disciples that he has risen from the dead" (Matt 28:5–7).

The call of the angel is with us still today. "Come and see; go and tell." In your heart and mind, come and see that the tomb is empty. Jesus is alive. As Christians, we do not serve a dead Savior; we serve a risen Lord. Get the facts. Get them in your head. The grave could not hold Jesus of Nazareth. He rose from the dead.

Once you have the facts cemented in your heart and mind, "go and tell." Do what the angel commanded the women to do. Do not be quiet about the fact that Jesus is alive. Tell your friends and family. Tell your story. Tell how you found yourself at the end of your rope, hanging on for dear life, when the hand of Jesus reached down from heaven and grabbed hold of you. If you have come to faith in Christ as Savior, tell someone. "Come and see; go and tell."

The grave may have been Jesus' final stopover on Earth, but it is not the final stopover for the 'Jesus story.' That continues with you and me. "Christ reconciled us to himself and gave us the ministry of reconciliation . . . entrusting to us the message of reconciliation. Therefore, we are ambassadors for Christ, God making his appeal through us" (2 Cor 5:18–20).

Daily, the stopovers beyond Calvary continue for you and me. Make every one meaningful. Make every one eternal. Be an ambassador for Christ and enjoy the significance of your exalted but gifted position. "Come and see; go and tell."

From the Upper Room to Joseph's Tomb

EPILOGUE

There is just something about Calvary, those crosses, and the Person dying on the middle one, that constantly brings us back to the foundation of our faith. While the plan for our salvation was conceived long before time began, it was during a less-than-twenty-four-hour period that the eternal plan of God unfolded. At Calvary, God's plan solidified. At Calvary, our Lord was crucified. At Calvary, God's wrath was satisfied. At Calvary, his love was magnified. And, at Calvary, for me, Jesus died.

At each stopover on Jesus' journey to Calvary, something awful happened to him. He was manhandled, falsely accused, spat on, beaten, slapped on the face, pummeled by brutal men, a crown of thorns was driven into his head, he was scourged within an inch of his life, and still, he had to carry the crossbeam of his own cross to the killing field of Calvary. That Friday was not a good day for Jesus, but it was a great day for us.

Today, I live confidently knowing that at Calvary, Jesus did all God required to pay the debt for my sin. I now live in the freedom of the cross. Because Jesus died in my place, I can live without fear or regret. I am forgiven. If this is also true for you, join me in remembering that day when Jesus died for you, remember and rejoice in his sacrifice through the words of Avis B. Christiansen's hymn.

> Up Calvary's Mountain One Dreadful Morn
> Walked Christ My Saviour, Weary And Worn
> Facing For Sinners Death On The Cross
> That He Might Save Them From Endless Loss.
> Blessed Redeemer, Precious Redeemer
> Seems Now I See Him On Calvary's Tree
> Wounded And Bleeding, For Sinners Pleading
> Blind And Unheeding, Dying For Me.
> O how I love Him, Savior and Friend,
> How can my praises ever find end?
> Thro' years unnumbered on heaven's shore,
> My tongue shall praise Him forevermore.

Endnotes

1. Clausen, *The Upper Room*; See also an update, "Hunting for the Upper Room in Jerusalem," *BAR*, April 08, 2020.
2. Bagatti, *The Church from the Circumcision*, 121.
3. Baldi, *Enchiridion Locorum Sanctorum*, 733.
4. ———, *Enchiridion Locorum Sanctorum*, 728.
5. ———, *Enchiridion Locorum Sanctorum*, 735.
6. Eusebius, *Church History* 3.11, 32:4ff.
7. Baldi, *Enchiridion Locorum Sanctorum* 732, 734, 739–741, 745–746.
8. ———, *Enchiridion Locorum Sanctorum*, 732.
9. Arculph was a seventh-century AD Frankish Bishop. He toured the Holy Land about the year 680 AD. In the *English Benedictine,* Venerable Bede's History of the Church in England (vol 15), Bede claimed Arculph was shipwrecked on the shores of the island of Iona, off the western coast of Scotland. Arculph was returning from a pilgrimage to the Levant. Bede records that Arculph was cordially received by the abbot of the island monastery whose name was Adomnán. Arculph divulged to Adomnán an exhaustive account of his travels. Subsequently, Adomnán produced *De Locis Sanctis* ("Concerning the Sacred Places"), a three-volume narrative of Arculph's journeys to Jerusalem, Bethlehem, and other places in Palestine, as well as Alexandria and Constantinople. When Bede came to know of *De Locis Sanctis*, he mentioned Arculph in his *Ecclesiastical History of the English People.*
10. Baldi, *Enchiridion Locorum Sanctorum*, 745.
11. van Esbroeck, "Une homélie sur l'Église," 86.
12. van Esbroeck, *Les plus anciens homiliaires Georgiens*, 314–315.
13. Jeremias, *Jerusalem*, 60–62.
14. Dalman, *Sacred Sites*, 264–267.
15. After discovering that the Kidron Valley was a place of sorrow, mourning, and death, how striking it is that one day this valley will be purified and ready for God's holy use. Jeremiah 31:40 makes this prophecy: "The whole valley of the dead bodies and the ashes, and all the fields as far as the brook Kidron, to the corner of the Horse Gate toward the east, shall be sacred to the LORD. It shall not be plucked up or overthrown anymore forever." Only the sovereign God can take a place of sorrow and mourning and remove the sadness and death for his eternal use.
16. Easton, "Gethsemane."
17. Kollek and Dowley, *Next Year in Jerusalem*, 1995.
18. See Curtis, "An Investigation," 137–138.
19. "What Really Happened at Gethsemane?" *Bible Review* 14:2, April 1998; see also

Endnotes

Murphy-O'Connor, "Pre-Constantinian Christian Jerusalem," 15–17.
20. *Wycliffe Bible Encyclopedia*, "Gethsemane," 675.
21. Easton, "Gethsemane."
22. Dalman, *Sacred Sites*, 320–321.
23. ———, *Sacred Sites*, 320–321.
24. From Adomnan, *De Locis Sanctis* 15.1–3; Wilkinson, *Jerusalem Pilgrims*, 99.
25. Finegan, *Archeology*, 105.
26. Kroll, *Auf den Spuren Jesu. Sein Leben*, 404.
27. ———, *Auf den Spuren Jesu. Sein Leben*, 410; see also Ratzinger, *Jesus of Nazareth*.
28. Kuchler, *Jerusalem: Ein Handbuch*, 826; see also Taylor, "The Garden of Gethsemane," 116–127.
29. See Corbo, *Ricerche archeologiche*, 1–57; Louis-Hugues Vincent and Felix-M Abel. *Jérusalem: recherches de topographie, d'archéologie et d'histoire. ii. Jérusalem nouvelle*, 335, fig. 147; and John Wilkinson, *Jerusalem as Jesus Knew It*, 1978, 127–131. For a complete history and physical description of the grotto see Joan E. Taylor, "The Garden of Gethsemane: Not the Place of Jesus' Arrest," *BAR* 21.4 (1995): 26, 28–31, 34–35.
30. For information about the archaeological excavations of this cave see Corbo, *Ricerche archeologiche al Monte degli Ulivi, Gerusalemme*, 1–57.
31. Edwards et al., "On the Physical Death of Jesus Christ," vol. 255, no. 11.
32. Schenck, Observationum Medicarum Rariorum, lib. iii, 458; Grafenberg, "Observ. Medic.," Lib. 3, 458.
33. Quoted in Stroud, *A Treatise The Physical Cause*, 86–87.
34. Zacchias, *Quaestiones Medico-legales*, 154.
35. Tissot, *Traité des nerfs*, 149.
36. Kannegiesser, *Institutiones medicinae legalis*, 354.
37. Pooley, "Bloody Sweat," 26: 357–365; Scott, "A Case of Hematidrosis," 1:532–533.
38. ———, "A Case of Haematidrosis," 1:532–533.
39. Holoubek, "Execution by Crucifixion," 26:1–16.
40. Ratzinger, *Jesus of Nazareth*, 157–166.
41. Huegel, *The Cross of Christ*, 56.
42. Although terribly abused and mistreated, Jesus was not scourged by the Jews, but by the Romans. Thus, he would not have been flogged here. Some of his disciples, however, quite likely were beaten here, if this is the location of the High Priest's palace. When Peter and the others were teaching about Jesus in the Temple, they were arrested and brought to the High Priest. Acts 5:40 informs us, "When they had called in the apostles, they beat them and charged them not to speak in the name of Jesus, and let them go." In all likelihood, these beatings were conducted at the residence of the High Priest.
43. Geva, Hillel, "Stratigraphy and Architecture," 1–90.
44. "Katros House–The Burnt House." GoIsrael.com Katros House–The Burnt House (archive.org).
45. Taylor, Justin, 2020. "Is This the High Priestly Palace Where Jesus Stood Trial?" *The Gospel Coalition* (blog). April 11, 2020,
46. The Qiao Family Compound belongs to a rich family in Shanxi Province, approximately 300 miles southwest of Beijing, China. This family compound was featured in the film "Raise the Red Lantern." The Qiao Family Compound was first built during the Qianlong Years (1736 – 1796 AD) of the Qing Dynasty. It is comprised of six big courtyards and twenty small courtyards, with three hundred and thirteen houses in total, covering an area of 8724 square meters (2.15 acres). Americans especially are familiar

Endnotes

with the Kennedy Compound, 24,000 square meters (5.93 acres) of waterfront property along Nantucket Sound in Hyannis Port, Massachusetts. This was the home of Joseph and Rose Kennedy and their children, including Senators Bobby and Ted Kennedy and U.S. President John F. Kennedy. There are three main houses on the compound. During the Kennedy administration, this compound became the Summer White House.

47. David W. Chapman and Eckhard J. Schnabel, *The Trial and Crucifixion of Jesus: Texts and Commentary*, 2. For the plausibility of an *ad hoc* meeting of the Sanhedrin, see Guido O. Kirner, *Strafgewalt und Provinzialherrschaft, Eine Untersuchung zur Strafgewaltspraxis der romischen Statthalter in Judea* (6–66 AD), 167–168, 259.

48. Edwin M. Yamauchi, "Historical Notes on the Trial and Crucifixion of Jesus Christ," *Christianity Today*, 9 April 1971, 9.

49. Ratzinger, Joseph, *Jesus of Nazareth*, 175–176. Ratzinger was elected pope, head of the Catholic Church, and sovereign of the Vatican City State from 2005 until his resignation in 2013. In my view, as an Evangelical Protestant, he was one of the keenest theologians produced by the Roman Catholic Church in generations.

50. Lane, *Mark*, 533.

51. Wilkinson, *Jerusalem as Jesus Knew It*, 136–137.

52. The modern translations of this word are all over the place, but they all refer to the same location. Here are some examples: CEV: "the courtyard of the fortress"; GNT: "the governor's palace"; HCSB: "courtyard (that is headquarters); JBP: "courtyard of the governor's residence"; KJV: 'the hall, called Praetorium"; MSG: "the palace (called Praetorium)"; MEV: "Praetorium Hall"; NASB, NCB, RSV, and NIV: "the palace (that is, the Praetorium)"; NKJV: "the hall called Praetorium"; NRSV: "the courtyard of the palace (that is, the governor's headquarters). It appears that the NLT attempted to cover all the bases with "the courtyard of the governor's headquarters (called the Praetorium)" To my mind, the TLB completely missed the point with "the barracks of the palace."

53. Mommsen, *The History of Rome*, 149, 362.

54. Campbell, "Praetorium,"11:775.

55. Berger, *Encyclopedic Dictionary of Roman Law*, 648.

56. Vincent, "Chronique: L'Antonia et la Prétoire," 83–113.

57. See de Sion, Marie Aline, "La Forteresse Antonia et la question du prétoire à Jérusalem."

58. Schürer, *A History of the Jewish People in the Time of Jesus Christ*, vol. 2, 55.

59. ———, *A History of the Jewish People in the Time of Jesus Christ*, 48–49. See also Josephus *Ant.* 17.10.2–3; *Wars* 2.17.8.

60. Gibson, *The Final Days of Jesus*, 91.

61. See Brown, "The Gospel According to John (13–21)," 845.

62. See Benoit, *Jesus and the Gospel*, vol. 1 168–182; Lane, *The Gospel According to Mark*, 549; Blinzler, *The Trial of Jesus*, 256–259; and Richard M. Mackowski, *Jerusalem, City of Jesus*, 104.

63. Magness, *The Archaeology of the Holy Land*, 158, 159.

64. Gibson, "*The Trial of Jesus*," 104.

65. Mommsen, *The History of Rome*, 149, 362.

66. See Lattey, "The Praetorium of Pilate," 180–182.

67. Berger, Adolph, *Encyclopedic Dictionary of Roman Law*. 10.23.4.

68. Eglash, Ruth, 2023. "Archaeologists Find Possible Site of Jesus's Trial in Jerusalem." *The Washington Post*, April 9, 2023.

69. See Toner, *Leisure and Ancient Rome*.

Endnotes

70. The author's notes from a class at Princeton on Greco-Roman Society and the Early Church, taught by Professor Metzger.
71. Hutton, 'There They Crucified Him,' 108–109.
72. Hoehner, *Herod Antipas*, 239.
73. The Hasmonean dynasty (Hebrew: חַשְׁמוֹנָאִים, Ḥašmonaʾīm) was the ruling dynasty of Judea during the period of classical antiquity. This dynasty was established by Simon Thassi some two decades after his brother Judas Maccabeus (יהודה המכבי *Yehudah HaMakabi*) defeated the Seleucid army during the Maccabean Revolt (167 BC–160 BC). There are more than ample sources that record these battles including 1 Maccabees, 2 Maccabees, and *The Wars of the Jews* by historian Flavius Josephus (37 AD–100 AD). The revolt began in opposition to the Seleucid leader Antiochus Epiphanes, who sacked Jerusalem and its Temple. The Hasmonean dynasty survived for 103 years before yielding to Herod the Great.
74. Wightman, "Temple Fortresses in Jerusalem Part II" The Hasmonean Baris and Herodian Antonia," 10:7–35.
75. Bahat, "The Western Wall Tunnels," 185.
76. Murphy-O'Connor, *The Holy Land*, 34–36.
77. Thurston, *The Stations of the Cross*, 55.
78. Murphy-O'Connor, *The Holy Land*, 37.
79. Vincent and Abel, *Jérusalem; recherches de topographie*, 626.
80. Early contributions to establishing the fourteen Stations of the Cross were made by John Pascha's Spiritual Pilgrimage (1563) and Christiaan van Adrichem (1585). For a complete history of the Stations of the Cross see https://www.udayton.edu/imri/mary/w/way-of-the-cross-history.php.
81. Kaiser, *Roman Urban Street Networks*, 160ff; Konrad, *Augusto Augurio*, 126ff.
82. These major Roman roads are thought either to have been constructed by the Roman emperor Hadrian (117–138 AD) or the Byzantine emperor Justinian (527–565 AD), with more scholars now leaning toward Justinian.
83. Gutfeld, "The Emperor's New Church, 31–42, 80–81.
84. Benoit, "The Archaeological Reconstruction, 87; also see *Wars*, 2:14:8.
85. In the Byzantine Period, the Via Dolorosa began in the western part of the city closer to the area of the Tower of David Museum. It was only after the thirteenth century that the beginning of the devotional walk was moved to the Antonia Fortress, the site of a former Roman military barracks.
86. Gibson, *The Final Days of Jesus*, 104–105.
87. *Wars*, 5:2.
88. Benoit, "The Archaeological Reconstruction, 87.
89. Gibson, *The Final Days of Jesus*, 104–106.
90. *Sanhedrin* 43a.
91. O'Reilly and Dugard, *Killing Jesus*.
92. Benoit, *The Passion and Resurrection of Jesus Christ*, 101.
93. Köstenberger, *John*, 542.
94. Plutarch, *Moralia* 554A-B: "Concerning Things Avenged Slowly by the Deity," §9.
95. Wilkinson, *Jerusalem as Jesus Knew It*, 150.
96. On the prisoner carrying his cross to the crucifixion site, see Luz, *Das Evangelium Nach Matthaus*; Evans, Mark 8:27–16:20, 499; and Michael Wolter, Das Lukasevangelium, 752.
97. Denny, *In the Shadow of the Cross*, 85. Adapted by the author.

Endnotes

98. Edwards et al., "On the Physical Death of Jesus Christ," *JAMA*. 255, 1455–1463.

99. "How Many Times Did Jesus Fall While Carrying the Cross?-Answers." 2023. Answers. August 19, 2023. One cross website in answer to the question, "How many times did Jesus fall when carrying the cross"? says, "We know of at least three times that he fell while he was carrying his cross. We know of this because we are the Catholic Church, which was established by Our Blessed Lord on the apostle Peter while Our Blessed Lord was still alive. The Church has the fullness of the truth, and only a fraction of that was committed to the Sacred Scriptures for reading at Mass."

100. Marinella, *Died He For Me*, 64.

101. Cavanagh, "Changes Fifty Bowie," 52–59.

102. Falcon Valley Music Ed., Stefano Vagnini, *Via Crucis*, Rome, 2002.

103. On the walls at St. Michael Parish of Canfield, Ohio, hangs a series of awe-inspiring mosaics depicting the Stations of the Cross. Call ahead for a visit.

104. Schilder, *Christ on Trial*, 370.

105. Brown, *The Death of the Messiah*, vol. 2, 912.

106. Tacitus, *Annals*, 2, 32; 15, 60; 14, 33; Plutarch, *Galba*, 9; Plautus, *Pseudolus*, 12.5.98.

107. Horace, *Epodes*, V, 99, and the scholia of Crusius; Pliny, *Naturalis Historia*. 36. 107.

108. Lipsius, *Iusti Lipsi De Cruce Libri Tres*.

109. Johnson, "Medical and Cardiological Aspects, 1978.

110. Brown, *The Death of the Messiah*, vol. 2, 912.

111. Murphy-O'Connor, *The Holy Land*, 50.

112. Kiehl, *The Passion of Our Lord*, 132.

113. For information about walking the Rampart Walk see https://www.touristisrael.com/ramparts-walk/7767/

114. For a complete discussion of the problems in identifying the "third wall" see Shanks, "The Jerusalem Wall That Shouldn't Be There," BAR, May-June 1987.

115. The following Bible translations also use the noun "Calvary": Wycliffe 1395, Tyndale 1524, Coverdale 1535, The Great Bible 1540, Matthew's Bible 1549, the Bishops' Bible 1568, the Geneva Bible 1557 to 1599, The Beza N.T. 1599, the Mace NT. 1729, the Worsley N.T. 1770, the Haweis N.T. 1795, the Thomson Translation 1808, Webster Bible 1833, The Revised English Bible 1877, The Clarke N.T. 1913, the New Life Version 1969, the NKJV 1982, the KJV 21st Century Version 1994, Worldwide English NT. 1998, The Third Millennium Bible 1998, The Revised Geneva Bible 2005, and others. Some versions, such as the Douay-Rheims 1582 and the Wycliffe Bible, all translate this word as "Calvary" in all four Gospels.

116. The Worldwide English New Testament [WE] translates all four Gospel accounts as they do Matthew 27:33, "They came to a place called Golgotha. That means, 'The place of a head bone.'"

117. Wilson, *Golgotha and the Holy Sepulchre*, 24–29.

118. Jeremias, *Golgotha*, 2.

119. Evans, "The Holy Sepulchre," 112.

120. Wilson, *Golgotha and the Holy Sepulchre*, 24–29.

121. Phillips, *The View from Mount Calvary*, 203.

122. Chrysostom, *Homilies on the Gospel of John*, 85, 756.

123. Schmidt, *A Scandalous Beauty*, 34.

124. Thiering, *Jesus and the Secret of the Dead Sea Scrolls*, 113–115.

Endnotes

125. Martin, *Secrets of Golgotha*, 10.

126. *Mishnah Parah* 3:6. "The red heifer, the goat for Azazel, and the red wool (used in the Yom Kippur service) are paid for using communal funds from the Temple treasury. The ramp for the heifer, the ramp for the goat, the thread between the goat's horns, the channel of water in the Temple, the Jerusalem city wall and its towers, and all city needs were paid for using money left in the treasury after the sacrificial needs were met. Abba Shaul said the kohanim paid for the ramp for the heifer using their own funds." *Shekalim* 4.2. Of the Talmudic books, Shekalim deals with the size and weight of the shekel. Thus, the discussion of paying for the ramp for the red heifer.

127. In Jewish thinking, the sages say, "Man was created from the very spot which atones for him" (*B'reishith Rabbah* 14:6). The exact location of the altar associated with the Holy of Holies has been established since eternity. King David and King Solomon built an altar on this site in the days of the First Temple. In the Second Temple Period, the altar was erected at the very same site. In Jewish belief, this is the very spot where Adam, the first man, was created. It was on this spot on Mount Moriah that Abraham, in a test of faith, built an altar and was prepared to sacrifice his only son, Isaac.

128. Martin, *Secrets of Golgotha*, 15.

129. ———, *Secrets of Golgotha*, 68b.

130. ———, *Secrets of Golgotha*, 24.

131. ———, *Secrets of Golgotha*, 85.

132. ———, *Secrets of Golgotha*, 82.

133. Charles George Gordon, the son of a Royal Artillery officer, entered the Royal Military Academy in 1848. In 1860, Gordon was posted to China as part of the Allied Expeditionary Force that was fighting the Second Opium War. Gordon became known as 'Chinese Gordon' in England. In 1884 when the Mahdi, a Muslim fundamentalist leader, led a revolt in the Sudan against Anglo-Egyptian rule, the British government appointed "Chinese" Gordon as Governor General of the Sudan. He arrived in Khartoum in February 1884. When the Mahdi besieged Gordon in Khartoum, the government was implored by everyone, including the Queen, to send a relief mission. They refused until October 1884. The relief column reached Khartoum two days after it fell to the Mahdi on January 26, 1885. Gordon was murdered at this battle or some point after it.

134. Gordon, *Reflections on Palestine*.

135. Conder, *Tent Work in Palestine*.

136. Claude Reignier Conder, *The City of Jerusalem*, 2005.

137. Jeffrey R. Chadwick, "Revisiting Golgotha and the Garden Tomb," 13–48.

138. Eusebius, *Onomasticon*, 74.

139. Jack Finegan, *The Archeology of the New Testament*, 110.

140. Michael Dumper and E. Stanley Bruce, *Cities of the Middle East and North Africa: A Historical Encyclopedia*, 2007.

141. Allyn Fisher-Ilan, "Punch-up at the Tomb of Jesus," The Guardian. London. (September 28, 2004).

142. Sarah El Deeb. "Christians Brawl at Jesus' Tomb," San Francisco Chronicle. Associated Press. (April 21, 2008).

143. See "Riot Police called as Monks clash in the Church of the Holy Sepulcher," *The Times*. London. November 10, 2008, and Toni O'Laughlin, "The monks who keep coming to blows in Jerusalem," *The Guardian*, November 10, 2008.

144. According to tradition, the Nuseibeh family took its name from a woman named Nusayba, who complained to the Prophet Muhammad about the unfair treatment of

Endnotes

women. Nusayba was an early example of women taking leadership roles in Islam. Since the Muslim conquest of Jerusalem in the seventh century, the Sunni Muslim family has held the key to the Church of the Holy Sepulchre. This arrangement emerged during the days of the second Muslim caliph, Umar Ibn al-Khattab. This caliph awarded the keys to the church the Nuseibeh family to avoid clashes among rival Christian groups for control over the church.

145. Arthur L. McMahon, "Holy Sepulchre." *Catholic Encyclopedia*, 1913.
146. See Justin Kroesen, *The Sepulchrum Domini Through the Ages*, 11.
147. James Fergusson, *A History of Architecture in All Countries,* vol. 1, 2010.
148. Dore Gold, *The Fight for Jerusalem*, 2007.
149. Henry L. Savage, "Pilgrimages and Pilgrim shrines in Palestine and Syria after 1095" vol 4, Madison, WI: University of Wisconsin Press, 1977, 37.
150. Gábor Ágoston, "Suleyman I" in the *Encyclopedia of the Ottoman Empire*, 541-545.
151. Marcel Serr and Dieter Vieweger, "Golgotha: Is the Holy Sepulchre Church Authentic?" *BAR*. May/June 2016.
152. Wynne-Jones, "Did Jesus die?" *The Daily Telegraph* (March 16, 2008).
153. Melton, *Religions of the World,* 55.
154. Valentine, *Islam and the Ahmadiyya Jama'at: History, Belief, Practice*, 28.
155. "The Japanese Jesus Trail," BBC (Sept 9, 2006).
156. Okamoto, *Pilgrimages in the Secular Age*, 109.
157. Jacobovici, Simcha, *The Jesus Family Tomb*, 2007; Tabor, (2007-03-27), "A Passover in 1980," The Jesus Dynasty Blog; (2007-02-27); "MyReflection-Archaeologist Amos Kloner Doesn't Buy the Jesus Christ's Coffin Story." n.d.; Andrey Feuerverger, "Statistical analysis of an archeological find." *The Annals of Applied Statistics.* (2008), 2 (1): 3–54; "Stephen Pfann, "The Improper Application of Statistics in the Lost Tomb of Jesus." n.d.; Heiser, Michael S., Logos Bible Software, Discovery Channel, Harper San Francisco, Israel Antiquities Authority, Jerusalem Post, Simcha Jacobovici, et al. n.d. "Evidence Real and Imagined: Thinking Clearly About the 'Jesus Family Tomb.'"
158. For a full description, see McBirnie, *Search for the Authentic Tomb of Jesus.* 1975, and Barkay, "The Garden Tomb."
159. Schick, "Gordon's Tomb," *PEQ,* 120–124.
160. Pappe, *A History of Modern Palestine,* 2006.
161. Conder, *Tentwork in Palestine,* 372.
162. ———, *Tentwork in Palestine,* 372–373.
163. ———, *Tentwork in Palestine,* 373.
164. Barkay, "The Garden Tomb," 50.
165. See Mazar, "Iron Age Burial Caves North of Damascus Gate Jerusalem," 1–8.
166. These suppositions were made by Ron Wyatt, a former nurse anesthetist who became an enthusiast of archaeology. Known for his "discoveries" (more than 100 of them) of Bible-related locations, including Noah's ark and the ark of the covenant, Wyatt's work has been dismissed by scientists, historians, biblical scholars, and by the entire academic community in general.
167. See also Davis and Kloner, "A Burial Cave, of the Late Israelite Period on the Slopes of Mt. Zion," 16–19, (in Hebrew).
168. Kloner, "A First Temple Period Burial Gave at Sobah," 71–71, (in Hebrew).
169. McRay, *Archaeology and the New Testament,* 207.
170. Barkayl, "The Garden Tomb".

Endnotes

171. Hachlili, *Jewish Funerary Customs.*
172. Kloner, "Did a Rolling Stone Close Jesus' Tomb?" 28.
173. ———, "Did a Rolling Stone Close Jesus' Tomb?" 28.
174. Barkay, "The Garden Tomb."
175. Conder, *PEQ*, 69–70.
176. Hanauer, *PEQ*, 199.
177. See Murphy-O'Connor, "The Holy Land, 21.
178. Boas, *Jerusalem in the Time of the Crusade*, 53.
179. McRay, *Archaeology and the New Testament*, 212.
180. Murphy-O'Connor, "The Garden Tomb and the Misfortunes of an Inscription," *BAR* 12:2, March/April 1986.
181. "Church of the Holy Sepulcher - Jerusalem 101." There is a beautiful website created by Galyn Wiemers that provides pictures, diagrams, and explanations of nearly every feature of the Church of the Holy Sepulchre.
182. Murphy-O'Connor, *The Holy Land*, 56, 59.
183. See Romey, "Jesus Burial Tomb Uncovered, October 31, 2016.
184. Goldman, "Tomb of Jesus Reopens to Public," 2017. Additional funding was provided by three denominations and a personal contribution made by King Abdullah II of Jordan.
185. See McMahon, "Holy Sepulchre"; Eusebius, *Life of Constantine*, 1999; Renner, "Is it the Tomb of Christ?" 1996.
186. Stephenson, *Constantine*, 206.
187. Bahat, "Does the Holy Sepulchre Church Mark the burial of Jesus?" 26–45.
188. Wilkinson, *Jerusalem as Jesus knew it*, 146.
189. For the history of the site of Golgotha, see Gibson and Taylor, *Beneath the Church of the Holy Sepulchre.*
190. The *nomen gentilicium* or "gentile name" designated a Roman citizen as a member of a particular *gens*—a "family" or "clan"—which constituted an extended Roman family, all of whom claimed descent from a common ancestor and shared the same nomen.
191. Speller, *Following Hadrian*, 218.
192. Wilkinson, *Jerusalem as Jesus Knew It*, 146–147.
193. For more information, see Serr and Vieweger, Archaeological Views, 42:03.
194. Klawans, "Site-Seeing: Archaeological Remains, 2017.
195. Major cities in which there are cathedrals dedicated to Alexander Nevsky include Warsaw and Łódź (Poland), Belgrade (Serbia), Yalta (Crimea), Tbilisi, (Georgia), and half a dozen Russian cities including St. Petersburg and Moscow.
196. See Drijvers, *Helena Augusta*, 1991; Thiede and d'Ancona, *The Quest for the True Cross*, 2000.
197. Eusebius, *Life of Constantine* 3.47.
198. On the Sessorian palace and Santa Croce, see Affanni, ed., *La Basilica di S. Croce in Gerusalemme*, 1997.
199. Drijvers, *Helena Augusta*, 1991.
200. *Epistula ad Constantius* 3, 33, 1168b.
201. *Catecheses* 4.10, 10.19, 13.4 PG 33, 467ff, 685–687, 777.
202. *Contra Galileos* 194c.
203. See Drijvers, *Helena Augusta*, 95–99; Borgehammar, *How the Holy Cross Was Found*, 7 ff.

Endnotes

204. Jeffery, *A Brief Description of the Holy Sepulchr*, 2.
205. González, "14—Official Theology: Eusebius of Caesarea," 129.
206. *Travels of Egeria* 37.1–7.
207. The first words of the Introduction to *The Pilgrimage of Etheria* by M. L. McClure are: "This book was discovered by Signor Gamurrini in an MS. Of the eleventh century at Arezzo, and he published it first in 1887." McClure, *The Pilgrimage of Etheria*, 7.
208. Jeffery, *A Brief Description of the Holy Sepulchre*, 4.
209. ———, *A Brief Description of the Holy Sepulchre*, 4.
210. Jerusalem, and the Church of the Holy Sepulchre in particular, was mentioned as the center of the Earth by Arculf, the seventh-century bishop who toured the Holy Land in around 680 AD and is called "the place called Compass" by Sæwulf.
211. Rhodes (2011) "Optically stimulated luminescence," 461–488.
212. Senthamil, Vilani, 2017. "Jesus Christ's Tomb at the Church of the Holy Sepulchre Older Than 4th C." *Architectural Digest India*, November 30, 2017.
213. See Grabar, *Les Ampoules des Terre Sainte*, 1958.
214. Meshorer, "Ancient Gold Ring," 46–48.
215. See Bahat, "Does the Holy Sepulchre Church Mark the Burial of Jesus?" 12:03
216. Geva, "Jerusalem/Tombs," 748.
217. Rousseau and Arav, *Jesus and His World*, 169.
218. ———, *Jesus and His World,* 167–68. The singular presence of the so-called "Herod family tomb" to the west of Jerusalem's Old City, on the grounds of the present-day King David Hotel, is explained by its distance from the Temple Mount—over 2,000 cubits, or 3,000 feet.
219. ———, *Jesus and His World*, 169.
220. Eusebius, *Life of Constantine* 3.26.
221. ———, *Life of Constantine* 3.27–28.
222. ———, *Life of Constantine* 3.46. For modern stories about Helena, see, e.g., Evelyn Waugh's *Helena*, and the recently published *Priestess of Avalon*, 2001.
223. An informative article on how the tomb of Jesus would have appeared in his day was written by archaeologist Jodi Magness entitled, "What Did Jesus' Tomb Look Like?" *BAR* 32:1, January/February 2006.

Bibliography

Adomnán. *De Locis Sanctis* 15.1–3. *Jerusalem Pilgrims Before the Crusades.* Warminster, England: Aris and Phillips, 1977.
Affanni, Anna Maria ed. *La Basilica di S. Croce in Gerusalemme a Roma quando l'antico è future.* Viterbo: Betagamma, 1997.
Ágoston, Gábor. "Suleyman I" in the *Encyclopedia of the Ottoman Empire.* New York: Facts on File, 2008.
Bagatti, Bellarmino. *The Church from the Circumcision.* Jerusalem: Franciscan, 1971.
Bahat, Dan. "Does the Holy Sepulchre Church Mark the burial of Jesus?" *Biblical Archaeology Review* 12, 1986.
———. "The Western Wall Tunnels." Ancient Jerusalem Revealed, *Israel Exploration Society*, 1994.
Baldi, Donato. *Enchiridion Locorum Sanctorum.* Jerusalem: Franciscan, 1982.
Barkay, Gabriel. "The Garden Tomb," *Biblical Archaeology Review*, March/April 1986.
Benoit, Pierre. "The Archaeological Reconstruction of the Antonia Fortress," in *Jerusalem Revealed: Archaeology in the Holy City, 1968—1974*, Yigael Yadin, editor. New Haven, CT: Yale University Press, 1976; also see *Wars*, 2:14:8.
———. *The Passion and Resurrection of Jesus Christ.* New York: Herder and Herder, 1970.
Berger, Adolph. *Encyclopedic Dictionary of Roman Law.* Clark, NJ: The Lawbook Exchange, Clark, NJ: The Lawbook Exchange, Ltd., 2014, q.v. "*Secretarium*," 693; Symmachus, *Epistulae.* 2014.
Blinzler, Josef. *The Trial of Jesus.* Westminster, MD: Newman, 1959.
Boas, Adrian J. *Jerusalem in the Time of the Crusades: Society, Landscape, and Art in the Holy City under Frankish Rule.* London: Routledge, 2001.
Borgehammar, Stephan. *How the Holy Cross Was Found.* Stockholm: Almqvist & Wiksell, 1991, 7 ff.
Bradley, Marion Zimmer and Diana L. Paxson. *Priestess of Avalon.* New York: Viking, 2001.
Brown, Raymond E. *The Death of the Messiah,* 2 vols. New York: Doubleday, 1994.
———, "The Gospel According to John (13–21)." *Anchor Bible* 29A. Garden City, NY: Doubleday, 1970.
Cameron, James and Simcha Jacobovici. "'A Passover in 1980,' the Jesus Dynasty Blog; James Cameron and Simcha Jacobovici - Search Videos." n.d. https://www.bing.com/videos/riverview/relatedvideo?q=%e2%80%9cA+Passover+in+1980%2c%e2%80%9d+The+Jesus+Dynasty+Blog%3b+James+Cameron+and+Simcha+Jacobovici+&&mid=837093BB2FF6AA783533837093BB2FF6AA783533&FORM=VAMGZC.

Bibliography

Campbell, B. "Praetorium," *Brill's New Pauly: Encyclopedia of the Ancient World*, 22 vols, 11:775. Leiden: E. J. Brill, 2002-2012.

Carroll, Sean M. *From Eternity to Here: The Quest for the Ultimate Theory of Time*. Boston, Dutton, 2009.

Cavanagh, David. "Changes Fifty Bowie," *Q Magazine*, 1997.

Chadwick, Jeffrey R. "Revisiting Golgotha and the Garden Tomb." *Religious Educator* 4, no. 1 (2003).

Chapman, David W., and Eckhard J. Schnabel. *The Trial and Crucifixion of Jesus: Texts and Commentary*. Peabody, MA: Hendrickson, 2019.

Chrysostom. *Homilies on the Gospel of John*, 85 (comments on John 19:16-18). Heidelberg, Germany: Zazzybee Verlag, 2017.

"Church of the Holy Sepulcher - Jerusalem 101." n.d. http://www.generationword.com/jerusalem101/52-holy-sepulcher.html.

Clausen, David Christian. *The Upper Room and Tomb of David: The History, Art and Archaeology of the Cenacle on Mount Zion*. Jefferson, NC: McFarland, 2016.

Conder, Claude Reignier. *Tent Work in Palestine: A Record of Discovery and Adventure*. New York: Wentworth, 2019.

———. *The City of Jerusalem*. Boston, MA: Adamant Media Corporation, 2005.

Corbo, Virgilio. *Ricerche archeologiche al Monte degli Ulivi, Gerusalemme*. Jerusalem: Franciscan, 1965.

Dalman, Gustaf H. *Sacred Sites and Ways: Studies in the Topography of the Gospels*. New York: Macmillan, 1935.

Davis, D. and Amos Kloner. "A Burial Cave of the Late Israelite Period on the Slopes of Mt. Zion," 1978, (in Hebrew).

Denny, Randal Earl. *In the Shadow of the Cross*. Kansas City, MO: Beacon Hill, 1995.

Dore Gold. *The Fight for Jerusalem: Radical Islam, the West, and the Future of the Holy City*. Washington, DC: Regnery Publishing, 2007.

Drijvers, Jan Willem. *Helena Augusta: The Mother of Constantine the Great and the Legend of Her Finding of the True Cross*. Leiden, Netherlands, Brill, 1991.

Edwards, MD., William D, Wesley J. Gabel, and Floyd E. Hosmer. "On the Physical Death of Jesus Christ." *JAMA*, (1986): vol. 255, no. 11.

Eglash, Ruth. 2023. "Archaeologists Find Possible Site of Jesus's Trial in Jerusalem." *The Washington Post*, April 9, 2023. http://www.washingtonpost.com/world/middle_east/archaeologists-find-possible-site-of-jesuss-trial-in-jerusalem/2015/01/04/6d0ce098-7f9a-45de-9639-b7922855bfdb_story.html.

Eusebius. *Life of Constantine*. Oxford: Oxford University Press, 1999.

Evans, Craig A. Mark 8:27–16:20, vol. 34B *Word Biblical Commentary*. Grand Rapids, MI: Zondervan Academic, 2015.

Evans, L. E. C. "The Holy Sepulchre," *Palestine Exploration Quarterly* 100, 1968.

Finegan, Jack. *The Archeology of the New Testament*. Princeton, NJ: Princeton University Press, 1992.

Geva, Hillel. "Jerusalem/Tombs," *The New Encyclopedia of Archaeological Excavations in the Holy Land*. Jerusalem: Israel Exploration Society & Carta, 1993.

———. "Stratigraphy and Architecture." Jewish Quarter Excavations in the Old City of Jerusalem IV." Jerusalem: *Israel Exploration Society*, 2020.

Gibson, Shimon and Joan E. Taylor. *Beneath the Church of the Holy Sepulchre, Jerusalem: The Archaeology and Early History of Traditional Golgotha*. London: Palestine Exploration Fund, 1994.

Bibliography

———. *The Final Days of Jesus: The Archaeological Evidence.* San Francisco: HarperOne, 2009.

———. "The Trial of Jesus at the Jerusalem Praetorium: New Archaeological Evidence," *The World of Jesus and the Early Church.* Peabody, 2011.

Goldman, Russell. "Tomb of Jesus Reopens to Public After $3 Million Restoration." The New York Times, March 22, 2017.

González, Justo. "14—Official Theology: Eusebius of Caesarea," *The Story of Christianity.* New York: HarperOne, 2010, 129.

Gordon, Charles G. *Reflections on Palestine.* New York: Wentworth, 2019.

Grabar, Andre. *Les Ampoules des Terre Sainte.* Paris: C. Klincksieck, 1958.

Grafenberg, J. S. "Observ. Medic," Lib. 3.

Gutfeld, Oren. "The Emperor's New Church on Main Street, Jerusalem," 80–81.

Hachlili, Rachel. *Jewish Funerary Customs, Practices, and Rites in the Second Temple Period.* Leiden, Netherlands: Brill, 2004.

Hanauer, J. C. *Palestine Exploration Fund Quarterly Statement,* July 1892.

Heiser, Michael S. Logos Bible Software, Discovery Channel, Harper San Francisco, Israel Antiquities Authority, Jerusalem Post, Simcha Jacobovici, et al. n.d. "Evidence Real and Imagined: Thinking Clearly About the 'Jesus Family Tomb.'" https://drmsh.com/michaelsheiser/Jesus%20Tomb%20article%20Heiser.pdf.

Hoehner, Harold. *Herod Antipas: A Contemporary of Jesus Christ.* Cambridge University Press, 1972.

Holoubek, Joe E. and Alice Baker Holoubek. "Execution by Crucifixion," *Journal of Medicine,* 1995.

"How Many Times Did Jesus Fall While Carrying the Cross? - Answers." 2023. Answers. August 19, 2023. https://www.answers.com/Q/How_many_times_did_Jesus_fall_when_carrying_the_cross.

Huegel, F. J. *The Cross of Christ—The Throne of God.* Grand Rapids, MI: Zondervan, 1946.

Hutchinson, N. F. "Further Notes on Our Lord's Tomb" in *Palestine Exploration Fund Quarterly* (July 1873).

Hutton, John A. *'There They Crucified Him.'* Edinburgh: T. and A. Constable, nd.

Jacobovici, Simcha and Charles Pellegrino. *The Jesus Family Tomb: The Discovery, the Investigation, and the Evidence That Could Change History.* New York: HarperOne, 2007.

Jeffery, George. *A Brief Description of the Holy Sepulchre in Jerusalem and other Christian Churches in the Holy City.* Cambridge: Cambridge University Press, 1919.

Jeremias, Joachim. *Golgotha.* Leipzig: Pfeiffer, 1926.

———. *Jerusalem in the Time of Jesus: An Investigation into Economic and Social Conditions during the New Testament Period.* Philadelphia: Fortress, 1969.

Johnson, Charles Duane. "Medical and Cardiological Aspects of the Passion and Crucifixion of Jesus, the Christ." *Boletin De La Asociacion Medica De Puerto Rico* 70, 1978.

Kannegiesser, Gottlieb Heinrich. *Institutiones medicinae legalis in usum auditorum concinnatae cum praefatione Andreae Eliae Büchneri.* Acad. Natur. Curios. Ann. 2 and Ann. 10. Kiel, Germany: Kiliae Holsatorum, 1777.

Kaiser, Alan. *Roman Urban Street Networks: Streets and the Organization of Space in Four Cities.* Abingdon-on-Thames, UK: Taylor & Francis, 2011.

Katros House – The Burnt House." GoIsrael.com Katros House-The Burnt House (archive.org).

Bibliography

Kiehl, Erich H. *The Passion of Our Lord*. Grand Rapids, MI: Baker, 1990.
Klawans, Jonathan. "Site-Seeing: Archaeological Remains, 2017."
Kloner, Amos. "A First Temple Period Burial Gave at Sobah," *Hadashot Archaelogiot* 78–79, 1982, (in Hebrew).
———. "Did a Rolling Stone Close Jesus' Tomb?" *Biblical Archaeology Review* 25, no. 5 (September/October 1999:28).
———. "myReflection - Archaeologist Amos Kloner Doesn't Buy the Jesus Christ's Coffin Story." n.d. https://web.archive.org/web/20080330043621/http://www.myreflection.com/Story.aspx?NewsID=1451.
Konrad, Christoph F. *Augusto Augurio: Rerum Humanarum Et Divinarum Commentationes in Honorem Jerzy Linderski*. Stuttgart, Germany: Franz Steiner Verlag, 2004.
Köstenberger, Andreas J. *John*. Grand Rapids, MI: Baker, 2004.
Kroll, Gerhard. *Auf den Spuren Jesu. Sein Leben - Sein Wirken - Seine Zeit*. Leipzig: St. Benno-Verlag, 1990.
Kroll, Woodrow Michael. *Roman Crucifixion and the Death of Jesus*. CRUCIFIXION: A Multidisciplinary Investigation of the Death of Jesus of Nazareth. Eugene, OR: Resource, 2023.
———. *Watching Jesus Die*. CRUCIFIXION: A Multidisciplinary Investigation of the Death of Jesus of Nazareth. Eugene, OR: Resource, 2023.
———. *The Trials, Crucifixion, and Burial of Jesus of Nazareth*. CRUCIFIXION: A Multidisciplinary Investigation of the Death of Jesus of Nazareth. Eugene, OR: Resource, 2024.
Kuchler, Max. *Jerusalem: Ein Handbuch und Studienreisefuhrer zur Heiligen Stadt (Orte und Landschaften der Bibel)*. Göttingen, Germany: Vandenhoeck & Ruprecht, 2007.
Lane, William L. *The Gospel According to Mark*. Grand Rapids: Eerdmans, 1974.
Lattey, Cuthbert. "The Praetorium of Pilate," 1930.
Lipsius, Justus. *Iusti Lipsi De Cruce Libri Tres: Ad Sacram Profanámque Historiam Utiles, Unà Cum Notis*. London: Forgotten Books, 2018.
Luz, Ulrich. *Das Evangelium Nach Matthaus* (MT 1-7) *Evangelisch-Katholischer Kommentar Zum Neuen Testament* (5th German Edition). Ostfildern, Germany: Verlagsgruppe Patmos, 2002.
Mackowski, Richard M. *Jerusalem, City of Jesus: An Exploration of the Traditions, Writing, and Remains of the Holy City from the Time of Christ*. Grand Rapids, MI: Eerdmans, 1980.
Magness, Jodi. *The Archaeology of the Holy Land*. New York: Cambridge University Press, 2012.
———. "What Did Jesus' Tomb Look Like?" *Biblical Archaeology Review* 32:1, January/February 2006.
Marinella, Mark A. *Died He For Me: A Physician's View of the Crucifixion of Jesus Christ*. Ventura, CA: Nordskog, 2008.
Martin, Ernest L. *Secrets of Golgotha*. Portland, OR: Associates for Scripture Knowledge, 1996.
Mazar, Amihai. "Iron Age Burial Caves North of Damascus Gate Jerusalem," *Israel Exploration Journal* 26, 1976.
McBirnie, William Steuart. *Search for the Authentic Tomb of Jesus*. Montrose, CA: Acclaimed Books, 1975.
McClure, M. L. *The Pilgrimage of Etheria*. London: SPCK, 1919.

Bibliography

McMahon, Arthur L. "Holy Sepulchre," *Catholic Encyclopedia*. New York: Robert Appleton Company; Eusebius, *Life of Constantine*. Oxford: Oxford University Press, 1999.

McRay, John. *Archaeology and the New Testament*. Grand Rapids: Baker Academic, 1991.

Melton, J. Gordon. *Religions of the World: A Comprehensive Encyclopedia of Beliefs and Practices*. Santa Barbara, CA: ABC-CLIO, 2010.

Meshorer, Yaakov. "Ancient Gold Ring Depicts the Holy Sepulchre," *Biblical Archaeology Review* 12.3, 1986.

Mommsen, Theodore. *The History of Rome*, vols. 1-5. Oxford: Benediction Classics, 2011.

Murphy-O'Connor, Jerome. "The Garden Tomb and the Misfortunes of an Inscription," *Biblical Archaeology Review*, March/April 1986.

———. *The Holy Land: An Oxford Archaeological Guide*. New York: Oxford University Press, 1998.

———. "The Holy Land: An Oxford Archaeological Guide from Earliest Times to 1700", *Oxford Archaeological Guides*, 2008.

———. "Pre-Constantinian Christian Jerusalem," *The Christian Heritage in the Holy Land*. London: Scorpian Cavandish, 1995.

Napier, Arthur Sampson. *History of the Holy Rood-Tree*. Boston, MA: Adamant Media Corporation, 2005.

Okamoto, Ryosuke. *Pilgrimages in the Secular Age: From El Camino to Anime*. Tokyo: Japan Publishing Industry Foundation for Culture, 2019.

O'Reilly, Bill, and Martin Dugard. *Killing Jesus*. New York: Henry Holt, 2013.

Pappe, Ilan. *A History of Modern Palestine: One Land, Two Peoples*. Cambridge: Cambridge University Press, 2003.

Pfann, Stephen. "The Improper Application of Statistics in the Lost Tomb of Jesus - Search Videos." n.d. https://www.bing.com/videos/riverview/ relatedvideo?q=+Stephen+Pfann%2c+%e2%80%9cThe+Improper+Application+of+Statistics+in+The+ Lost+ Tomb +of+Jesus&&mid=F7351B39A937A79428BDF7 351B39A937A79428BD& FORM =V AMGZC.

Phillips, John. *The View from Mount Calvary*. Grand Rapids, MI: Kregel, 2006.

Pilkington, Ed, and Rory McCarthy. 2017. "Is This Really the Last Resting Place of Jesus, Mary Magdalene - and Their Son?" *The Guardian*, November 26, 2017. https://www.theguardian.com/world/2007/feb/27/religion.israel.

Pooley, J.H. "Bloody Sweat." *The Popular Science Monthly*. 26: 357–365, 1884–1885.

Ratzinger, Joseph. *Jesus of Nazareth. Holy Week: From the Entrance into Jerusalem to the Resurrection*. San Francisco: Ignatius, 2011.

Renner, Gerald. "Is it the Tomb of Christ? A Search for Evidence." *Hartford Courant*, 1996.

Rhodes, Edward J. (2011). "Optically stimulated luminescence dating of sediments over the past 200,000 years." Annual Review of Earth and Planetary Sciences. 39.

Romey, Kristin. "Jesus Burial Tomb Uncovered: Here's What Scientists Saw Inside," *National Geographic*, October 31, 2016.

Rousseau, John J. and Rami Arav. *Jesus and His World: An Archaeological and Cultural Dictionary*. Minneapolis, MN: Fortress, 1995.

Savage, Henry L. "Pilgrimages and Pilgrim shrines in Palestine and Syria after 1095." *A History of the Crusades: The Art and Architecture of the Crusader States*, volume 4. Madison, WI: University of Wisconsin Press, 1977.

Schenck, Joannes. Observationum Medicarum Rariorum, lib. iii. Lugduni (Lyon, France): Huguetan, 1644.

Bibliography

Schick, Conrad. "Gordon's Tomb," *PEQ*, 1892.
Schilder, Klaas. *Christ on Trial*. Minneapolis, MN: Klock & Klock, 1978.
Schmidt, Thomas. *A Scandalous Beauty*. Grand Rapids, MI. Brazos, 2002.
Schürer, Emil. *A History of the Jewish People in the Time of Jesus Christ*. Edinburgh, Scotland: T & T Clark, 2014.
Scott, Charles T. "A Case of Haematidrosis," *British Medical Journal*, 1918.
Senthamil, Vilani. 2017. "Jesus Christ's Tomb at the Church of the Holy Sepulchre Older Than 4th C." *Architectural Digest India*, November 30, 2017. https://www.architecturaldigest.in/content/jesus-christ-tomb-church-holy-sepulchre-jerusalem-archaeology-discovery/.
Serr, Marcel, and Dieter Vieweger. Archaeological Views: "Golgotha: Is the Holy Sepulchre Church Authentic?" *Biblical Archaeology Review* 42:03.
Shanks, Hershel. "The Jerusalem Wall That Shouldn't Be There," *Biblical Archaeology Review* 13:03, May-June 1987.
———. "The Garden of Gethsemane," *Where Christianity Was Born*, Herschel Shanks, editor. Washington, DC: Biblical Archaeology Society, 2006.
de Sion, Marie Aline. Aline*"La Forteresse Antonia et la question du prétoire à Jérusalem"* (a Sorbonne thesis). Jerusalem: Ex typis PP. Fransiscalium, 1955.
Speller, Elizabeth. *Following Hadrian: A Second-Century Journey Through the Roman Empire*. New York: Oxford University Press, 2004.
Stephenson, Paul. *Constantine: Roman Emperor, Christian Victor*. New York: Overlook, 2010.
Stroud, William. *A Treatise on the Physical Cause of the Death of Christ: And its Relations to the Principles And Practice of Christianity*. London: Palala Press, 2016.
Tabor, James. (2007-03-27). "A Passover in 1980," The Jesus Dynasty Blog; James Cameron and Simcha Jacobovici. (https://www.jesusfamilytomb.com/press-release.html).
Taylor, Joan E. "The Garden of Gethsemane: Not the Place of Jesus' Arrest," *BAR* 21.4 (1995).
Taylor, Justin. 2020. "Is This the High Priestly Palace Where Jesus Stood Trial?" *The Gospel Coalition* (blog). April 11, 2020. https://blogs.thegospelcoalition.org/justintaylor/2012/08/28/is-this-the-high-priestly-palace-where-jesus-stood-trial/.
Taylor, Vincent. *The Cross of Christ*. London: Macmillan, 1956.
Thiede, Carsten Peter, and Matthew d'Ancona. *The Quest for the True Cross*. New York: Palgrave, 2000.
Thiering, Barbara. *Jesus and the Secret of the Dead Sea Scrolls*. San Francisco: Harper, 1992.
Thurston, Herbert. *The Stations of the Cross*. London: Burns and Oates, 1906.
Tissot, Samuel Auguste André David. *Traité des nerfs et de leurs maladies*. Charleston, SC: Nabu Press, 2012.
Toner, J. P. *Leisure and Ancient Rome*. Cambridge: Polity Press, 1995.
Vincent, Louis-Hugues. "Chronique: L'Antonia et la Prétoire," *Revue Biblique* 42 1933.
Vincent, Louis-Hugues and Felix-M Abel. *Jérusalem: recherches de topographie, d'archéologie et d'histoire. ii. Jérusalem nouvelle*. Berkley, CA: Gabalda, 1914.
Waugh, Evelyn. *Helena*. London: Chapman & Hall, 1950
Wilkinson, John. *Jerusalem as Jesus Knew It*. London: Thames and Hudson, 1978.
———. *Jerusalem Pilgrims Before the Crusades*. Warminster, England: Aris and Phillips, 1997.
Wilson, Sir Charles William. *Golgotha and the Holy Sepulchre*. London: PEF, 1906.

Bibliography

Witherington, Ben III. "Biblical Views: The Turn of the Christian Era: The Tale of Dionysius Exiguus," *BAR* 43.6 (2017).

Wightman, Gregory J. "Temple Fortresses in Jerusalem Part II" The Hasmonean Baris and Herodian Antonia." *Bulletin of the Anglo-Israeli Archaeological Society.*

Wolter, Michael W. Das Lukas-evangelium. *Handkommentar zum Neuen Testament,* 5. Tübingen: Mohr Siebeck, 2008.

Yamauchi, Edwin M. "Historical Notes on the Trial and Crucifixion of Jesus Christ," 9 April 1971.

Zacchias, Paulus. *Quaestiones Medico-legales, lib. iii.* London: Palala, 2015.

Name Index

Abdullah II, King of Jordan, 202
Adrichem, van Christiaan, 198
Alexander, Cecil Frances, 104
Arav, Rami, 190
Avigad, Nahman, 49, 150

Bach, Johann Sebastian, 92
Bagatti, Bellarmino, 7
Bahat, Dan, 169, 192
Barkay, Gabriel, 117, 141, 146, 147, 152, 161, 162
Beckholt, Karl, 143
Benoit, Pierre, 84, 87
Biagent, Michael, 110
Blake, William, 105
Blinzler, Josef, 52
Boldensele, von Wilhelm, 23
Bolen, Ted, 121
Borop, Niles, 92
Bowie, David, 92
Brown, Dan, 110
Brown, Raymond C., 52, 97, 130
Bunyan, John, 105

Cameron, James, 140
Chapman, David W., 52
Christiansen, Avis B., 194
Claudel, Paul, 92
Clausen, David, 5, 6, 11
Cohen, Rabbi, 165
Condor, Claude, 118, 142, 143, 145, 162
Corbo, Friar Virgilio Canio, 23
Curtis, John Briggs, 18

Dalman, Gustaf, 21, 22
Defoe, Daniel, 105
Denny, Randal Earl, 89
Donne, John, 106
Drijvers, Jan Willem, 177
Dupré, Marcel, 92
Dyer, Charles, xii, xvii

Edwards, William D., 89
Esbrœck, von Michel, 23

Finegan, Jack, 24
Fox, George, 105

Gabel, Wesley J., 89
Gibson, Shimon, 58, 62, 63, 85, 140
Gordon, General Charles, 118, 119, 142, 143, 200

Heusler, Erika, 52
Hoehner, Harold, 69
Hosmer, F. E., 89
Huegel, F. J., 31
al Ghodayya, 123
Hull, Edward, 119
al Husseini, Joudeh, 123
Hutchinson, R. F., 114

Jacobovici, Simcha, 140
Johnson, Charles Duane, 97

Kannegiesser, Gottlieb Heinrich, 28
Kennedy, Senator Bobby, 197
Kennedy, President John F., 197
Kennedy, Joseph and Rose, 197

Name Index

Kennedy, Senator Ted, 197
Kenyon, Dame Kathleen, 146
Klawans, Jonathan, 173
Kloner, Amos, 140, 146, 147, 158, 159
Köstenberger, Andreas J., 88
Krafft, Adam, 78
Kroll, Gerhard, 24
Kroll, Woodrow Michael, xii, xv, 32
Kuchler, Max, 25

Lang, Anton, 89
LeBec, A., 28
Liszt, Franz, 92
Lucado, Max, 182
Luther, Martin, 126

Macleod, George F., 96
Magness, Jodi, 140, 203
Maldonato, Joannes, 26, 29
Marston, Sir Charles, 146
Martin, Ernest L., 110–16
Mattox, F. W., xiv
Mazar, Benjamin, 185
McIntyre, John, 107
McRay, John, 164
Melton, J. Gordon, 138
Meshorer, Yaakov, 186
Metzger, Bruce, 66
Mommsen, Theodor, 55, 63
Montgomery, James, 105
Montgomery, Sir William, 230
Moropoulou, Antonia, 185
Morrison, Frank, 19
Murphy-O'Connor, Jerome, 19, 44, 86, 164, 175

Nevsky, Alexander, 174–76, 202
Nuseibeh, Wajeeh, 124, 200, 201

Pascha, John, 197
Patmore, Hector, 84
Pellegrino, Charles, 140
Petrie, Sir Flinders, 146
Pfann, Stephan, 140
Pinkerfeld, Jacob, 6, 7
Pixner, Bargil, 44
Pooley, J. H., 28
Pope
    Benedict XVI, 197
    Nicolas IV, 126
    Sixtus V, 27
    Urban II, 126
Price, Jonathan, 140

Ramsay, Sir William, 17
Ratzinger, Joseph, 30, 197
Reed, Jonathan, 89
Re'em, Amit, 62
Reubens, Peter Paul, 80
Rippon, John, 105
Ritmeyer, Leen, 49
Romey, Kristin, 169, 192
Rousseau, John, 190

Sandys, George, 120
Schenck, Joannes, 26
Schick, Conrad, 119, 129, 141, 142
Schilder, Klaas, 95
Schmidt, Thomas, 107
Schnabel, Eckhard J., 52, 81
Schürer, Emil, 57, 58
Schwabe, Moshe, 7
Scott, C. T., 29
Scott, Sir Walter, 56
Serr, Marcel, 129
Seymour, Diane, 92
Shanks, Hershel, 140
Spafford, Horatio, 142, 143
Sprague, Billy, 92

Taylor, Vincent, xiv
Tenedora, Norman, 113
Testa, Emmanuele, 7
Thenius, Otto, 119, 143
Thiering, Barbara, 107–9
Tissot, Samuel A. A. D., 17
Thou, de Jacque-Auguste, 27
Tristram, Canon Henry Baker, 119

Vagnini, Stefano, 92
Valenti, Michael, 92
Valentine, Simon Ross, 138
Vincent, Peré Louis-Hugues, 57, 129
Vermes, Géza, 110
Vieweger, Dieter, 129
Vos, Geerhardos, 30

Name Index

Wagner-Lux, Ute, 129
Warren, Sir Charles, 118, 142
Watts, Isaac, 105
Wesley, John, 105
Wesley, Susanna, 105
Whitaker, Ryland, 28
Wilkinson, John, 54, 170, 173
Wilson, Sir Charles, 53, 118

Wyatt, Ron, 201

Yamauchi, Edwin M., 52
Yaroulavitz, Alexander, 174

Zacchias, Paulus, 27
Zias, Joe, 140
Zugibe, Frederick T., 90

Subject Index

1948 War of Independence, 6, 127, 169
Aaron, 135
Abbot Daniel, 183, 184, 191
Abu Badd Stone, 156, 157, 160
Abu Gosh. *See* Kiriath Jearim
Acropolis, 168
Adam's Skull, 105
Adomán, 13, 23, 24, 195
Aedicula. *See* Edicule
Aelia Capitolina, 85, 99, 101, 125, 127, 172, 173, 175
Agrippa and Bernice, 50
Agrippium, 59
Alexander Hospice, 87
al-Hakim bi-Amr Allah, Caliph, 42, 125
al-Khattab, Omar ibn, 46, 201
Altar of the Cross, 122
Altars
    Burnt Offering (Brazen), 112
    Earthen. *See* Burnt Offering
    Golden. *See* Incense
    Great. *See* Burnt Offering
    Incense, 112
    Inner. *See* Incense
    Outer. *See* Burnt Offering
    Table of the LORD. *See* Burnt Offering
    Third, 111–15
Akiva, Rabbi, 189
Ambrose, 104, 178
American Colony, 142, 143
Ananias, House of, 39, 50
Ananias and Sapphira, 135
Anastasis, 122, 169, 187

Angel(s), 3, 145, 154, 156, 167, 179, 183, 187, 193
Annas, 33–35, 47, 49–51, 54, 55, 72, 73, 90
Antonia Fortress, 57
Apostles, 7–9, 51, 180, 196
Aramaic, 22, 49, 87, 90, 103, 104, 129, 135
Archaeology, 49, 62, 85, 117, 129, 141, 147, 159–61, 186, 201
Arcosolia, 137, 139, 149, 187
Arculph, Bishop (Gaul), 8, 195
Aretas IV, King, 67, 68
Aristotle, 26, 29
Armenia, 46, 51
Armenian
    Apostolic Church, 51, 123, 165
    Compound, 46, 47, 48
    Monastery of Jerusalem, 45
    Monks, 123
    Palace of the High Priest, 45
    Patriarch of Jerusalem, 46, 47, 51
    Pilgrims, 46
    Quarter, 46, 47, 51
    Refugees, 47
Assumptionist Catholics, 42
Alpha and Omega, 142
America, Americans, xvii, 171, 196
Antonia Fortress, 57, 58, 60, 61, 70, 74, 81, 84, 85, 103, 185, 198
Ashland, Nebraska, xv, 171
Athanasius, 166
Augustine, Bishop of Hippo, 106
Austro-Hungarian Hospice, 77

Subject Index

Babylon, Babylonian, 36, 39
Bahri Mamluk Dynasty, 126
Baldwin II, King of Jerusalem, 183
Bar Kochba Revolt, 172
Batnit, Saul ben Abba, 49
Battle of Hattin, 126
"Battle of the Ice," 174
Bas Relief(s), 42, 77
Basil the Great. *See* Bishops
Basilica, 169, 175
Bethlehem, 95, 178, 195
Bethphage, 157
Bethsaida, 96
Beyond the Jordan, 96
Bible, xii–xv, 16, 18, 22, 38, 46, 79, 104, 105, 110, 112, 114, 116, 154, 159, 160, 181, 199, 201
Bishops
    Basil the Great, 106
    Caesarea, 19, 169, 178
    Constantinople, 106
    Cyprus, 7
    Cyril, Bishop of Jerusalem, 178
    Francia, 8, 24, 195, 203
    Gobat, Samuel, Bishop of Jerusalem, 119
    Jerusalem, 8, 47, 119, 125, 169
    Lyon, 7
    Macarius, Bishop of Jerusalem, 125, 169
Bloody Sweat, 26, 28, 29
Bone Hill. *See* Bunhill Fields
Boneyard, 105
Bordeaux Pilgrim, 19, 24, 45, 191
The Braggart Warrior. See Miles Gloriosus
Bread and circuses, 65, 66
British Mandate, 127, 169
British Museum, 185
Bunhill Fields, 105
Burji Mamluk Dynasty, 126
The Burnt House, 49
Byzantine. *See* Periods: Byzantine
Byzantine
    Basilica, 6
    Christians, 147
    Church/Basilica, 8, 11, 41, 42, 163

Cross(es), 45
Emperor, 198
Empire, 125
House, 185
Jerusalem, 41
Monastery, 156
Oil Presses, 152
Shrine, 41

Caesar Traianus Hadrianus Augustus, 172
Caesarea Maritima, 63, 69, 84
Caesarea Philippi, 96
Caiaphas, 8, 17, 33–35, 41–45, 50–55, 72, 73, 90
Callirhoe. See Chaereas
Calvaria, 104
Calvary, xiii, xv, 2, 11, 17, 34, 38, 54, 64, 67, 72, 73, 79, 81, 87–91, 93, 99, 104–6, 117, 119–22, 136, 143, 145, 146, 157, 166, 170, 171, 176, 183, 191–94, 199
Calvary Event, The, 95, 107, 116
Campus Esquilinus, 97, 107
Capernaum, 23, 95, 96, 121
Cardo Decumanus, Jerusalem, 82–86
Cardo Maximus, Jerusalem, 9, 82, 82–85, 176
Carnifex Servorum, 97
Cathedral of Our Lady, Antwerp. *See* Churches
Cedron. *See* Kidron
Cemetery of Hesban, 157, 158
Cenotaph, 5, 6
"Center of the World," xxi, 117, 128, 203
Centurion, 87, 115–17
Cerveteri Necropoli della Banditaccia, 134
Chaereas, 88
The Chamber of the Hewn Stone, 51–55, 72, 112, 113
Chapel of the Angel, 167
The Charcoal Woman Carbonaria, 88
chi sigma, 141
China, 142, 196, 200

Subject Index

Christian Church, 109, 177
Christians, xiii, xiv, 6, 6, 40, 44, 99,
    127, 138, 144, 146, 147, 165,
    172, 178, 184, 190, 192, 193
Chrysostom, John, 106, 191
Church of England, 105
Church History, 178, 176
Churches/Basilicas
    Alexander Nevsky Church, 174, 176
    Armenian Church of Jerusalem, 51
    Basilica of Agony, 20, 24
    Basilica Heleniana, 177
    Cathedral of Our Lady, Antwerp, 80
    Chapel of Simon of Cyrene, 77
    Church of All Nations, 18, 20, 21, 23
    Church of the Apostles, 7, 8
    Church of the Anastasis. *See* Church of the Resurrection
    Church of the Ascension, 19
    Church of the Condemnation, 76
    Church of the Flagellation, 76
    Church of the Holy Archangels, 47
    Church of the Holy Face and St. Veronica, 77
    Church of the Holy Sepulchre, 19, 80, 99, 100, 103, 105, 116, 121–27, 129–32, 140, 145, 165–67, 169–71, 173–76, 178, 179, 181–85, 187, 188, 190–93, 201–3
    Church of Mary Magdalene, 20
    Church of the Resurrection, 122
    Dormition Abbey, 6, 44
    Ecce Homo Church, 76
    Egeria's Church (*ecclesia elegans*), 24
    Hagia Sophia, Istanbul, 168
    Hagia Zion, 6, 8–10, 168
    Holy Zion, 6, 11, 48
    Lutheran Church of the Redeemer, 171, 173–75
    Santa Croce in Gerusalemme, 177
    Santa Maria Maggiore, Rome, 10
    St. George's Cathedral, 157
    St. James Cathedral, 47
    St. Peter in Gallicantu, 41, 42, 44, 45, 48
Cistern(s), 23, 44, 45, 48, 59, 142, 150–52
Citadel, 70, 86, 101
Cities
    Alexandria, Egypt, 195
    Athens, Greece, 134, 168, 185
    Beijing, China, 38, 196
    Constantinople, 24, 51, 106, 195
    Damascus, Syria, 46, 121
    Faisaliyah, Jordan, 156
    Jerusalem, Israel, xii, xv, xxi, 1, 3, 4, 7–9, 11–13, 18–21, 33, 34, 36–41, 45–49, 51, 54–63, 67–70, 74, 75, 78, 79, 81, 83–88, 90, 92, 93, 96–101, 104–7, 110, 111, 113–16, 118–30, 133–46, 148, 150, 151, 155–58, 162–66, 169, 171–78, 180–89, 191, 192, 195, 198, 200
    Madaba, Jordan, 8, 9
    Oberammergau, Germany, 89
    Shingō, Japan, 138
    Srinagar, India, 137
    Washington, D.C., 74, 134
City of David, 34, 101
City of the Dead, 134, 189
City Road, London, 105
De Civitate Dei, 106
Cleopas, 134
"Cock's Crow." *See* Rooster, 44
Codex Aretinus, 182
Column of Flagellation, 8
Concerning the Sacred Places, 195
Constantinople, 24, 51, 106, 195
Convent of the Sisters of Zion, 74
Coptic Church of Egypt, 123
Council of Nicea, 7
Countries
    Belgium, 80
    Bulgaria, 174
    Croatia, 82

Subject Index

Egypt, 24, 120, 123, 125, 126, 134, 159, 162, 182
France, 82, 174, 181
Germany, 89, 126
Iran, 125
Israel, xi, xii, xvii, 7, 14, 38, 49, 50, 54, 68, 85, 97, 98, 112, 113, 126, 127, 146, 151, 152, 175, 188
Italy, 120, 182, 184
Jordan, xiii, 8, 9, 127, 156, 183, 202
Russia, 9, 174
Scotland, 23, 195
Turkey (Türkye), 46, 47, 182
United Kingdom, 119
Court of the Priests, 112
Cross, the, xiii, xiv, xxi, xxii, 17, 28–31, 42, 43, 54, 71, 73–81, 85, 87–92, 96–98, 106, 109, 122, 125, 129, 133, 135, 138, 142, 157, 172, 175, 177, 178, 182, 183, 191, 192–94, 198, 199
Crown of Thorns, 57, 76, 184, 194
Crucify, Crucified, xxii, 30, 61, 76, 79, 86–89, 94–98, 104–7, 114, 119, 121, 129, 133–36, 151, 153, 163, 166, 171, 173, 190, 193, 194
Crucifixion, xvii, xxi, 3, 7, 16, 17, 19, 25, 27, 31, 41, 50, 51, 61, 64, 73, 86–92, 95, 97, 99, 103, 107–12, 117–19, 121, 125, 127, 132, 138, 147, 155, 163–65, 174, 184, 190, 193
Cumanus, Prefect, 60
Curtain. *See* Veil

Les Dames de Sion. See Convent of Sisters of Zion
Daughters of Jerusalem, 38, 75, 78, 133
David, King, 5, 6, 13, 14, 34, 37, 39, 62, 83, 84, 86, 87, 91, 100, 101, 105, 106, 114, 139, 157, 173, 198, 200, 203
David Street, Jerusalem, 83, 87, 173

The Da Vinci Code, 110
Day of Preparation, 34, 136
Dead Sea Scrolls, 107, 108, 110
Death of Jesus, xiv, xvii, xxi, 21, 26–29, 35, 41, 52–54, 58, 61, 73, 79, 81, 86–89, 91, 95, 98, 99, 106, 107, 110, 116, 121, 122, 133–35, 139, 144, 147, 170, 173, 180, 187, 189, 192, 194, 195
De Locis Sanctis. See Concerning the Sacred Places, 23, 195
Declamations, 94
Demonstratio Evangelica, 7
Descent from the Cross, 80, 183
Disciples, xi, 1–3, 7, 11–13, 17, 18, 21–25, 42, 110, 133, 135, 154, 156, 193, 196
  Bartholomew, 51
  James, Son of Zebedee, 47
  John, 2, 4, 16, 17, 22, 25, 34, 63, 85, 98, 103, 136, 153, 159
  Judas, 2, 15, 17, 19, 21, 23–25, 54, 134, 139
  Matthew, 4, 52, 106, 116, 139, 154, 159
  Peter, 2, 4, 17, 22, 41–45, 50, 51, 80, 196, 199
  Thaddeus, 51
  Thomas, 2
"DOMINE IVIMVS," 127
Demonstratio Evangelica, 7

Early Church, 6, 106, 198
Earthquake(s), 3, 115, 116, 122, 125, 154, 156, 167
East Jerusalem, 127, 143, 188
Easter, 122, 182,
Eastern Orthodox Church, 51, 122, 165, 177
Ecce Homo Arch, 76, 175
Ecclestiscal History of the English People, 195
École Biblique et Archéologique Française de Jérusalem, 164
Edict of Milan, 125, 169
Edicule, 80, 158, 167–70, 184

Subject Index

Egeria, pilgrim, 8, 19, 24, 45, 169, 181, 182, 191
Egypt, 24, 120, 123, 125, 126, 134, 159, 162, 182
Elders, 14, 52
Eli Eli Lema Sabachthani, 3, 155,
Emmaus, 134
Epiphanius, Bishop of Cyprus, 7, 162
Epiphanius of Salamis, 106
Essene Community, 102, 108
Ethiopian Orthodox Tewahedo Church, 123
Eucherius, Bishop of Lyon, 7
Eudocia, Empress, 164
Europe, European, xxi, 5, 80, 117, 128, 142, 184, 185
Eusebius, Bishop of Caesarea, 7, 19, 99, 121, 169, 173, 177–79, 181, 190, 191
Evangelical(s), 52, 192, 197
Exactor Mortis, 87

Fatimids, 125, 126
Firman(s), 123
Fortress of Antonia. *See* Antonia Fortress
Franciscan White Sisters Convent, 143

Galilee, xxi, 12, 22, 23, 43, 67–69, 95, 96, 109, 171
Gamurrini, Gian Francesco, 203
Garden of Eden, 112
Garden of Gethsemane, xii, 11, 19, 21–25, 30, 73, 153
Garden Tomb, 104, 116, 119–21, 130–32, 140–53, 156, 157, 160–65, 170, 187, 191–93
Garden Tomb Association, The, 143, 149
Gardener, 153, 154
Gates, 37, 63, 85, 87, 88, 96, 97, 99, 111, 135, 141, 176
  Damascus, 83, 121, 143, 147, 163, 201
  Essenes, 102
  Eastern, 19, 24, 112, 113, 163
  Garden, 32
  Gennath, 89, 103
  Golden, 11
  Jaffa, 51, 58, 69, 83, 85, 174
  Jerusalem, 98
  Lion, 74, 84, 163
  St. Stephan, 163
  Triple, 185
  Zion, 51
Gaul, 7, 68
Gelasius, Bishop of Caesarea, 178
Gemara, 86
German Archaeologists/Scholars, 23, 28, 30, 78, 119, 129, 141, 143
German Protestant Institute of Archaeology, 129
Gessius Florus, prefect, 39, 60, 61
Gihon, (village), 11
God-man, 90
Golf Digest, 171
Golgotha, xii, 16, 31, 32, 74–77, 79, 81, 83, 86, 87, 89, 90, 97–99, 103–7, 110–12, 115, 117–19, 121, 122, 124, 125, 129, 130, 133, 135, 136, 138, 140–43, 157, 166, 167, 169, 170, 171, 173, 176, 178, 180, 181, 183, 184, 187, 190, 192, 199
Good Friday, 47, 67, 92, 109
Gordon's Calvary, 117, 119–21, 143, 157, 170
Gospel (narratives), xiii, 53, 57, 61, 63, 71, 75–77, 81, 83, 91, 97, 98, 103, 104, 109, 110, 116, 133, 140, 155, 192, 199
Gospel (Good News), 7, 92, 140
Graffito, Graffiti, 6, 7
Greek (language), xiv, xv, 3, 5, 7, 53, 87, 98, 103, 104, 139, 141, 142, 155, 159, 178
Greek (nationality), 26, 104, 106, 124, 127, 142, 168, 169, 172
The Grotto of the Betrayal, 24
The Grotto of Gethsemane, 20, 23

Haboob, 188
Hakim, Caliph, 42, 125

Subject Index

Halacha Law, 134
Hall, 50, 53, 56, 57, 63, 87, 90, 113, 192
"The Hall Beside the Xystus," 53
Hashemite Kingdom of Jordan, xiii
Hasmonean(s), 69, 70, 198
Hasmonean Palace, 40, 70, 72
Heavenly Father, xxi, 15, 20, 25, 96
Hebrew (language), xv, 13, 18, 22, 45, 49, 76, 103, 107, 108, 139
el Heidhemiyah, 120, 146
Helena, Constantine's mother, xiii, 99, 103, 125, 145, 169, 177, 178, 181, 182–84, 191
Helena, Queen of Adiabene, 145
Hematidrosis, 25–29
Herod. *See* Herods: Herod the Great
Herodian Mansion, 49
Herodias, 67, 68
Herods
    Herod Agrippa I, 47, 90
    Herod Antipas, 66, 68, 69, 71, 72, 192
    Herod the Great, 36, 39, 58, 60, 61, 66, 68–70, 83, 85, 198
    Herod Philip II, 68
Herod's Palace, 57, 58
Hezekiah, King, 14, 15, 101, 144
High Priest, 33–38, 43, 49, 50, 51, 52, 54, 70, 96, 111, 112, 155, 196
High Priest's Residence, 39, 40, 44, 45, 73, 90
Hippos, 152
Historia sui Temporis. See History of His Own Time, 27, 29
Holy Blood and the Holy Grail, 110
Holy City, 1, 5, 12, 13, 36, 38, 42, 74, 86, 95, 98, 100, 125, 126, 133, 134, 162, 184, 192
Holy Fire, 122
"Holy and Glorious Zion," 9
Holy of Holies, 36, 53, 112, 113, 190, 191
Holy Place, 53, 112
Holy Sepulchre Ring, 185, 187
Holy Spirit, xiv, 2, 7–9
Holy Trinity, 31

Holy Week, 19, 122, 182
Hattin, Battle of, 126
House of Ashes, 114
Hungarian, 90, 146
Hurva Square, Jerusalem, 50

Idols, 14, 179
Ἰησοῦς, 141
"The Immovable Ladder," 124
Imposition of the Cross, 76
In the Footsteps of Jesus: His Life. His Work. His Time, 24
In the Shadow of the Cross, 89
"The Invention of the Cross," 184
Iona, Island, 23, 195
iota sigma, 141
Isaac, 136, 200
Ishmael, 136
Isukiri, 138, 139
Israel, xi, xii, xvii, 7, 14, 49, 50, 54, 68, 85, 97, 98, 112, 113, 126, 127, 139, 146, 151, 152, 167, 174, 188
Israel Antiquities Authority (IAA), 11, 49, 62, 139, 167
Israel Exploration Society, 49
Israel's Supreme Court. *See* Knesset, 54
Istanbul, Turkey, 168
It Is Well With My Soul, 142
Itinerarium Burdigalense. See Bordeaux Pilgrim
Itinerarium Egeriae. See Egeria

Jeremiah's Grotto, 119, 120, 146
Jericho, 31, 36, 96
Jerome, 7, 105, 162, 191
Jerusalem, xii, xv, xxi, 1, 3, 4, 7–9, 11–13, 18–21, 33, 34, 36–41, 45–49, 51, 54–63, 67–70, 74, 75, 78, 79, 81, 83–86, 88, 90, 92, 93, 96–101, 103–7, 110, 111, 113–16, 118–23, 125–30, 133–36, 139–46, 148, 150, 151, 155–58, 162–66, 169, 171–78, 180–89, 191, 192, 195, 196, 198, 200, 201, 203

Subject Index

Jerusalem Syndrome, 37
Jesus, xi–xiii, xv, xxi, xxii, 1–8, 11–13, 15–25, 29–31, 33–39, 41–45, 47, 50–58, 61, 63–69, 71–81, 83–101, 103–12, 116, 117, 119–22, 125, 127, 129, 130, 132–44, 146–58, 162–67, 169–77, 179, 183–85, 187, 194
Jesus Christ, 7, 28, 51, 73, 93, 105, 113, 116, 122, 148, 155, 172
Jesus of Nazareth, xiv, xvii, xxii, 30, 87, 97, 110, 118, 130, 133, 140, 145, 148, 173, 193
Jesus and the Secret of the Dead Sea Scrolls, 107
Jesus the Man, 110
Jewish Authorities, 53
Jewish Festivals/Feasts, xxi, 9
Jewish Quarter, 40, 48–50, 70, 176
Jew(s) 13, 34, 36, 40, 60, 61, 63, 76, 87, 95, 99, 100, 127, 134, 138, 145, 162, 163, 188, 189, 196, 198
John. *See* Disciples: John
John the Baptist, 68
Jordan River, xxi, 68, 96
Jordan Valley. *See* Valleys: Jordan
Jordanian Jerusalem, 127
Josaphat. *See* Valleys: Jehoshaphat/Josaphat
Joseph of Arimathea, xxi, 122, 133, 136, 137, 145, 147, 148, 166, 176, 187
Joseph's Tomb, xxii, 137, 153, 156, 157, 163, 192
"The Joy of All the Earth," 36
Judea, 49, 52, 58, 60, 61, 67, 69, 95, 109, 172, 198
Jupiter, 99, 125, 169, 172, 173
Juvenal, 65, 66

Kapoustin, Archimandrite Antonin, 175
al Kattab, Omar Ibn, Calif, 46
Kerameikos of Athens, 134
Khartoum, Sudan, 142, 200

Khosrau II, 125
Kidron, Brook, 13, 195
Killing Field, 95, 97, 105, 194
Killing Squad, 87, 91
King David Hotel, 157, 203
King of the Jews, 76, 87
Kinsman Redeemer, 36
Kiriath Jearim, 158
Kishle, 62
Kiyomaro, Takeuchi, 139
Knesset, 54
Knights Hospitaller, 171
Kokh, Kokhim, 139, 145, 149, 187, 188
Kulio, 159

Lamb of God, 36
Last Supper, xiii, xxi, 1, 2, 4–6, 21–23, 48, 90
Law of Moses, 37, 52, 71, 114, 134, 135, 153, 162
Library of Celsus, Ephesus, 82
Life of Constantine, 173, 178, 181
Lipsius, Justus, 97
Lithostrotos, 76
De Locis Sanctis. *See*: *On Holy Places*, 23, 24
"The Lost Tomb of Jesus," 140, 201
Lower City, The, 36, 37, 39, 101
Lucan, Marcus Annaeus Lucanus, 26
Luke (person), 2, 4, 16, 22, 25, 26, 69, 71, 98, 104, 116, 154, 159

Maccabees, 39, 101, 198
Machpelah, Cave of, 136
Madaba Map, 9, 10, 175, 176
Mahdi, 137, 200
Man of a Lie, 108
Mark (person), 2, 4, 61, 62, 71, 116, 154, 159
Mary Magdalene, 109, 140, 153, 187
Master, 25, 31, 43
Matthew. *See* Disciples: Matthew
Mediterranean Sea, 18, 188
mégas, 2, 154–56, 160, 161
Megiddo, 157, 158
Messiah, xiv, 36, 69, 86, 114, 137, 138

Subject Index

St. Michael Parish, Canfield, Ohio, 199
Middle Ages, 5, 77
Middle East, 4, 5, 20, 117, 136
Midras's Tomb, 157, 161
Miles Gloriosus, 88, 97
Mishnah, 39, 53, 54, 112, 115, 119, 163, 189, 200
Miyuko, 138
Mohammad, 46, 124, 137
Monastery of St. Étienne, 146, 147, 164
Monument of the Fuller, 103
Moralia, 88
Mosaic Law. *See* Law of Moses
Moses, 71, 98, 111, 114, 133, 135, 157
Mosque, 5, 19
Mostellaria, 88
"Mother of All Churches," 6, 9
Mount
    Ararat, 46
    Calvary, 104
    Carmel, 157
    Corruption, 18
    Gerizim, 152
    Hor, 157
    Nebo, 157
    Olives, 7, 12, 18–22, 24, 31, 36, 38, 52, 110, 111–15, 117, 157, 178, 189
    Scopus, 18
    Temple, 36–38, 49, 53, 69, 70, 74, 81, 83, 84, 101, 112, 115, 150, 185, 190, 203
    Transfiguration, xxi, 133
    Zion, 5, 6–8, 11, 37, 38, 39, 41, 42, 44, 45
Muristan, 127, 171, 173, 174

Nablus Road, 121, 142, 143
Nazareth, xiv, xvii, xxii, 8, 30, 68, 87, 95, 97, 110, 118, 130, 133, 138, 140, 145, 148, 173, 193
Nebi Samuel, 162
Necropolis(i), 134, 189
Nehemiah, 14, 39, 101

New Testament, xv, 4, 11, 12, 17, 63, 66, 77, 103, 107, 110, 135, 140, 153, 155, 159, 164, 175, 199
Nicodemus, 189
Noah's Ark, 46, 201

Oil Press, 18, 21, 22, 24
Old City, 5, 11, 48, 51, 81, 83, 84, 99, 100, 103, 127, 129, 134, 139, 142, 143, 171, 173, 191, 203
Old Testament, 19, 14, 18, 38, 39, 108, 114
Olive Grove, 25, 141
Olive Press, 18, 21, 22, 24, 152
On Holy Places, 23, 195
Onomasticon, 19, 121
Optical Simulated Luminescence (OSL), 184, 185
Origen, 106
Ormanyan, Archbishop Maghakia, 47
Ottoman, 126
    Empire, 100
    Period, 62, 126
    Turks, 84
"Outside the Camp," 96, 97, 99, 11, 112, 135

Palatial Mansion, 49, 50
Palestine, 118, 119, 125, 126, 142, 145, 169, 172, 177, 181, 184, 195
Palestine Exploration Fund. *See* Society
Palestine Exploration Society, 118, 142, 145
Parah, tractate, 115, 200
The Passion, xiii, 19, 73, 103
Passion Play, 89
Passion Week, 76, 133
Passover, xxi, 2, 11, 12, 17, 34, 66–69, 95, 166, 189
Patibulum, 79, 87, 88, 90, 91
Patrologia Graeca, 106
Pentecost, 2, 9
Peregrinatio, 19
Perea, 12, 67–69

Subject Index

Periods
    Ayyubid, 126
    Byzantine, 6, 8, 11, 41–43, 45,
        125, 145–47, 152, 156, 163,
        184, 187, 198
    Crusader, 6, 47, 85, 126, 152,
        161–63, 174, 185, 187
    Herodian, 48, 49, 146, 152, 188
    Iron Age, 147, 148, 188
    Iron Age II, 146, 147, 150
    Mamluk, 126
    Ottoman, 62, 84, 100, 123, 126,
        144
    Roman, 46, 50, 83, 125, 134, 190
    Second Temple, 19, 40, 43, 53,
        100, 140, 147–50, 158, 200
    Persian Empire, 125
Pesher, 108, 110
Pilate, Pontius, 53–55, 57, 62, 63,
    66–69, 71–73, 75, 76, 80, 81,
    85–87, 85, 95, 96, 133, 137
Pilgrim's Progress, The, 105
The Place of the Skull, 74, 94, 97, 104,
    105, 170
Plautus, 88, 97
Pontius Pilate. *See* Pilate
Praetorium, 55, 56, 58, 61–63, 75, 81,
    84, 89, 90, 197
Priests, Jewish, 14, 25, 35, 45, 48, 49,
    52, 67, 71, 87, 112, 113
Procula, Pilate's wife, 55, 63
Protestant(s), 119, 129, 197
Publius Aelius Hadrianus, 172

Qianlong Years, 196
Qing Dynasty, 196
Quarry Oaks Golf Course, 171
*Questiones medico-legales. See
    Medical and Legal Questions*,
    27
Quintilian, 94

Rabbah. *See* Samuel bar Nahami, 96
"Raise the Red Lantern," 196
Red Heifer, 112–15, 200
Reflections on Palestine, 118

The Resurrection of Jesus, 1, 7, 43, 67,
    110, 121, 122, 127, 130, 158,
    164, 165, 167, 179, 180, 184,
    187, 190–93
Robinson Crusoe, 105
Rock of Agony, 19, 21
Rock of Golgotha, 167
Rolling Stone, 145, 157, 158, 160, 161
Roman
    Army/Soldiers, xi, 44, 58, 60, 62,
        86, 87, 90, 91, 98, 125, 198
    Building(s), 44, 82, 151
    Crucifixion, xiv, xxi, 88, 105, 107,
        129
    Emperor, 52, 56, 68, 125, 127,
        164
    Empire, 36, 97, 145, 172, 177, 181
    Law/Justice, 95, 96, 98, 134
    Poet/Scholar, 26, 65, 88, 94, 97,
        104
    Prefect/Governor, 1, 5, 40, 49, 52,
        55, 56, 58, 60, 61, 63, 69, 71,
        84, 85, 95, 97
    Religion, 172, 173,
    Society, 61, 66, 99, 125, 167, 172,
        202
    Streets/Roads, xi, xiv, 9, 11, 12,
        76, 82, 84, 85, 151, 176, 198
    Warfare, 21
Roman Catholic Church, 8, 20, 77,
    78, 197
Roman Emperors
    Caligula, 68
    Claudius, 88
    Constantine the Great, xiii, 125,
        170, 179–81, 183, 187, 190
    Constantine II, 178
    Constantine IX Monomachos,
        126
    Hadrian, 7, 99, 125, 127, 172,
        175, 190, 198
    Julian, 178
    Justinian, 198
    Theodosius I, 8, 9, 48
    Theodosius II, 164
    Rooster, 22, 41, 42, 44
Rotunda, 80, 122, 167, 169

Subject Index

Russian, 174, 175, 183, 202
Russian Ecclesiastical Mission, 175
Russian Orthodox Church, 20, 175

Sabbath, 97, 135, 140, 148
Sabine people, 181
Sackcloth, 13, 14
Sæwulf, 184, 203
Saladin, 126
Samuel, 162
The Sanhedrin, 34, 35, 41, 51–54, 69, 90, 113, 146, 197
Sanhedrin Tombs, 146
Sarcophagus(i), 141, 145, 147
Savior, xiv, 7, 11, 30, 31, 67, 87, 92, 107, 133, 148, 155, 192–94
Sawaguchi, Sajiro, 138, 139
Scribes, 52, 67, 71
Sea of Galilee, 23, 43, 96, 126
Secretarium, 63, 205
Secrets of Golgotha, 110, 115
Seljuk Turks, 126
Seneca the Younger, 26
Sermon on the Mount, xxi
Sermons de Passione, 106
Sessorium, 97
Shanxi Provence, 196
Shin, Hebrew letter, 13
Shroud, Linen, 3, 80, 136, 137, 154
Siloam, Pool of, 101, 102
Siloam, Village of, 11, 150
Silwan. *See* Siloam
Simon of Cyrene, 75, 77, 78, 88, 91
Sion. *See* Zion
Sirocco. *See* Haboob
Skull, 74, 79, 94, 97, 104, 105, 118, 120, 121, 170
S. S. Ville du Havre, 142
St. Étienne Tombs, 147, 164
Star of Bethlehem, 110
State of Israel, 85, 127
Stations of the Cross, 43, 74, 75, 79, 92, 198, 199
Status Quo, 123, 124
Stipes, 79
Stone of Anointing, 80, 166
Straton's Tower, 70

Streets
  Via Appia, Rome, 74, 134
  Via Dolorosa, Jerusalem, 57, 63, 64, 72–81, 84, 86, 87, 90–93, 122, 133, 173, 175, 192, 198
Suleiman the Great. *See* Suleiman the Magnificient
Suleiman the Magnificient, 100, 101, 126, 127, 144
Synagogue, 5, 6, 12, 138
Syria Palistina, 172
Samuel bar Nahami, Rabbi, 96
Shephelah, 161
Solomon, 13, 34, 36, 101, 139, 200
Sophia, Bulgaria, 174
"Spirit of the Paraclete," 7
Stephen, 98, 135, 140, 163
Sudan, 20, 200
Sufi Mystic, 138
Superman, 90
Sussita. *See* Hippos
Sweat Drops of Blood, 25–29
Sybaris, 58
Sychar, 96
Synoptic(s), 17, 22, 117, 154, 157, 158
Syria, 120, 126, 182
Syrian Orthodox Church of Antioch, 123

Tabernacle, 111, 112
Tagus River, 82
Taiping Rebellion, 142
Tallinn, Estonia, 174
Talmud, Babylonian, 36, 49, 96
Talpiot Tomb, 139, 140
Tannery, 189
Teacher of Righteousness, 108
Temple of Jerusalem, xxi, 33, 35, 36–40, 45, 49, 52, 53, 57–60, 69–71, 74, 80, 81, 83, 84, 101, 102, 110, 113–16, 119, 125, 150, 169, 170, 185, 190, 196, 198, 200, 203
Temple Police, 17, 25, 33, 35
Temple of Jupiter, 125, 169, 172
Temple of Venus, 125, 169, 173, 190
Tentwork in Palestine, 145

Subject Index

Tertullian, 162
The Land and the Book, xii, xvii, 20
"THE THING," 115
Theophrastus, 26
Tiridates III, King, 46
Titulus, 86, 91
Titus Flavius, 125, 148
Tomb of Jesus, 80, 122, 125, 130, 132, 133, 138, 140, 142, 143, 145–47, 150, 157, 165, 167, 169, 170, 179, 184, 185, 187, 203
"Tomb of the Kings," 146, 157, 161
Tomb of the Virgin Mary, 20
Torai Tora Daitenku, 138
"The Torrent of the Kidron," 19
Tower of David, Jerusalem, 62, 84, 86, 87, 139, 198
Tower of David Museum, 62
Tractate 35, Matthew, 106
Trial, xi, 17, 34, 35, 41, 43, 51, 52, 54, 57, 61, 63, 66, 73, 75, 76, 85, 92, 95, 96, 133
Traité des nerfs et de leurs maladies. See *Treatise on the Nerves and Nervous Disorders*
The Transfiguration, xxi, 133
The Travels of Egeria, 182
Treatise on the Nerves and Nervous Disorders, 27
Tri-leaf-globe, 138
Triple Gate, 185
Triumphal Entry, xxi, 4
"True Cross," 125, 178, 181, 183, 191
Tyre, 14, 96
Tyropean Valley, 37, 39

UNESCO World Heritage Site, 100
Universities
    Albright Institute of Archaeological Research, 62
    Bar-Ilan University, 146
    Hebrew University, 49, 141, 146, 185
    Institute of Archaeology, Hebrew University, 49
    University of Groningen, 178
    National Technical University of Athens, 168, 185
    University of the Holy Land, 146
    University of Munich, 8, 9
    University of North Carolina, Chapel Hill, 62
    University of North Carolina, Charlotte, 6
    Studium Biblicum Franscanum, 7
    Wheaton College, 164
The Upper City, 12, 36–41, 44, 58, 60, 63, 70, 101
Upper Marketplace, 60
Upper Room, xi, xii, xv, xvii, xxii, 1–11, 17, 18, 21, 69, 90, 155, 192
Upper West Side, New York City, 38
Usha, 152
Uzza, 136
Uzziel, 135

Valleys
    Cheesemakers. See Tyropean Valley
    Cheesemongers. See Tyropean Valley
    Hinnom, 13, 146, 157
    Jehoshaphat/Josaphat, 19
    Jezreel, 157
    Jordan, 18, 31, 36, 67, 157
    Kashmir, 137
    Kidron, 11–15, 146, 157, 195
    Tyropean, 37, 101
Veil, 80, 112, 113, 115–17
Venerable Bede, 105, 195
Veronica, 75, 77, 78
Vestments, 70, 183
Via Appia, Rome, 74, 134
Via Dolorosa, Jerusalem, 57, 63, 64, 72–81, 84, 86, 87, 90–93, 122,Via Appia, Rome, 74, 134
Via Dolorosa, Jerusalem, 57, 63, 64, 72–81, 84, 86, 87, 90–93, 122
Via Crucis. *See* Streets: Via Dolorosa
Vineyard, 141, 152–154

"Walk Where Jesus Walked," xiii, xv

Subject Index

Walls. *See* Jerusalem's Walls
Warren's Shaft, 118
The Wars of the Jews, 60, 118
The Way, 92
"Way of the Cross." *See* Streets: Via Dolorosa
"Way of Sorrows." *See* Streets: Via Dolorosa
"Way of Suffering." *See* Streets: Via Dolorosa
Weeping Chamber, 141, 149
Wesley's Chapel, 105
West, Western World, xiv, 31

Wicked Priest, 108, 110
Wilson's Arch, 53, 118
World Monuments Fund, 168
World War I, 47, 127
World War II, 31, 139

Xystus, 40, 53, 70

YHWH, 36, 37, 162

Zion, 5-9, 11, 33, 37-39, 41, 42, 44, 45, 48, 51, 74, 100

www.ingramcontent.com/pod-product-compliance
Lightning Source LLC
Chambersburg PA
CBHW050350230426
43663CB00010B/2065